SERVICE SAVVY
HEALTH CARE
ONE GOAL AT A TIME

Wendy Leebov, Susan Afriat, Jeanne Presha

AHA
Press

American Hospital Publishing, Inc.
An American Hospital Association Company
Chicago

Cover design by Jeanne Calabrese

Library of Congress Cataloging-in-Publication Data
Leebov, Wendy.
        Service savvy health care : One goal at a time / Wendy Leebov, Susan H. Afriat, Jeanne Presha.
            p.   cm.
        Includes bibliographical references and index.
        ISBN: 1-55648-225-6
        1. Health facilities—Administration. 2. Total quality management. 3. Customer relations. 4. Benchmarking (Management).
I. Afriat, Susan H. II. Presha, Jeanne. III. Title.
        [DNLM: 1. Health Facilities—organization & administration.
2. Quality of Health Care—organization & administration.   WX 153
L482s 1998]
RA971.L374   1998
362.1'068—dc21
DNLM/DLC   97-50160
for Library of Congress   CIP

Item Number: 042101

Contents

About the Authors

Wendy Leebov is currently associate vice president of human resources for the Albert Einstein Healthcare Network in Philadelphia, where she is responsible for organizational learning and performance enhancement strategies.

Previously, Wendy was founder and president of the Einstein Consulting Group, a subsidiary of Albert Einstein Healthcare Network that received international recognition for leadership and expertise on service and quality improvement strategies in health care. Wendy is a nationally recognized speaker, author, and consultant, having written five books on service and quality improvement, including *The Healthcare Manager's Guide to Continuous Quality Improvement* (with Clara Jean Ersoz, MD), *Service Quality Improvement: The Customer Satisfaction Strategy for Health Care* and *Healthcare Managers in Transition* (with Gail Scott), and *Patient Satisfaction: A Guide to Practice Enhancement* (with Gail Scott and Michael Vergare, MD). Wendy has her BA degree from Oberlin College, as well as her master's and doctoral degrees in education from the Harvard Graduate School of Education.

Susan Afriat is currently director of organization development and team services for the Albert Einstein Healthcare Network in Philadelphia, where she is responsible for quality-improvement team support, organization development, and team-building strategies for the multihospital system's Department of Organization and Staff Development (a part of human resources).

Susan was formerly senior consultant with the Einstein Consulting Group, responsible for design and implementation of comprehensive service quality improvement programs in hospitals, ambulatory care facilities, and managed care organizations. Before that, she was training specialist for ambulatory care facilities in a regional training program serving five states. Susan coauthored with Wendy Leebov "Customer Service Excellence in Ambulatory Care Organizations," *Journal of Healthcare Marketing,* 1989.

Susan has her BA degree in social welfare and her MEd in health education from Temple University.

Jeanne Presha is currently director of performance enhancement in the department of human resources for the Albert Einstein Healthcare Network in Philadelphia, where she directs adult basic education and literacy programs, on-site college programs, and alignment of performance management tools with the network's values. She also manages values alignment initiatives and develops and implements train-the-trainer and management development programs. In addition, Jeanne created the "At Your Service" training program for frontline employees.

An experienced manager in health care and other service industries, Jeanne has developed a comprehensive system of work redesign and skill-building strategies to help health care employees tool up for effectiveness in the dynamic health care environment. Previously, Jeanne worked at Thomas Jefferson University Hospital in Philadelphia for three years, where she consulted to university and hospital departments on internal organization development, designed and implemented hospitalwide education programs, collaborated in design of competency development programs, and provided management and supervisory development programs.

Jeanne has her BS degree in marketing education from Temple University and her MS degree in organizational behavior from the University of Pennsylvania.

Preface

In the Albert Einstein Healthcare Network in Philadelphia, we've been engaged in a far-reaching, long-term strategy to become a value-driven organization. We have identified and articulated a set of shared values—including compassion, professionalism, teamwork, quality, hospitality, and more—and have been doing a wide variety of interventions to help staff at all levels to align their everyday behaviors and decisions with these values.

As we explore our shared values with our workforce of more than four thousand people, the greatest challenge has been to find ways to help people go beyond rhetoric and generalities and apply the values concretely to everyday behavior and decisions with their *particular* work teams and their *particular* customers.

We established a multihospital, multidisciplinary team called the alignment team to figure out how to move the values to the work team level and help teams align with these values in their unique work in a way that was consistent from team to team throughout our network.

To accomplish this, the alignment team developed a process that is consistent with both the Japanese approach to Hoshin Planning and the 10-step performance improvement process of the Joint Commission for the Accreditation of Healthcare Organizations. They proposed that all work teams throughout the organization follow this process in collective pursuit of one organizationwide values objective at a time. Their idea was to select one important values objective and have every team and every individual—at every level and in every job—work toward that *same* objective at the same time in a synchronized fashion. Adoption of a shared objective and a shared process would glue the organization together while still allowing, even ensuring, that each work team had the flexibility to define and pursue its own particular team-specific, job-specific, and person-specific subgoals.

The alignment team decided to call these overarching objectives *breakthrough objectives* because if everyone worked toward the same objective at the same time and made even incremental improvements toward it, all of the incremental improvements would add up to a breakthrough—a major shift in the quality of performance.

To select our first objective, they applied these criteria:

- The goal had to be important to our network's customers.
- It had to relate to a gap between our stated values and our everyday performance—a gap between the ideal and the real.
- Every person, no matter what his or her job, had to be able to participate in it and contribute to it.
- The objective had to be attainable, concrete enough for everyone to understand, behavioral enough for everyone to make some changes, and within people's power to make those changes.
- And if everyone contributed to it, the results would have to be impressive and noticeable to customers—in short, a breakthrough.

Applying these criteria, the alignment team selected as our network's first values objective "first impressions last," with the goal of improving the process of meeting and greeting customers in every nook and cranny of our network. In the next four months, a first impressions steering committee built and disseminated a process by which every work team in our network of more than four thousand people developed or improved the *job-specific* greeting protocols they used to greet their particular customers. Also, the alignment team developed and promoted *"universal"* greeting protocols that everyone would use in public areas like hallways, elevators, the cafeteria, the parking lots, and so on.

To support people's efforts, the network's Organization and Staff Development Department, in conjunction with the "first impressions last" steering committee, developed a "tool kit" that detailed the process that work teams needed to follow, along with many resources to help them on their journey. We sponsored training for managers and staff on skills needed to approach the objective. We held rallies.

We developed recognition strategies for all teams to use. And we set up help clinics where teams and individuals could come for help with any and all problems they faced as they proceeded to improve the greeting processes in their work teams. The "first impressions last" steering committee sponsored an awareness-raising scavenger hunt, the First Impressions Dare (a mystery guest audit in contest form), and other events to keep awareness of greeting processes on the top of people's minds and also to celebrate what were by then obvious, visible improvements.

In hallways, elevators, and the cafeteria, people smiled and said "hello" to others. When you called another department, you could expect a friendly hello. The people who answered introduced themselves and asked how they could help. If you witnessed a patient entering an outpatient area, you would typically see the staff members welcome the patient and introduce themselves. The results were not perfect, but they were dramatic. We realized how much *easier* it is to promote behavior change when *everyone* in the organization is working on the same behavior, when there is one *single, simple focus.*

Since then, we have been identifying one values objective at a time and pursuing it as a network—all of us together. We've found this approach to be refreshing and effective. It does not overwhelm people because they have a single, easy-to-describe focus. And it does align people's efforts. All teams move in synch in the same direction—not at cross-purposes—and there is a powerful contagion related to the pursued objective that sweeps through the organization. Also, you can efficiently provide help, resources, and support along the way because everyone is working on the same process step at the same time. And, people learn from each other because one team's insights and tools are clearly adaptable to another's. And finally, you can see the results.

About This Book

We decided to write this book because of our excitement about this one-objective-at-a-time approach. It's powerful. It is a way to align many, many people's efforts, and that's not easy today when fragmentation, scattered attention, and multiple demands are the norm. We're hoping that people in hospitals, networks and systems, HMOs and other managed care organizations, alternative and complementary medicine programs, medical practices, ambulatory care centers, wellness and prevention services, long-term care facilities, and every other type of health care service can adapt the materials and approach described here to their goals and customers.

This book is a guide to help others pursue one service objective at a time, so that other organizations attracted to this approach don't have to reinvent the wheel. We recognize that not all organizations have the benefit of an Organization and Staff Development Department or other internal or external consultants or staff to develop and support strategies like these from scratch. Therefore, we provide here both a structure for one-goal-at-a-time strategies, and also the concrete resources and tools needed to pursue three specific goals key to service improvement and customer satisfaction in health care. Specifically, you'll find here the resources to pursue objectives relating to meeting and greeting, providing great explanations, and handling complaints effectively.

We hope the idea catches on with a vengeance and that everyone who tries it will then swap resources and approaches. Imagine the tool kit we would be able to build! So, if you decide to embrace one service objective at a time, please stay in touch and help grow the body of know-how to improve service one goal at a time for the sake of grateful customers. Address your questions and share your learning and results by writing to Wendy Leebov, Albert Einstein Healthcare Network, 5501 Old York Road, Philadelphia, PA, 19141, or by calling 215-456-7067 or faxing to 215-456-8353.

Acknowledgments

Many wonderful people helped us prepare to write this book, and many more supported us in the process. Thanks to all of the people of the Albert Einstein Healthcare Network team who paved the way and helped us learn from pursuit of breakthrough objectives within our values strategy. Gratitude to the leaders of the Einstein Network who supported the values work and helped to create its ripple effects throughout our network, particularly Martin Goldsmith, Janine Kilty, Susan Bernini, Ray Uhlhorn, and Jack Dembow.

Special thanks to Terry McGoldrick, who spearheaded the alignment team that first developed our one-goal-at-a-time approach and made sure the approach itself aligned with the JCAHO performance improvement process. Thanks to the creative, magic-making organization and staff development team: Kelly Yeager, Wes Hilton, Cynthia Jackson, Ron Kalstein, Ken Pugh, Denise McGill Boensch, Jackie Riley, Bill Johnson, and Ruth Fyne; thanks also to everyone on the first impressions team, the great explanations team, the respect team, and the tooling up for the future team who helped to develop and implement our one-goal-at-a-time strategies so far.

Thanks also to the many people who, over the years, have helped us to learn about service improvement, including colleagues in and clients of the Einstein Consulting Group, and the many, many change agents in health care organizations nationwide who have persistently pursued service quality improvement for the sake of patients and members.

Thanks also to our favorite editor, Audrey Kaufman of AHA Press, who sees promise in every seedling idea for a book and helps to grow it into something worth sharing.

And finally, thanks to our families and friends Florence and Mike Leebov, Nikki Gollub, Casey Goldston, Linda Goldston, Richard Presha, Steve Hyman, Mary Ellen Barnett, Joe and Gertrude Bowman, Lynne Kornblatt, John O'Hara, Julie Scenna, Fitzgibbons, and especially Julie Hyland for their enthusiasm, levity, inspiration, and encouragement throughout the writing process.

Wendy Leebov
Susan Afriat
Jeanne Presha

PART ONE

• • •

The Pursuit of Service Improvement

• • •

This section provides the rationale and frame-work for improving service one goal at a time.

- In chapter 1, "Using Breakthrough Objectives to Drive Service Improvement," you'll find an explanation of the concept of breakthrough objectives and the features that cause them to be powerful drivers of service improvement.

- In chapter 2, "Tools for Planning Your Service Improvement Pursuits," you'll find simple step-by-step processes that help you select and plan for one objective at a time. You'll learn how to use a decision matrix to pick the next objective on which you want to focus. Also, we will describe alternative ways you can provide leadership and coordination for your strategy—depending on the size and scope of your organization—so that your strategy reaches every nook and cranny of your organization or service.

- In chapter 3, "The 10-Step Service Improvement Process," we'll introduce you to a generic process that you can apply to any objective you choose. You'll also find a description of several powerful ways to support individuals and teams as they follow this process in pursuit of their objectives. And specifically, we'll describe in generic terms the kinds of concrete tools you'll find in part 2, where we present do-it-yourself kits for pursuing three specific service objectives. We'll describe tools that help you provide training, practice, and coaching to teams and individuals in need of it, and tools that help you recognize and reinforce individuals and teams who implement improvements and achieve positive results.

Chapter 1

· · ·

Using Breakthrough Objectives to Drive Service Improvement

Health care organizations have focused in the last few years primarily on cost reduction, reengineering, mergers and acquisitions, and repositioning for managed care. Because these changes have been wrenching and distracting, they have threatened the quality of service delivered by the organizations and their people, with consequences on patient and staff satisfaction. As costs have evened out and consumer choice has remained a hallmark of our emerging managed care system, health care leaders are once again concerned about increasing their organization's competitiveness by achieving distinctive *service*—service that attracts payers and consumers.

While many health care organizations—including hospitals, ambulatory care centers, medical practices, networks, systems, managed care organizations, nursing homes, home care agencies, and the like—have occasionally focused staff attention on service improvement, even those most advanced in their approaches recognize the need to focus attention on service improvement repeatedly and redundantly. If you ever let up, service slips, consumers protest, and the organization loses favor in the eyes of its customers.

Yes, But . . .

In today's turbulent environment, health care professionals and administrators are on serious overload. Understandably, managers and staff alike resist going all out to improve service. They resist

3

implementing complex strategies to improve service because these strategies demand so much energy, time, and attention. If people *don't do* all of what they need to do, the strategy falls apart. And if they *do* all that they need to do, they don't get their other important work done. They have too little time available to carry out their multiple responsibilities and achieve the great productivity expected of them. There are throngs of people in health care who want to be wonderful to patients and other customers. When faced with carrying out plans to improve service, however, they often feel frustrated, conflicted, and even guilt stricken because they value the effort but can't find the time. Also, when strategies are complex, people become confused about what they're supposed to be doing, so they don't do it.

So, given work overload combined with the wrenching changes health care services and employees are experiencing, how can you continue your relentless pursuit of service quality without further aggravating the feeling of oppression that so many employees are already experiencing?

Improve service in a manageable, doable way by focusing everyone's attention and energy on *one simple aspect of quality service at a time.* Build on the concept of "breakthrough objectives" developed by Japanese thinkers within the framework of Hoshin Planning.

What Is a *Breakthrough Objective?*

A breakthrough objective is an objective that *everybody* can contribute to, no matter what their job. It is the shining metal compass that points direction toward one unifying objective. And, if everyone makes even a small incremental improvement toward that objective, it adds up to a breakthrough because of the *cumulative impact* of everyone making an improvement on the same thing. If everyone in the organization is focusing on reducing cycle time and speeding up service, for example, and if every step in a service process is shortened by even five minutes, the cumulative effect of all those five-minute savings is a substantial reduction in the length of the overall process; this will have a positive impact on cost and customer satisfaction. You would not see that impact if different teams were focusing on different service dimensions.

In the book *Breakthrough Leadership,* Mara Melum and Casey Collett describe Hoshin Planning approaches in detail. They cite five features of Hoshin Planning that explain why breakthrough objectives are so powerful:

1. Focus
2. Alignment
3. Collective knowledge
4. Empowered employees
5. Enhanced teamwork[1]

Focus

Let's look at these one at a time, starting with *focus*. A breakthrough objective is by definition a focus for the organization. Employees in most organizations have too much to do and too little time in which to do it. As a result they burn out and complain about being over-stretched and disrespected. By selecting one goal at a time, management helps people move forward without feeling overwhelmed. Having a single-minded focus enables people to remember what they're working toward and simplifies the demands on their attention. Also, by having to choose one focus at a time, management is pressured to select what's most important—to stop saying, "I want it all" and say instead, "I want from you this *one* important thing!"

You've probably heard about the Pareto principle. It started out as an economic principle describing how wealth was distributed (that 20 percent of the people had 80 percent of the money), but has since been implied in an intuitive way to all sorts of situations. For instance, according to the Pareto principle, 20 percent of your effort leads to 80 percent of your impact. Twenty percent of staff create 80 percent of customer dissatisfaction. Twenty percent of your life experiences probably led to 80 percent of your learning. Application to many other situations seems intuitive. Applied to service improvement in a health care organization, the Pareto principle suggests that focusing on 20 percent of the aspects of service that customers care about will lead to 80 percent improvement—if the 20 percent that you work on reflects the "vital few" service features that matter to customers, not the "trivial many." By adopting one breakthrough objective at a time, you force yourself to focus on the vital few. This increases your opportunity to create a powerful impact.

Alignment

Breakthrough objectives also help to align the organization. Imagine that the arrows in the following diagram reflect people's energy. If some people's energies go in one direction and other people's energies go in different directions, look at how the energy dissipates.

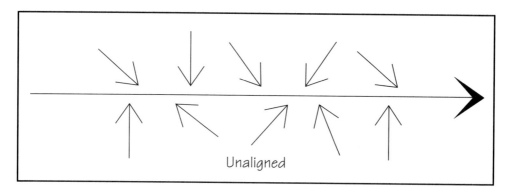

On the other hand, if everyone's energies are focused in the same direction, the energy is cumulative and powerful, as shown in the diagram below.

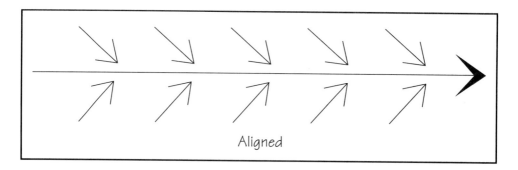

The same diagrams could apply as well to systems or networks. Some entities or facilities or teams might be going in one direction, and others might be taking different roads. Or, people in different roles might be moving in various directions. For instance, hospitality service personnel might be working on a service goal like better meeting and greeting, while nurses are minimizing its importance when they compare this to the goals they are pursuing. When people in different entities, different jobs, and different levels adopt one objective together, the destructive aspects of pecking orders diminish and people see each other as all one team. When this occurs, people show unity in their values and focus.

Collective Knowledge

A wonderful thing about pursuing one breakthrough objective at a time is that people can help each other and learn from each other because everyone is working on the same thing. Why, after all, should every manager have to reinvent the wheel? If you think of a great approach, knowing about it would probably help me, too. For instance, if you develop a great evaluation device, others probably can benefit by using or adapting it. We would end up with a better outcome because we contributed to each other's effectiveness along the way. When all personnel in a health care organization pursue a breakthrough objective together, group learning happens naturally through organized meetings where people share problems and approaches. Teams create pools of collective wisdom that become resources to the organization immediately and forever—all because people are pursuing the same objective.

Empowered Employees

When everyone is working on the same objective, goals and accountability are in everyone's minds. Because of the public commitment to the goal, when employees take initiative to make an improvement, it is that much less likely that their supervisor will challenge their initiative and actions by saying, "Who told you to do that?" or "Why didn't you get my permission?" The goal is public. People know what they can and cannot do. People share responsibility for getting there. And this helps employees feel empowered to take action and initiative to contribute.

Enhanced Teamwork

Clear expectations and clear communication lead to trust, and trust leads to teamwork. By adopting one breakthrough objective at a time, all the employees know what's expected of them *and* what they can expect of each other. They are less likely to work at cross-purposes and less likely to question one another's behavior and motives. When there are handoffs from one staff person to another, as are rampant in health care, enhanced teamwork results in people having the same objective driving their behavior. There is more continuity from person to person and less dropping of the ball. By working together toward the same end, they have common goals, engage in strategies in common, and share results of mutual interest. All of this breeds trust and harmony.

Visible Results

We want to add a sixth compelling feature of breakthrough objectives to Hoshin Planning's five, and that is "visible results." When people are working on many different goals, it is less likely that there will be any whopping results for any individual effort. Also, there's a lot going on at once, and all of it is competing for people's attention. With breakthrough objectives, because everyone is already focused on the objective, people notice the results without others having to demand or command their attention. The shared goal heightens people's awareness, and they notice without being hounded to pay attention. Then, as people notice the results, they are further encouraged. Everyone gets to see and celebrate success, and this sparks people's energies even further. Positive ripple effects occur. Visible successes breed more successes. And staff see and feel, "We do make a difference!"

Conclusion

Focus, alignment, collective knowledge, empowered employees, enhanced teamwork, and visible results—all attributes of service improvement strategies that focus on breakthrough objectives lead to benefits for customers, benefits that overpower those that accrue from different people pursuing different goals.

Reference

1. Mara Minerva Melum and Casey Collett, *Breakthrough Leadership: Achieving Organizational Alignment through Hoshin Planning* (Chicago: American Hospital Publishing, 1995), p. 5.

Chapter 2

• • •

Tools for Planning Your Service Improvement Pursuits

So, how do you begin? Start by picking your service objectives. To pick high-impact objectives, you'll need to pinpoint priorities—objectives with the greatest potential impact or the "vital few among the trivial many." Here's a straightforward process for doing this:

How to Pick Objectives

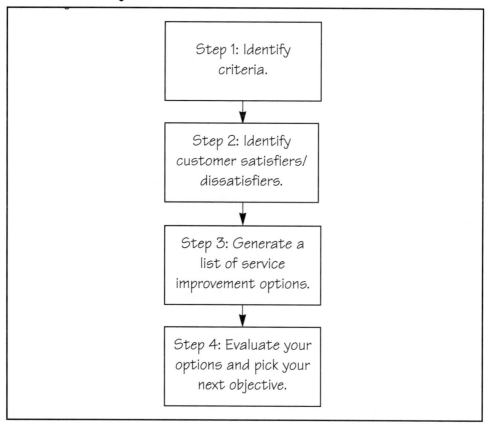

Step 1: Identify criteria.

Step 2: Identify customer satisfiers/dissatisfiers.

Step 3: Generate a list of service improvement options.

Step 4: Evaluate your options and pick your next objective.

Step 1: Identify Criteria for Selecting Which Objective You Want to Pursue

Depending on the size of your team and the nature of your organization, you should be able to do this in a short discussion with the people on your management team and/or your staff. Propose a list of possible criteria to get people thinking. Then, ask them to discuss and fix the list to their liking. Here's a list of possible criteria for picking one out of many possible objectives:

Possible Criteria for Picking an Objective

- The objective should be one that everyone can contribute to, no matter what their job. Physicians, housekeepers, nurses, finance people, and everyone else should *all* be able to contribute to this objective.
- The objective should be one that is *important to customers.* If we become *great* at it, customer satisfaction will increase.
- The objective should be one that affords *plenty of room for improvement.*
- The objective should be *tangible and definable.* You should be able to describe it in specific or behavioral terms. It can be defined so that everyone has the same understanding of it. It doesn't mean different things to different people (like "improve staff attitudes").
- We will be able to *know if we make improvements* on it. Improvements on it are somehow measurable.
- If everyone makes improvements on the objective, even small ones, it will add up to a big, noticeable improvement.
- The objective is *doable.* People on the team should have the power and ability to make changes on it. ("Move facility to different neighborhood or city" would score low here.)

Step 2: Identify Customer Satisfiers and Dissatisfiers

Learn from customers what satisfies and dissatisfies them. Ask them about their priorities. Ideally, first conduct customer focus groups or interviews with customers in which you *listen, listen, listen* to what's important to them. Find out their improvement priorities for your service by asking questions like the following:

- What about your experience with us was important to you?
- What impressed you during your experience with us?
- What distressed you? What caused you worry or anxiety or frustration or stress?
- What is your wish list of improvements we need to make in order to improve the experience of our future patients/members?
- Looking at this list, if we could make improvements in only two or three of these, which two or three would you hope we would improve, because they are the most important?

If your organization has access to marketing, market research, customer service, or quality improvement specialists, consider doing a quantitative survey in which you propose the options to many more health care consumers (both former patients and prospects). Do a correlation study of which service factors are most highly correlated to people's overall satisfaction with their health care experience. This will give you a good idea of what a more representative group thinks your service's improvement priorities should be. Look also at the satisfaction surveys you already do and especially scrutinize the repetitive complaints your service receives from customers. These methods will produce for you a list of service improvement options that you then need to evaluate using the criteria for picking a good, powerful breakthrough objective.

Step 3: Generate a List of Service Improvement Options

Drawing on what you learned from contacts with customers (in interviews, focus groups, analysis of complaints, and satisfaction surveys) *and* drawing on discussion with staff about what they think needs to improve in the way of service, make a list of options—objectives it would make sense for your team to pursue.

Sample Service Improvement Options

- Improve meeting and greeting
- Improve privacy and confidentiality
- Decrease noise
- Increase responsiveness to customer requests

- Improve written communications
- Improve handling of complaints
- Speed up service
- Make it easier for people to find their way
- Improve internal customer relationships

Step 4: Evaluate the Options and Pick Your Next Objective

Once you have your criteria, make a decision matrix and use it to get a quick reading from your team on which objectives win when evaluated against your criteria.

Sample Decision Matrix

Criteria: (Rate 1 to 4 with 1 = weak, 4 = strong)						
Options	All can contribute	Important to customers	Room to improve	Doable	Could impress!	Totals
Meet/greet						
Privacy/ confidentiality						
Noise reduction						
Responsiveness to requests						
Written communications						
Complaint handling						
Service speed						
Way finding						

To make a decision matrix, follow these six steps:

1. In the left column of a sheet of paper or piece of flipchart paper, list your service improvement options.
2. Along the top, write in your criteria for evaluating the options.

3. Figure out a scoring system, for instance: Rate each option on each criterion using a 4-point scale, with "1" being the lowest score ("weak" on that criterion) and "4" being the highest score ("strong" on that criterion).
4. Include a "Totals" column on the right.
5. Copy this chart so everyone can fill it in independently. Engage lots of people because the more investment you have in the objective you choose, the better, Explain the decision chart and ask people to fill it in. Then, tally up everyone's individual ratings into a group profile such as the one below:

Sample Group Profile of Service Improvement Goal Preferences

Tally of Four Employees for a Possible Total of 80						
Options	All can contribute	Important to customers	Room to improve	Doable	Could impress!	Total
Meet/greet	16	16	16	16	16	80
Privacy/ confidentiality	13	10	10	12	10	55
Noise reduction	16	8	10	8	8	50
Responsiveness to requests	16	16	13	10	16	71
Written communications	10	12	16	12	12	62
Complaint handling	13	16	12	8	16	65
Service speed	16	16	16	8	16	72
Way finding	16	16	12	14	13	71

6. Then, have your team look at the results and react to them. Sometimes, the results strike people as "right" and they say, "Let's go ahead with the winning objective." Other times, the results don't sit right with people, and they move the group to a deeper discussion often leading to the addition of an important criterion that needs to be on the chart. Or, someone may want to influence people's ratings on one dimension or another. Encourage group discussion until the group reaches consensus on a good objective.

How to Organize Your Work on a Breakthrough Objective: Alternative Leadership Structures

Your challenge is to structure your strategy so that it reaches and embraces every person in your organization, no matter what your organization's size. Needless to say, this is a lot more difficult the bigger your organization is. Before launching a service objective, establish a leadership structure that enables you to reach everyone. This is a big and important decision.

To begin, identify leadership for your effort: whether this is an individual, a steering committee, or a multilevel structure. Strategy leaders will need to digest, discuss, and tailor your service improvement activities. Then they will plan the details, including who to involve, when to involve them, and the timeline for your approach. They will also need to figure out the division of labor, including who will facilitate meetings, who will communicate, and how every part of the strategy will be coordinated and disseminated. The goal of all this is to reach everyone and draw them into the process in meaningful ways.

The next sections discuss the three functions that must be served by your project leadership structure and are followed by several examples of such structure in action.

Project Manager

Have one person serve as project manager—someone who oversees the pursuit of your objective by organizing people who need to be involved in the planning process; amassing needed resources; doing ongoing communications; troubleshooting; and being the point person for problems, needs, plans and follow-up. You probably know who the right person is for this role. Perhaps it's you. In a medical practice or service (like a heart center, cancer center, imaging center, or so on), it might be a physician champion or office manager or nurse enthusiast. In a hospital or network, it might be someone in training or organization development, patient relations, marketing, or human resources. Or perhaps an administrator or line manager who is a service enthusiast would be the appropriate choice. It needs to be someone who can plan, organize, coordinate, follow through, and motivate.

Steering Committee or Team

In a small service (if your team has 10 people or fewer), this might be the only other infrastructure you need. This group figures out your specific plan, schedule, and activities. They plan and implement the needed communications with others in your service. And they locate and make available needed resources. Then, as people proceed through the steps in your approach, they collect results, monitor what's going on, troubleshoot, report, and focus people's attention on the improvements. The best members to choose for this group are people who first of all are *willing* to do this because of some degree of enthusiasm for helping people make change and pursue your breakthrough objective. In addition, make sure the steering committee consists of opinion leaders—people who have some pied piper ability to attract a following—to engage people as allies in pursuing the objective. In short, select people with the power to motivate. You'll also need people with different competencies, such as writing, resource finding, creativity, and organizational skills, so they can help to do the work that's involved in spearheading a breakthrough objective. And, if your organization is hierarchical, don't forget to include people from different levels.

Subgroups within the Team

You might also want to form committees, subcommittees, or miniteams to focus on particular aspects of the plan to pursue the objective. There are several different ways to organize these subcommittees. You can form them by *task,* such as having a subcommittee for protocol design, a subcommittee for recognition, and a subcommittee to plan an awareness-raising rally. You can also form them by *position* to work on job-specific protocols. Or maybe you want to form subcommittees by *customer group* so that people in different positions who relate to the same customers can coordinate their efforts. In a larger organization, you can form subcommittees by *supervisor* so that a supervisor or designee is responsible for the work of his or her respective work teams. Yet another option is to have a manager be responsible for the design and evaluation process steps, invite staff input and reactions, and help staff during implementation.

Examples of Project Leadership Structures

The following three scenarios describe the project leadership structure in three different types of organizations: a hospital department, a clinical service, and a medical practice.

- A hospital's materials management department consists of linen, mail room, storeroom, and print shop. A representative (or subgroup) from each section served on the materials management steering committee for pursuit of the objective: better meeting and greeting. These subgroups were the development teams who worked on improvements for their own specialty areas: one for linen, one for mail room, one for storeroom, and one for print shop.
- In a clinical service, the director and an enthusiastic nurse together formed a steering committee to champion and lead the process of improving confidentiality. The steering committee at times formed ad hoc subgroups to involve different staff in design work or such initiatives as a mystery visitor miniproject (see chapter 7 for an example) and implementation of a recognition method.
- The office manager and a physician champion of a medical practice worked together to steer a strategy to improve explanations to patients. They formed a committee of three others—people from billing, registration, and nursing—and worked out the plans and resources. The five of them then divided up the work and ran the process.

Project Leadership Structures in a Large Organization: A Case Study

In a large organization, such as an entire hospital, nursing home, or health care system, a more complex structure than those presented in the previous examples is needed. Albert Einstein Healthcare Network developed a structure that proved highly effective. It consisted of a project manager, a steering committee, core group leaders, core groups, buddies, and a team of people from the network's Organization and Staff Development Department. Here's how it worked.

Strategy Infrastructure for a Large Organization

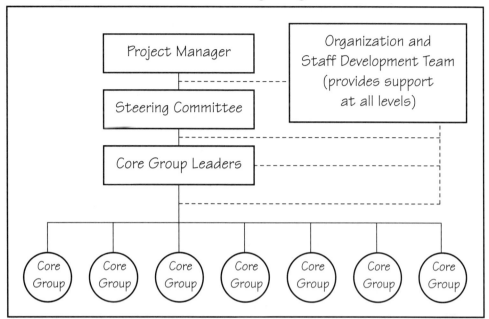

The *project manager* from the network's Organization and Staff Development Department led the whole strategy, organizing a steering committee, convening its meetings, keeping watch over timelines, delegating work, overseeing production of materials and scheduling of events, and managing communications.

The *steering committee* consisted of a mix of 15 or so people enthusiastic about the service objective and also representative of the different organizational entities and divisions of this network. The steering committee served as the main planning team for the entire strategy by developing the creative aspects, planning for rallies and events, guiding the development of needed tools and training, and actively disseminating communications throughout the organization.

Then, every department and/or work team identified *a core group leader or two.* Core group leaders were responsible for leading their department or work team through the strategy. They served as liaison between the steering committee and their work team. They formed subcommittees, facilitated team meetings, and provided leadership and support to people within their teams working on design and implementation of team-specific improvements. Usually, department directors selected a highly respected supervisor or energetic, influential line staff person to serve as core group leader.

In conjunction with the steering committee, the network's Organization and Staff Development Department provided up-front orientation and training for core group leaders. The team gave them an overview of the strategy and plan, specific expectations of them, the steps involved in the process for their work teams, and the kinds of support available to them to help them lead their work teams through the process.

Most core group leaders, especially those with large work teams or departments, then formed core groups within their work areas. These groups worked like subcommittees, coordinating and implementing the improvement process with their coworkers on the work team. The organization and staff development team also provided an orientation session for core group members so they would have a clear overview of the entire approach, an understanding of their relationships with the core group leader, their roles as core group members, and knowledge of available support and resources. Then, at different stages of the 10-step process, the organization and staff development team reconvened core group leaders for progress reports, an orientation to the next several steps in the process, and sharing of lessons learned and mutual advice.

This model worked well because the ultimate leaders of the strategy at the work team level were frontline people and/or respected supervisors. By encouraging department managers to select as core group leaders and core group members people suited to leadership, respected by peers, and interested in the objective at hand, the core group structure served to mobilize people effectively as they tackled department-specific priorities.

Conclusion

Before you launch into a breakthrough service objective, convene a group of key people and figure out the best infrastructure for *your* service improvement strategies. Be sure to include enthusiasts in key roles as well as opinion leaders—highly respected staff members who, when they lead, others follow.

Chapter 3

$\bullet\ \bullet\ \bullet$

The 10-Step Service Improvement Process

If you plan to pursue one strategy after another, adopt a generic process that you'll apply to every objective—an iterative process. By applying the same process to every objective, you and your team will benefit from a learning curve. You will all become familiar with the approach and need less guidance as the steps become clearer and more predictable.

Because some of your organizations and services are subject to review by the Joint Commission for the Accreditation of Healthcare Organizations, we're recommending a service improvement process that is highly consistent with the performance improvement process advocated by the Joint Commission. By using this, you kill two birds with one stone: You have a comprehensive, repetitive, and soon familiar approach to improvement, and you also can present your breakthrough objectives projects as case studies of performance improvement when the Joint Commission pays you an accreditation call.

Here's the process we recommend. It's a road map for every work team to follow in hot pursuit of a breakthrough objective. By instituting this process as the skeletal framework for your strategy, you can effectively mobilize everyone to pursue the shared goal in a synchronized and coordinated way.

The 10-Step Service Improvement Process

Step 1: Focus people on your service objective and build commitment.

Step 2: Take stock of current performance and set priorities and targets.

Step 3: Attack priorities and design the improvements.

Step 4: Communicate improvements and new expectations to all staff.

Step 5: Equip staff with needed tools and skills.

Step 6: Do a trial run, assess performance, and use feedback to improve the improvements.

Step 7: Institute the improvements and build new habits.

Step 8: Check performance against targets.

Step 9: Share experiences and results. Learn from each other and celebrate successes.

Step 10: Institute ongoing methods for sustaining top-notch performance.

In the following sections we describe each step of the process in detail. We also describe the kinds of tools that aid in the fulfillment of each. Concrete examples of these tools can be found in the next three chapters, which are "do-it-yourself" kits that deal with three specific service improvement efforts.

Step 1: Focus People on Your Service Objective and Build Commitment

Leaders and staff need to get on board with your service objective. Of course, their input into *selection* of the objective will go far to develop their investment in the objective. In addition, leaders will need to take steps to focus *themselves* squarely on and educate themselves about the objective. Then, they/you need to focus staff on the objective, using memos, campaigns, staff meetings, and any creative awareness-raising methods your team can dream up.

To help you implement this step, we provide helpful tools for each objective addressed in this book. We suggest engaging and informing your boss and other key people who are outside of your service but who nonetheless affect it of your selected objective and rationale. To accomplish this, we provide a meeting format and the handouts you need for a meeting of everyone in management and supervisory positions so that they can unite around the objective, understand the plans, and prepare to help their work teams get involved. We also provide a staff meeting format and all necessary materials that team leaders can use to orient all staff to the new service objective. We provide a "service improvement alert," which is a written fact sheet you can distribute to everyone to reinforce facts about your rationale for selecting the particular goal, a definition of the goal, and a summary of your approach. And, we suggest an "energy builder"—an activity designed to generate enthusiasm for the objective among staff.

Step 2: Take Stock of Current Performance and Set Priorities and Targets

To begin this step, you need a measure of baseline performance. How effective are people's current practices related to this objective? And what quantitative goal do you strive to meet through your improvement efforts? To accomplish this, use any measures you currently have in place, such as pertinent patient survey questions. But, in case you have no such measures in place, the following chapters provide a simple service report card you can use to establish a baseline level of performance.

Then, although your overall goal might be clear, each work team needs to examine the overall goal as it affects their particular customers and their particular practices with these customers. Every work team needs to figure out how, where, and when the overall objective applies to their work. They need to pinpoint their own specific priorities or subgoals needed for their customers and functions. To help work teams set such priorities, a variety of methods can be used, including focus group protocols, staff meeting formats, and other analytical tools for pinpointing job- and team-specific priorities. No matter what the method, questions like these help teams set their own priorities.

Where Are Our Opportunities to Work on This Goal?

- Which customers are involved?
- Which staff are involved with those customers?

- What functions do the staff perform when involved with these customers?
- Which steps in the service process are we talking about?
- How are we currently doing with each of these key customer groups on this goal?
- What are *our specific needs* related to this goal? What do *we* need to improve? Given our jobs and our team's contributions to service delivery and customers, what should our priorities be?

Consider as an example a women and children's services team that has as its objective improving the quality of explanations given to customers. At this step in the process, the team must figure out which staff members play a role in meeting each customer group's information needs, and in which circumstances. They also need to pinpoint the specific work contexts in which improvements need to be made. Once they do this, they can identify the customers involved and what these customers want. So they might pinpoint mammography patients and new parents whose satisfaction with staff explanations fails to meet established targets. They decide that, while other patient information needs are important, explanations related to these two customer groups should receive top priority for improvement. They then focus on subgoals within the overall goal that are meaningful to them in their particular jobs, such as better explaining mammography to a person experiencing one for the first time, better explaining the need for uncomfortable pressure during a mammogram, better explain breast-feeding and options in the event of problems.

Step 3: Attack Priorities and Design the Improvements

After setting priorities for improvement, teams need to do design work. They need to rethink the processes that need improvement. In the case of improving explanations, they need to examine the explanations used currently and either refine them or develop a new version that better serves customer needs. Staff need to identify customers' information needs, learn from customers how best to meet these needs, and redesign the materials or face-to-face explanations they think need improvement. They need to decide exactly how key explanations should be delivered from then on and develop the actual materials or write down protocols as job aids for the appropriate staff.

For this design phase, we provide what we call "universal protocols," which are guidelines for top-notch performance related to the specific objective. For instance, related to improving explanations, we provide a universally applicable framework for structuring a good explanation—the "Anatomy of a Great Explanation." And we provide protocols for writing a good explanatory memo, writing effective patient education materials, explaining procedures to colleagues, and several other tasks. We also provide a step-by-step approach for helping staff develop job-specific protocols, which go farther than universal protocols by applying to specific customer needs within particular jobs and functions. For instance, a human resources generalist might have a protocol for explaining insurance benefits to employees; a physician might have a protocol for explaining preoperative informed consent; a phone operator might have a protocol for explaining how a visitor can travel to the health center from a variety of starting points.

We also provide job aids, or suggest a format for producing them, so that staff can have at their fingertips cards, signs, or other reminders of the new protocols, scripts, or steps they are to follow in order to make the improvements.

Step 4: Communicate Improvements and New Expectations to All Staff

Once the design work is done and the improvements are ready to "go live," you, your steering committee, or your team leaders need to convene everyone and communicate the changes/improvements and the reasons for them, as well as exactly what role each person is expected to play to implement the improvements. If the goal is to improve explanations, each staff member needs to know the explanations that have been developed and which ones they need to use with which customers and in which circumstances. The team distributes the "new" protocols (which by then should not be new to people, as they should have helped design them), and communicates that, starting on a particular date, *everyone* is expected to start using them with *every* appropriate customer. The following list offers some general tips for communicating expectations effectively:

Communicating What's Expected

- Say it to the team, all together.
- Make a big poster, "Don't forget: From today on, we're all supposed to _____."
- And say it in a memo, too. By stating your expectations for changed behavior in a memo, you have the documentation you need *in case* you ever need to follow through in a progressive discipline process. The person in question cannot defensibly say, "I wasn't clear about what you expected."
- Have supervisors talk with each person who reports to them, inviting and discussing questions and concerns. This is an excellent way to head off resistance and generate enthusiasm and involvement.

The "do-it-yourself" kits also provide a staff meeting format for communicating new expectations.

Step 5: Equip Staff with Needed Skills and Tools

Since we're talking about changing people's ways, many people might need to build new skills. This might involve polishing the use of protocols in specific customer interactions or learning to use judgment and discretion in more situations. During this step, use training, coaching, support groups, and practice exercises using case scenarios. We provide in the *do-it-yourself kits* three kinds of aids: help clinics, management prompts, and skill builders.

Help Clinics

Help clinics are "just-in-time" and "just-for-you" opportunities to seek help from skilled resource people. Who can staff the help clinics? Advertise skills you think you'll need and ask for volunteers. For instance, when pursuing the improvement of explanations, find volunteers to help edit new materials, react to protocols during trial runs, format written explanations and job aids on computer, print signs for public areas, and much more. Then advertise specific help clinics focusing on particular skills. In order to attract people with a broader range of problems or requests, hold open-ended help clinics staffed by the steering committee. If your service is part of a larger organization, seek specialists there accessible to you for this purpose, such as writers, marketing people, trainers, and the like. If not, identify people on your team with special talents and a willingness to help others. Formalizing this helping opportunity by calling it a *help clinic* and scheduling times for it makes it much more likely that people will write it in their calendars and show up with their problem defined and with the motivation to solve it. We suggest these in the do-it-yourself kits to support particularly challenging steps in the improvement process.

Management Prompts

These are reminders and props designed to help every member of your management team engage in key actions that boost staff morale and help them stay on course. People with authority over others in your service need to pay attention by indicating interest in what people are doing, asking questions, giving feedback about processes, and recognizing people for their efforts. If they do, staff remain all the more energized to persist in their improvement work. Management prompts are specific instructions that tell managers exactly what they need to do at pivotal moments in your service improvement process.

Skill Builders

These are short training workshops that can be delivered during staff meetings to build skills key to staff effectiveness related to the objective at hand. We provide a series of these associated with each breakthrough service objective so that team leaders, members of your steering committee, or someone available to you with facilitation skills can help staff tool up for top performance and sustain it over the long run.

Step 6: Do a Trial Run, Assess Performance, and Use Feedback to Improve the Improvements

The changes are now designed, and they need to be tested in an experimental implementation period during which you identify and iron out the kinks. You invite people to try them out and see how they work and feel. You scrutinize the changes and trouble-shoot them.

For this step, we provide examples of "ticklers"—written reminders that show people how many days they've been at the changes and how many days they have to go. We suggest another round of global customer feedback using a service report card as well as feedback related to improvements specific to each work team. We provide reinforcement and coaching methods to boost people along. In addition, we provide meeting formats for use with work teams to help them examine customer response to the changes and use this feedback to refine their improvements.

Step 7: Institute the Improvements and Build New Habits

Following the idea that it takes 21 days of persistent behavior change to build a new habit (to become semiautomatic in a task), we adopted a 21-day habit-building period in our network. Old habits die hard, and this period gives people the opportunity to develop the required new habits through practicing them consistently. Many well-designed changes are deemed failures when the real problem was that they were never consistently or fully implemented! Maybe people adopted the change at the start but then regressed to their previous behavior. Had the changes been implemented persistently, they would have certainly produced positive results. That's why this step explicitly focuses on *holding the gains,* on persistent implementation that requires self-discipline, considerable pushing, nudging, reminders, feedback, and oversight. If your objective is to improve explanations, it's at this step that you expect staff to begin using their newly improved explanations with each and every appropriate customer. The goal is to make improved explanations automatic.

Step 8: Check Improvements against Targets

At this step, use either the global service report card again or the pertinent quantitative measures of performance related to this objective. Compare scores with their targets for improvement, going back to the drawing board to make further improvements if you do not see progress. In the next chapters we provide a memo and staff meeting format in which next steps are announced and data about performance are compared to performance targets.

Step 9: Share Experiences and Results, Learn from Each Other, and Celebrate Successes

At this step, people working on various teams—or even individuals working in various positions—get together to share results, compare notes, and discuss their perceptions of the changes, high points, low points, and learning along the way. This provides a chance for the group to learn from their collective experience. A straightforward approach like the following one does the trick.

Learn from the Experience

Convene your team and help them process their experience and learn from it. Ask such questions as:

- What were the high points in the process we used to make the improvements?
- What was frustrating?
- Based on what worked in our process this time, what about the process should we repeat with our next objective?
- Based on our process this time, what changes would you suggest for next time? What would make us more effective?

Here we suggest report formats, bulletin board displays, story sharing, and recognition methods that help to call attention to your goal and people's accomplishments in a dramatic way.

Step 10: Institute Ongoing Methods for Sustaining Top-Notch Performance

Even if all went well and you have measurable improvements that everyone feels good about, you can't rest on your laurels. Plan for ongoing monitoring and feedback so that you can make sure people hold the gains and if not, make course corrections. This step is essential in order to avoid a one-time fix-it campaign and instead install a *continuous* improvement process.

We recommend three other follow-through actions as well:

1. Build into your hiring process a method for screening applicants so that you hire people good at this service objective. If you hire people good at it, you don't have to train, train, train or address performance problems later.
2. Add to all job descriptions and your performance appraisal process an explicit expectation related to this objective. Since these objectives were selected partly because everyone *could and should* contribute to them in order for the organization to provide impeccable service, the defined standards of performance should really become job expectations. We provide job description statements and wording for incorporation of the service standards into your performance review process.
3. Keep awareness high. Remember the old saying, "Out of sight, out of mind." For this step, we provide awareness campaigns and "skill builder" modules for staff meetings to help coach staff to first of all remember to pay attention to this service attribute and also to enhance their skills over time.

These methods provide ongoing impetus to keep people's attention on the service aspects of their jobs—and this is essential to producing lasting results.

Conclusion

While it is work for your steering committee to develop tools and process support for work teams, it increases the probability that work teams will agree with the improvement process and take responsibility for moving it forward. If there are too many demands on their time, many people become disheartened by trying to figure out on their own how to do every step of the process, and they end up dismissing it as just another burden. All of the above process tools cut down on demands you're making on staff time and creative energy. These tools prevent people from getting bogged down in developing processes. Instead, by providing support and tools throughout the process, you protect people's time, leaving the maximum available for them to do the actual improvement work.

PART TWO

• • •

Do-It-Yourself Kits
for Pursuing Three Specific
Service Objectives

• • •

The next three chapters are do-it-yourself kits for pursuing the following three service objectives:

- Improving First Impressions
- Improving Explanations to Customers
- Improving Service Recovery (Complaint Management)

Each do-it-yourself kit provides you with a step-by-step guide and the concrete resource you need to pursue the specific breakthrough objective with your team. Each kit follows the 10-step improvement process outlined in chapter 3.

Step 1:   Focus your people on your service objective and build commitment.

Step 2:   Take stock of your team's current performance and set priorities and targets for improvement.

Step 3:   Attack priorities. Design improvements.

Step 4:   Communicate improvements and new expectations to staff.

Step 5:   Equip staff with needed tools and skills.

Step 6:   Do a trial run, assess performance, and improve the improvements.

Step 7:   Institute the improvements and build new habits.

Step 8:   Check performance against targets.

Step 9:   Share experiences and results. Learn from each other and celebrate successes.

Step 10:   Institute ongoing methods for sustaining top-notch performance.

For each objective, you'll find background information, including its rationale, benefits, and definition. Then, after an overview of the 10-step service improvement process *tailored* to the objective at hand, you'll find instructions for proceeding through each step. These instructions include key actions and the tools needed to complete them.

Respecting how busy you and your colleagues are, we have developed these do-it-yourself kits so that they require a minimum of customization. Hopefully, you'll be able to use most of the recommended tools as is. But inevitably, in some cases, you and your steering committee will need to modify and adapt the tools to your own people and circumstances. And in other cases, you'll find that you'll be able to omit key actions such as "focus managers in an orientation meeting," especially if your service is small and does not have a layered authority structure.

So, we hope you, your project manager, and your steering committee will read through each do-it-yourself kit thoroughly and pick and choose exactly what you will do, adapting and customizing as needed as you go along.

Why these objectives? These objectives are important to health care customers and widely applicable to all types of health care services.

If your process of selecting important objectives results in selection of *different* objectives than those we chose to address, you can still benefit greatly from these do-it-yourself kits. By examining the tools provided here, you'll quickly see that they are adaptable to other objectives.

Chapter 4

• • •

Do-It-Yourself Kit for Improving First Impressions

"Improving first impressions" is a great *first* objective, not only because your team can address it quickly, but also because it is so concrete that everyone understands it. For these reasons, it provides an easy way to teach people about breakthrough service objectives and also demonstrates the powerful, visible impact of having everyone work together in an aligned way in pursuit of the same objective.

Background Information on First Impressions

The "first impressions" objective stems from a recognition of the power and importance of building rapport immediately in relationships with customers. There is research indicating that customers form first impressions within the first six seconds of interactions with a service provider. And the first impressions they form are stubbornly resistant to change. If a customer perceives a service provider as warm and welcoming, the customer relaxes and expects other interactions with that person and others in the chain of service delivery to be positive and helpful. On the other hand, if a customer perceives a service provider initially as unfriendly, impersonal, or unprofessional, the customer immediately becomes watchful and begins to distrust the service they're about to receive. Immediately, they lose a degree of confidence in the team providing the service.

While some might consider a focus on the first few seconds of an interaction trivial, it isn't, because of the power first impressions have over subsequent interactions. Does every individual on your team greet every customer with warmth, a welcoming manner, and obvious professionalism and respect? If not, there is not only room for improvement, but an opportunity to exert a powerful positive influence on customer experiences and perceptions of your service.

So, in summary, the better the first few seconds of an interaction, the more positive and harmonious the interactions that follow. And this makes the business at hand easier to accomplish, the service easier to deliver, and the customer easier to satisfy. And not only that, when staff make consistently positive first impressions on customers, customers are bedazzled, because they don't expect this. And they go tell their friends about how *surprisingly nice* and welcoming everyone was to them. They develop a warm, fuzzy feeling about the service team, the kind of feeling that breeds loyalty and makes people choose to give that team their future business. From this impressive behavior that exceeds customer expectations comes true competitive advantage.

What's Involved in Creating Positive First Impressions?

Because service improvement should be driven by customer expectations, improving first impressions must be guided by a shared understanding of what customers consider a great greeting. While health care teams need to identify their specific customers and learn from them what they prefer in the way of greetings by staff, focus groups with health care consumers show certain basics that customers want (and don't want) when staff members greet them. Consider the following suggestions for good greetings:

How to Impress Customers with a Greeting

- Acknowledge them immediately.
- Say a warm hello—with a smile and eye contact.
- Introduce yourself by name, and if there's any doubt, by position too.
- Call the customer by name if at all possible.
- Offer help, or state what you'll do next for the customer.

These behaviors are in contrast to what health care consumers *expect* when greeted by staff. They *expect* a wide variety of greetings that fall short of providing these basics and are unimpressive, like the following examples:

Greetings that Dissatisfy Customers

- "Hi, what can I do for you?" This leaves the customer in the dark about who is serving them. Customers want staff to be willing to introduce themselves because it shows that they're willing to be accountable.
- "Next!" Customers find this to be a blatantly rude greeting.
- "Hello, your name please." This strikes customers as mechanical or bureaucratic. They feel that staff are treating them like a number.
- "Hello, Admissions." Customers complain that this kind of greeting is abrupt and that it leaves the burden for the interaction completely on the customer.

To make greetings great then, you and your team need to value great greetings, rethink and redesign how staff greet customers, and install these redesigned, impressive greetings as the standard for staff behavior every day.

Preliminary Planning

The following list shows some of the important steps that you should take before beginning this process improvement effort:

- If you haven't yet figured out the leadership structure for your strategy, do so now, considering the alternatives described in chapter 2.
- Familiarize yourself with this breakthrough objective and exactly how it relates to your organization's mission and values. Prepare to articulate this rationale and the process steps well.
- With the leadership you choose, examine the recommended process, tools, and materials in this manual and decide whether you think these will work as is, or whether you must otherwise tailor them to your team and situation.
- Develop a timeline to guide your first impressions process. Determine the number of weeks you'll devote to each step in this process and create a calendar that serves as a timeline for work teams to follow.
- Then, get started!

Needless to say, you will need to customize these steps and tools with your team and organizational culture in mind.

10 Steps to Improving First Impressions: The Process in a Nutshell

This process helps you to lead your team through the steps needed to rethink, redesign, and institute wonderful greetings extended consistently to every customer of your service. The following table lists the 10 steps, as well as the key actions to accomplish them. Then, each section of this chapter deals with one step in detail, explaining the key actions and offering tools to help implement each step.

The 10-Step Process for Improving First Impressions

Step 1: Focus people on the power of first impressions and on your plans. Build commitment.
—Inform and engage your boss and other key people outside of your service.
—Orient everyone on your management team to the first impressions goal and plan.
—Distribute a fact sheet to staff.
—Orient staff to your service objective.
—Generate enthusiasm for the objective with an energy-building activity.

Step 2: Assess people's current approaches to greeting customers and set priorities and targets for improvement.
—Scan existing data about the quality of staff greetings and first impressions.
—Design and use assessment tools to fill information gaps about the current effectiveness of staff greeting behavior.
—Hold a staff meeting to review results and set priorities for redesign work.

Step 3: Attack your priorities. Design the improvements.
—Review and adapt the universal greeting protocols.
—Design and improve greetings in line with priorities.
—Produce job aids.
—Provide help to people in their redesign efforts.

Step 4: Communicate new greeting protocols and expectations to staff.
—Communicate expectations.

Step 5: Equip staff with skills needed to implement greeting protocols in a professional, genuine, and nonmechanical manner.
—Clarify managers' roles.
—Provide protocol practice in work teams.
—Troubleshoot with staff.

Step 6: Do a trial run of the protocols, assess their effectiveness, and improve them based on feedback.
—Assess your greeting protocols.
—Provide resources for troubleshooting.

Step 7: Institute the refined protocols and build new habits.
—Equip staff with job aids.
—Remind people daily to use their new protocols, since repetition is a habit builder.
—Recognize and reinforce people's efforts.

Step 8: Check the implementation and effectiveness of the protocols against your targets.
—Check implementation.
—Check effectiveness using a service report card and protocol-specific devices.

Step 9: Share experiences and results. Learn from each other and celebrate successes.
—Help staff share their experiences and learning.
—Recognize teams for their contributions to improvement.
—Celebrate successes.

Step 10: Institute ongoing methods for sustaining top-notch greetings of customers.
—Institute an ongoing way to monitor the effectiveness of greetings.
—Build into your hiring process a screening method that helps you hire people who make a good first impression and orient them to the appropriate greeting protocols.
—Add effectiveness in greeting customers to job descriptions and the performance review process.
—Keep awareness high.

Focus People on the Power of First Impressions

 ### Key Actions

- Inform and engage your boss and other key people outside of your service.
- Orient everyone on your management team to the first impressions goal and plan.
- Distribute a fact sheet to staff.
- Orient staff to your service objective.
- Generate enthusiasm for the objective with an energy-building activity.

Inform supervisors as well as the staff who interact with customers every day of the process improvement initiative you are about to undertake. Move your objective forward by planning ways to generate excitement and provide people with incentives to participate. Use the following actions and the tools that accompany them to take this crucial first step toward improving greetings in your organization.

 ### Inform and Engage Your Boss and Other Key People Outside of Your Service

If your service is part of a larger organization, you probably report to someone. Also, there are likely to be other people (for example, managers and physicians) who work with your service or are served by it, but who are not directly members of your team. Let them know about your team's new objective and about your plans. Leave room for participation and contribution if they are so inclined. Address their questions and concerns. Show them the benefits of what your team is doing so that you and your team will have their support and interest.

 ### Orient Everyone on Your Management Team to the First Impressions Goal and Plan

Before presenting your objective to staff, get people in authority positions on board, able to articulate the reasons for the strategy and their understanding of your plans and approach. One way to do this is by using an orientation agenda like this one.

Management Team Orientation to First Impressions

1. Start with a statement such as the following: "We're meeting to discuss our next breakthrough service objective. It's hopefully an easy one, 'Creating Positive First Impressions.' To warm up to this topic, let's quickly look at our instinctive ways of meeting and greeting someone we don't know. Turn to someone near you. Imagine this is a customer you haven't met before. Quickly, greet them as you would greet a customer you don't know. Then, switch roles and have the other person take a turn."

2. Afterward, ask "How did people greet their customers? What were the behaviors and words people used?" List them on a flipchart or whiteboard. Acknowledge the variety of behaviors and words and also ask people if they really greet customers that way when they're busy doing other things and aren't focusing on how they greet people.

3. Say "You have just participated in our next breakthrough objective—to make consistently positive first impressions on all of our customers."

4. Introduce meeting agenda:
   —To familiarize you with this objective . . .
   —To get commitment for your involvement . . .
   —To review the process . . .
   —To answer your questions . . .

5. Ask people to react to the idea of focusing on this service objective and to identify the benefits they see it producing for customers and the organization. Point out that, as leaders, they will need to articulate these benefits to their staff throughout the course of the strategy.

6. Lay out your plans for improving first impressions and the leadership structure and timeline. Distribute them and ask people to walk through the tool kit you want managers or supervisors to use with their work teams.

7. Describe the next steps.
   —Ask people to examine the plan for the staff orientation and make it clear who (you, a facilitator, an appropriate staff member) will conduct this meeting with their work teams.
   —Provide the details of who, what, where, and when.
   —Discuss the key role of managers and supervisors as role models in the process—that managers and supervisors must model commitment to the goal and also make personal improvements in their own greetings of customers.

8. Answer questions.

Distribute a Fact Sheet to Staff

Distribute a fact sheet like the one shown here, signed by you or your steering committee, before the orientation session for staff so that they have time to think about what's coming.

Fact Sheet for Staff on Creating Positive First Impressions

Our next service objective is to improve the first impressions we make on our patients, other customers, and coworkers. How? By consistently extending to them warm, polished, welcoming greetings at the start of every interaction.

Why Focus on First Impressions?

It's a well-documented fact that people develop opinions about other people in the first six seconds of interacting with them. Following are some of the reasons we want to create positive first impressions in our interactions with customers and coworkers:

- *Improving how we meet and greet our customers:* To help our patients and other customers feel welcome and comfortable with us and to earn their respect, we need to start by excelling in our first interactions with them. If we excel in these first moments with each customer, our hospitality triggers a positive chain reaction. People go from one interaction to the next with confidence in us, a feeling that they are welcome and respected, and with a cooperative attitude.
- *Improving how we meet and greet each other:* Also, to create a warm and welcoming work atmosphere throughout our service and improve the quality of our everyday work life, we need to meet and greet coworkers, including people we don't know, in a friendly and helpful manner. We are, after all, one another's "internal" customers; we rely on each other to reach our work goals.

By improving first impressions throughout our service, we better serve our customers. We demonstrate warmth and hospitality, and also set our interactions with our customers off to a good start.

Our Approach

To excel in creating positive first impressions, we need to think through and redesign our methods of meeting and greeting customers.

Some staff do a great job of meeting and greeting, because that's their personality or it's the normal way of doing things on their work team. But for many of us, the meeting and greeting step in the service cycle is one that we have not fully examined or designed. The result, unfortunately, is that we are inconsistent and sometimes unimpressive.

Our aim in these next four months is to make consistently positive first impressions by paying concerted attention to improving our meeting and greeting performance. Specifically, we will design and institute *protocols* for meeting and greeting—standardized methods of two types.

1. Universal greeting protocols—universal because they apply to *all of us* in the following situations:
   —In public areas like hallways, elevators, lounges, and cafeterias
   —When we enter patient rooms
   —When people visit our work areas
   —When we answer the phone
2. Job-specific protocols within each team or department. These relate to each staff member's specific role and the needs of their specific customers.

Watch for the details and get involved!

 ## Orient Staff to Your Service Objective

In a staff meeting or special workshop, you, steering committee members, or appropriate others should address all staff or talk with each work team to explain the objective and develop the rationale for improving first impressions servicewide. Then, solicit staff help to do the following:

• Identify functions and work processes in which there are "greeting" moments.
• Identify customers and the expectations these customers have of staff when they are greeted by them.
• Identify the positions involved in meeting each customer group.

Use this agenda for a staff orientation to the objective in a department meeting or a workshop.

Sample Plan for Staff Orientation to "Creating Positive First Impressions"

1. Facilitator welcomes people and explains purpose of meeting: To plan this team's approach to the first servicewide goal of improving first impressions.

2. Review the idea of breakthrough service objectives pursued by the whole team.

> "As you know from me, from coworkers who've been involved in the planning, and from the memo you received last week, we're starting up an effort to improve the satisfaction of our customers by working all together on one service improvement goal at a time. The plan is for everyone, no matter what their job, to all work on the same goal at the same time. This goal is to create consistently positive first impressions on all of our customers every day. We'll take on this goal for about ___ months/weeks, working hard on it—long enough to make improvements and form new habits that we then follow without having to think much about them.
>
> "Throughout our service, we'll all work to design and institute better ways to meet and greet customers in public areas like hallways, elevators, in patient rooms, and in our own areas, such as in person and on the phone.
>
> "The great thing about having *all* of us work on first impressions at the same time—all together—is that we can have a huge impact. Picture it! Everyone throughout our services being *consistently* warm, welcoming, helpful, and professional in hallways, elevators, and our specific jobs!
>
> "As we take on one service goal after another, we'll make our service quality truly impressive to customers over time and build customer loyalty that makes us unbeatable in our competitive marketplace.
>
> "So what does this mean for our team? It means that we will look at all the situations in which we have the opportunity to make a first impression by meeting and greeting our customers and each other. (Give examples such as the following: 'When a new patient arrives, which staff member greets them first and in what manner? When the receptionist hands off the customer to a care-

giver, how does that happen? What does the caregiver say to greet the person, and what does the receptionist say to hand off the customer to that caregiver? Are our current ways of doing these things effectively creating positive first impressions of every individual on our team?")

"We know that standards of behavior vary from position to position in this team and that our customers expect different things from us depending on our particular jobs. So, in order to design meeting and greeting standards that will move us toward improved first impressions, we need first to identify our different customers, determine what each group needs or wants from us, and then figure out which behaviors can best meet their needs to create great first impressions."

3. Post a flipchart page for the position "front desk receptionist" and demonstrate the process you'll be asking people to follow to identify greeting situations and related customer expectations.

—Ask people to brainstorm the greeting situations a front desk receptionist handles and write them on the left column of the flipchart page.

—Then, focusing the group on one greeting situation at a time, ask people to empathize with that customer group and identify what they think are the greeting behaviors on the part of staff that would impress that customer group.

Position: Front Desk Receptionist

Greeting Situations	Greeting Behaviors that Would Impress!
(Example) Greets new outpatient at desk	Says "hello," introduces self, and asks, "May I help you?"
Greets patient's friends/family	
Greets on phone	
Greets coworkers	

4. Now divide the whole team into groups of two or three (by "like" position where there is more than one person in a position or by combinations of positions if there is only one person in a position).
   —Pass out paper and ask small groups to make a similar chart for their position.
   —Have small groups report back to the large group.

5. Explain the next steps and set dates for the following:
   —Groups will develop (or revise) greeting "protocols" for each of their key customer groups by (date).
   —The group will reconvene to review the newly explicit greeting protocols and practice them on (date).
   —There will then be a trial run on (date) during which people will try out their new protocols, find out from customers how effective they are, and make any needed refinements. The group will then institute the new protocols during a 21-day habit-building period to make them everyday routine.

6. Organize people into teams responsible for developing specific protocols (or a subcommittee that will do all of them). Give each team one or more assignments and deadlines for development. Provide this "Input Worksheet" for people to use to solicit input from others in the group or position before crystallizing the new protocols they're responsible for.

Input Worksheet

Check the protocol assigned to your group:

____ Phone greetings ____ Greeting coworkers
____ Greeting inpatients

What behaviors that we do now work very well (are welcoming, hospitable, professional, minimally demanding of people's time or attention, and good for our image)? These are the "dos."

What behaviors are problematic at times (are *not* welcoming, hospitable, professional, minimally demanding of people's time or attention, or good for our image)? These are the "don'ts."

What advice do you have for your coworkers who are developing greeting protocols for this customer group and situation?

7. Close the meeting.
   —Invite one-line reactions to two questions:
     –What did you think about this meeting?
     –What are your feelings about our plans for improving first impressions?
   —Remind staff of the next steps:
     –First impressions team(s) will develop job-specific greeting protocols and distribute them by a certain date, with a deadline for feedback.
     –Team(s) will refine protocols based on feedback and convene another meeting at which they'll present the universal and job-specific protocols, with a schedule for implementation, evaluation, and habit building.
   —Thank everyone for coming and giving their ideas.

 ### Generate Enthusiasm for the Objective with an Energy-Building Activity

Engage your steering committee in creative thinking to develop an energizing activity. Such an activity can be simple, such as holding a competition in which people bring video clips of "the best greeting" and "the worst greeting" and show these at a staff meeting, voting for the best and worst and giving prizes. Or, you can use a more elaborate activity like this competition-inspiring scavenger hunt used in the Albert Einstein Healthcare Network to generate enthusiasm for their "first impressions last" objective. Or, your steering committee can develop your own motivational event or approach. Events like this spark enthusiasm for first impressions work.

First Impressions Scavenger Hunt

Rules

- Hunting must not interfere with patient care but can be completed during work time.
- Turn in your results by (date) to any steering committee member.
- The team with the highest points wins. In case of a tie, a tie-breaker question will be delivered to the team captains with instructions.
- Results/winners will be announced at the staff meeting on (date).
- The most original team name that ties in with first impressions (to be decided by steering committee) will receive 50 extra points.

Prizes

☐ First prize: $25 gift certificate for each team member

☐ Second prize: $10 gift certificate to _____ for each team member

☐ Third prize: $5 certificate for lunch at _____ for each team member

All participants will receive a coupon for a free frozen yogurt; team captains will receive a T-shirt.

Items and Tasks

1. Create two buttons that you wear: One showing a positive greeting; another showing a negative greeting. Value: 20 points for each button; total 40 points

2. Find a sign related to our services that does not give a positive impression. Value: 50 points. Bonus for attaching a photograph of the sign: 25 points

3. Gather guest relations orientation material from a local hotel—materials used to train new employees on positive guest relations. Value: 100 points

4. Interview three customers in our waiting area. Ask them what their first impression of our service was. Value: 50 points

5. Go to a patient care area (not your own) and observe for five minutes whether any employee knocks prior to entering a patient's room. Note: Try to be invisible, but if asked what you are doing, simply state you are conducting research on first impressions. Value: 100 points

6. Create a poster depicting meeting and greeting. All creative efforts, including cartoons, will be welcomed! Value: 150 points

7. Observe three employees who are stars at meeting and greeting. Tell them what a great job they are doing. Record names and greetings. Value: 100 points

8. Interview a physician, nurse, secretary, manager, and one other coworker. Ask them: "When you are having a bad day, what do you do so that you don't communicate your bad day to others?" Value: 100 points

9. Create a meeting-and-greeting limerick, and be prepared to recite it at the staff meeting on (date). Value: 75 points

10. Create a meeting-and-greeting song using a tune that people will recognize. Submit an audiotape that will be played at the staff meeting on (date). Value: 100 points

11. Bonus item: Create a videotape of your team demonstrating superior meeting-and-greeting behaviors. All videos will be shown at staff meeting. Value: 250 points

Reprinted, with permission, from Albert Einstein Healthcare Network © 1994.

 Tips

- Take the time to involve champions, enthusiasts, and opinion leaders in this step. You are going public with your strategy and need people to launch it who are most likely to generate enthusiasm in others.
- Take the time you need at this step, so that people don't say, "We're working on *what??*" and feel left out of the loop.

Step 2: Assess People's Current Approaches to Greeting Customers and Set Priorities and Targets for Improvement

 Key Actions

- Scan existing data about the quality of staff greetings and first impressions.
- Design and use assessment tools to fill information gaps about the current effectiveness of staff greeting behavior.

• Hold a staff meeting to review results and set priorities for redesign work.

How do staff greet customers now? How does this current practice differ from the ideal? Step 2 will show you how to answer questions like these using the assessment tools already in place and will offer ideas for developing new tools. You will also learn how to discuss the results with your staff and plan the next steps in the process improvement effort.

Scan Existing Data about the Quality of Staff Greetings and First Impressions

Scan relevant satisfaction survey items or other evidence of the effectiveness of people's greetings currently. Do you have in your patient survey a question that asks customers to rate the friendliness and courtesy of staff? Chances are the ratings will tell you something about the current perceptions of staff greetings, since these set the tone for the ensuing interactions.

Design and Use Assessment Tools to Fill Information Gaps about the Current Effectiveness of Staff Greeting Behavior

Collect specific information about how greetings are done currently and how effective they are. Options include having staff observe staff, asking customers, and using a specifically designed customer survey tool.

Method: Have Staff Observe Staff
Have members of your steering committee each observe 10 different staff members extending greetings to customers. Orchestrate this so that the members aren't all observing the same people. Have them record the exact greeting behaviors they see and hear so they can identify current greeting patterns.

Method: Ask Customers
In areas where customers convene (such as reception areas) have steering committee members stand outside and say to customers on their way in, "Excuse me. My name is _____ and I am a

(position) here. I'm on a team working on improving the way our staff treat our customers. Would you be willing to help by noticing how you are greeted when you enter this service area, and checking off on this sheet the behavior you see on the part of our staff? We'll use the results to make improvements here for our customers' sake."

Another way to ask customers is by providing a survey tool like this one.

Please Tell Us about Our First Impressions

Dear Patient,

We want to know how you feel about the manner in which each of our team members greeted you. Please take one minute to tell us. Fill this out and put it in the box on the reception desk. Thank you.

	Yes	No	Not Applicable
Did our staff smile, make eye contact, and say "Hi" as soon as they met you?			
Did they call you by your name?			
If you had anyone with you, did they greet them in a friendly manner?			
Did they tell you their names?			
Did they tell you what they would do for you?			

What impression did our staff first make on you?

___ very good ___ pretty good ___ fair ___ pretty poor ___ very poor

What could we have done to make your visit more personally satisfying?

Hold a Staff Meeting to Review Results and Set Priorities for Redesign Work

This meeting provides another chance to refocus staff on your first impressions objective, focus attention on their work revising or developing greeting protocols, and provide data that shows room for improvement.

The staff meeting is for the purpose of setting priorities and should include the following actions:

- Remind people of your first impressions objective.
- Have the steering committee report on all available data about how staff greet customers and how customers perceive these greetings.
- Invite staff to comment about what they view as the team's priorities, given this data.
- Share with staff the plans and methods for working on the priorities, forming teams, or allocating tasks as needed depending on what the data says about greetings.
- Invite and address questions again now, since people's design work is about to begin.

Step 3: Attack Your Priorities and Design the Improvements

 Key Actions

- Review and adapt the universal greeting protocols.
- Design and improve greetings in line with priorities.
- Produce job aids.
- Provide help to people in their redesign efforts.

Now that you've identified how greetings need to be improved in your organization and set your targets, follow through and begin creating the tools that will help your staff achieve this objective. The following ideas and concrete tools will aid in this step.

 Review and Adapt the Universal Greeting Protocols

Universal greeting protocols will hopefully save you time. We designed these to lay out in behavioral terms how all staff, regardless of their specific job, should greet people on the phone and in hallways, elevators, and patient rooms. Consider the following universal protocols:

Universal Greeting Protocols

In the Public Eye

1. Make eye contact, smile, and say "hello."
2. Wear your name badge where others can see it.
3. Hold doors and yield to patients, visitors, wheelchairs, and stretchers.
4. If someone looks lost, help them find their way.
5. Offer help, even if it's not your job.

In Patient Rooms

1. Knock before entering.
2. If the curtain is closed, announce yourself.
3. Introduce yourself to anyone who doesn't know you.
4. Call patients and their guests by their last name, unless invited to do otherwise.

On the Phone

1. Take a breath before answering the phone.
2. Put a smile in your voice.
3. Greet the caller and identify yourself and your department.
4. Say "May I help you?" or "How may I help you?"

In Your Unique Role

1. Acknowledge customer's presence right away, even if you're on the phone.
2. Make eye contact, smile, say hello.
3. Introduce yourself and state your role and purpose.
4. Use a welcoming line, like "How may I help you?"

Given your setting, have your steering committee or a subcommittee of staff review these and decide whether they need to be modified to suit your setting and service mission. Make the necessary changes.

 ### Design and Improve Greetings in Line with Your Priorities

With the universal greeting protocols as guides, have staff pairs or teams design *job-specific* greetings and concretize them into job-specific protocols.

Method

If you have a team working on this for *all* positions, not just one specific position, use the following method:

1. For each key customer group, draw a flowchart of each customer group's pathway through your services.
2. Pinpoint each step along their pathway where they meet a new staff member.
3. Clarify the greeting protocol for each staff member who routinely greets the customer. In a nuclear medicine department, for instance, a person who goes for a stress test might follow the pathway shown below. The people at each step need a meeting and greeting protocol. Be sure the protocol includes how each person should "hand off" the customer to the next person.

Sample Customer Pathway

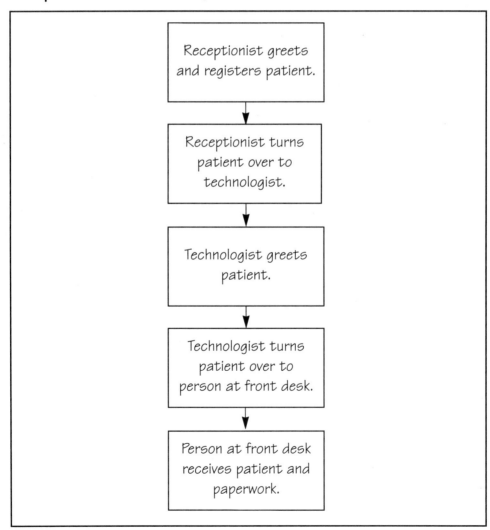

After you've created protocols for greeting each customer group at each key meeting point along their service route through your department, cluster the protocols by position. Assemble those that apply to *each* position, so you can give the relevant protocols to people in each position.

Method

If you develop protocols one job at a time, use the method outlined here:

1. Brainstorm every routine opportunity for meeting and greeting in that job.

Brainstorming on First Impressions

The director of Inpatient Admissions asked staff to brainstorm ways the department could better satisfy customer expectations when patients walk into Admissions. The department had already identified (through interviews) that patients want courtesy, answers, and immediate assistance. The next task was to determine concrete ways to provide prompt, courteous service.

1. *Generate alternatives:* The director printed on newsprint "How We Can Provide More Prompt, Courteous Service When We First Meet Our Patients." She recorded their ideas verbatim:
   —Smile and say "hello" immediately.
   —Turn desk around to face patients.
   —Offer immediate help.
   —Don't leave area without getting coverage.
   —Post "rest room" signs so patients won't be embarrassed.
   —Request phone coverage by others when busy with patient.
   —If you're on the phone, acknowledge patient's arrival with a smile and gesture to indicate you'll be right with them.
   —Make small talk to break the ice, especially if you expect the patient may have to wait for a while, for example, "What a lovely bracelet" or "What a winter this has been!"
   —Address adults by their last names with the correct preface.
   —Don't say "honey," "sweetie," or "dear."
   —Install mirrors in the office so that no matter where staff are, they can see patients coming in.

2. *Clarify:* The team leader then invited people to clarify any unclear ideas, but there weren't any.
3. *Evaluate ideas:* For example, "Requesting that phones be covered by other staff" was deemed beyond this team's control, so this item was tabled. The team decided to table "making small talk" too.

The other ideas went to the admissions subcommittee for incorporation into the protocols they were developing for greeting patients.

2. Design a protocol for *each* greeting situation.
3. Ask "What do we need to do to meet customer expectations and professional standards of care?" Answer this question in behavioral terms, for instance, "We must look up, smile, and acknowledge our customers immediately."

 ## Produce Job Aids

Job aids are handy references (printed cards, signs, or sheets) that you give to staff to help them remember what they're supposed to do. For this breakthrough objective, give each staff member a job aid like the one following, with their protocols on them. You also need to create and provide job aids with people's job-specific protocols on them and give these to the relevant employees at that same meeting.

Distribute job aids on cards or plaques or key chains, so staff have a reminder in hand of the steps they are supposed to follow in their job-specific greetings.

Job Aid Examples

Receptionist Greeting Protocol

Situation: When Handing Patient over to Technologist

1. Right away, smile, make eye contact, and say "hi" to the technologist and any other staff or visitors close by.
2. Call the technologist by name.
3. Introduce the patient to the technologist, referring to the patient as Mr., Mrs., Miss, or Ms. ("Lee, this is Ms. Marsh. Ms. Marsh, this is Lee Mason.")
4. If others are with the patient, introduce them to the technologist too.

5. Turn to the patient and say what the technologist will do for them. (For example, "Lee will take you for your X ray.")
6. Say something reassuring, like "With Lee, you're in good hands!"

Housekeeping Aide Greeting Protocol

Situation: When Cleaning a Patient's Room

1. Before entering, knock and announce yourself. (For example, knock and say: "It's Helen Hammond from Environmental Services. May I come in?")
2. Make eye contact, smile, give a greeting, and state your name. (For example, make eye contact, smile, and say: "Hi, I'm Helen Hammond, and I'm here to clean your room.")
3. Before you leave, ask if everything is OK and give a pleasant departing remark. (For example, "That does it for today unless you see anything I missed. Hope today goes well for you.")

Physical Therapy Secretary Protocol

Situation: Greeting Outpatients

1. Look up, make eye contact, smile, and say: "Good morning/afternoon, I'm _____. Can I help you?" Use a friendly tone of voice.
2. Say "May I have your name please? . . . Just a moment and I'll see if your therapist is ready for you. . . . Do you know the way to station A/B?" or "I'm sorry, (therapist's name) is not quite ready for you. Please come in and have a seat here on the right. It will be about ____ minutes."
3. When it's time for the patient to go to therapy, go out to the waiting area, address the patient by name, and say: "Mr./Mrs./Ms. _____. (therapist's name) is ready for you now. Do you know the way to station A/B?"
4. Whenever possible, walk the patient back to the therapy area or request an aide, especially if it is the patient's first visit or if the patient isn't clear where to go.
5. If you can take the patient to the therapist, introduce the patient to the therapist, calling the patient by name and saying the patient's name first. For example, "Mrs. Jones, this is (therapist's name) and (she or he) will be your therapist today. You'll be in good hands with (therapist's first name). OK? . . . Have a good day."

Provide Help to People in Their Redesign Efforts

With your steering committee, anticipate which individuals and which work teams might need help and link them with resource people who can help them. Line up a series of individuals with special skills to aid people who show up for help during designated help clinic hours. Here are three kinds of help that people appreciate as you pursue this objective.

- *Help clinic on protocol design:* Have one or more protocol pros on hand to help people develop job-specific meeting and greeting protocols for their position/service. Invite them to bring questions, confusion, rough drafts, raw materials—and to get help!
- *Protocol polishing service:* Identify an experienced writer or two who will polish people's job protocols, make suggestions, and then print protocols into spiffy job aids for staff.
- *Help clinic on measurement:* Have a colleague with measurement savvy available on a given day to help teams develop or polish the checkup methods they'll use to evaluate protocol use and effectiveness.

 ### Tips

- This design phase doesn't have to take a long time. Some organizations prefer creating a one-time work session during which all staff working on protocols come together and help each other. The design process can be done in one fell swoop.
- It helps to have models of protocols floating around. Ideally, the steering committee will take the first models developed by any work team and ask their permission to circulate it to others. This lets the others see that a team has already done its work and also allows everyone to learn from completed protocols.

Step 4: Communicate New Greeting Protocols and Expectations to Staff

During this step, present the universal and job-specific protocols to staff, proclaiming why they're important and how they were developed. Make it very clear that performance in accord with these protocols is a job requirement. And, explain the process the whole organization will follow to make better meeting and greeting (and as a result, better first impressions) a habit throughout the organization.

You can communicate expectations in several ways:

- Hold a staff meeting and talk with all staff at once.
- Have each supervisor communicate these expectations to his or her direct reports in a group. Or, have each supervisor meet with each individual and discuss the protocols appropriate to their customers in particular and work out any concerns raised.
- If you used a subcommittee to develop job-specific protocols, have each person on the subcommittee take responsibility for communicating expectations to a few people. Or, hold a meeting where the subcommittee presents the protocols and you clarify that they are now expected of everyone.
- Regardless of the option you choose, include the elements listed below in the communication with staff.

Communicate Expectations: Key Elements

- Clarify the overall goal of improving first impressions through better meeting and greeting. Review with staff the benefits of improved first impressions for customers, staff, and the organization. Describe the focus on greeting protocols as the main approach to creating more consistently positive first impressions.
- Distribute and walk people through the newly crystallized greeting protocols, including both the universal protocols and the job-specific protocols, and describe how your team's job-specific protocols were developed.
- Describe the schedule and approach for making these behaviors reality, including the trial run and refinement, 21-day habit building, and celebration of successes.
- Make it clear that everyone is expected to follow these protocols—that they are from now on job expectations. Make the point that people can use their own language, but that their greetings need to include the elements identified in the protocols. Have team leaders demonstrate how simple it is.
- Invite and address questions.

Tips

- With this objective in particular, some staff don't think you're seriously expecting them to consistently greet customers according to protocols. At this step in the process, reemphasize the importance of the first few seconds of interactions in building rapport with customers and assert that excellence doesn't occur by accident. Excellence in greetings is a matter of design. People have taken the time and care to design really good greeting protocols, and it's important that everyone use them. Reinforce that this is a key aspect of providing excellent service and that excellent service, not just people's technical skills, is a job requirement.
- You will probably be met with resistance from people who advocate spontaneity with customers and balk at following protocols because this might make them appear mechanical and phony. Emphasize that the protocols identify the key elements important to effective greetings and that there is indeed room for people to use their own words and own style, *as long as they include the key elements in their greetings*. Don't back down.

Step 5: Equip Staff with Skills Needed to Implement Protocols in a Professional, Genuine, and Nonmechanical Manner

 Key Actions

- Clarify managers' roles.
- Provide protocol practice in work teams.
- Troubleshoot with staff.

Now that your staff have been introduced to the redesigned protocols for improved greetings, help them internalize the changes and make their effective, friendly greetings automatic without seeming forced or artificial.

Clarify Managers' Roles

Help managers and team leaders to exemplify first impressions and also to use their influence and authority as leaders to encourage staff in the direction of better greetings. Discuss managers' roles at a meeting or provide written guidelines in the form of a "prompt for managers" such as the one that follows:

Prompt for Managers: Encouraging Great First Impressions

1. From this minute on, use your power and visibility as leader to be an exemplary role model of meeting and greeting. Follow our universal protocols. Don't give anyone grounds to accuse you of a double standard.
   —Greet people you know and people you don't know in public areas like hallways and elevators.
   —Follow our telephone protocols.
2. In your work area, make great greetings a reality.
   —Greet every person you pass.
   —When someone comes to your office for a meeting, give them a warm welcome (and perhaps a handshake) before delving into the business at hand.
   —Invite coworkers to give you feedback about your meeting and greeting behavior—to point out missed opportunities and more effective behaviors.
   —Give your coworkers feedback on their meeting and greeting style.
   –Compliment people on their meeting and greeting style when you think it's effective.
   –Provide constructive suggestions.
3. Be a greeter at a main employee entrance at the start of their shift:
   —Greet employees as they arrive to work, welcoming them and giving them a warm hello.
4. Schedule yourself for walks through hallways you don't usually frequent, greeting people in an exemplary fashion. The best times to do this are during the trial run.

5. Schedule yourself to drop in for 30 minutes to each of the teams that report to you. Say "hello" to all staff. Ask how they're doing with the first impressions goal. The best times to do this are during the trial run and habit-building periods.

6. Coach your direct reports on how you want first impressions to work. Start asking how they're doing *now* and ask frequently hereafter. (Show how much this is on your mind.)

 ## Provide Protocol Practice in Work Teams

While the protocols will be explicit and recorded on paper, they must be delivered effectively in order to work. At two successive staff meetings (or one if you have a meeting that is long enough), address with staff the dos and don'ts of effective greetings and also provide skill practice. Facilitate this yourself, or select someone who you think can effectively facilitate these mini-training sessions.

 ### Skill Builder: Address with Staff the Dos and Don'ts of Effective Greetings

The purpose of this skill builder is to share an understanding of what helps and hinders our effectiveness when we greet customers. Follow these six steps:

1. Explain the human/business model: This model suggests that there are two sides of every interaction with customers, the human side and the business side. The business side involves the tasks you need to accomplish. The human side has to do with connecting to the person at a human level, communicating your concern and dedication to them. A good greeting needs to address both sides.

2. Ask staff to describe greetings that are "all business."

3. Ask staff to describe greetings that are "all human."

4. Invite them to identify the problems with each.

5. Now, post a piece of flipchart paper divided into two columns and ask staff to identify the dos and don'ts in delivering effec-

tive greetings if the goal is to do the business at hand while connecting to the human being who is your customer. List every idea that people suggest. Probe for both verbal and non-verbal behavior (for example, eye contact, robotic voice tone).

6. Make a closing statement, being sure to do the following:
   —Emphasize the importance of both the business side and the human side.
   —Remind people that they have new greeting protocols and thank the people involved in their development.
   —Encourage people to keep this model in mind as they try out their new greeting protocols and work on becoming effective with them.

 Skill Builder: Calling People by Name
Since customers are impressed when staff call them by name in a greeting, engage staff in skill building on using names.

1. Ask people to note what their greeting protocols say about introducing themselves to customers and also calling customers and each other by name. Invite reactions and attempt to unearth resistance to this (which is inevitably there).

2. As people balk at the concept of introducing themselves to customers, ask for their reasons and list them on a piece of flipchart paper. Then, ask people to express their concerns about calling people by name and list those.

3. Go through one at a time and ask group members to respond to each. Help them talk through the benefits of introducing themselves and the costs of not doing so. Help them talk through the difficulties of calling customers by name and agree on the appropriate names to use. Use and distribute items like the handout shown here.

Volume 1, Issue 1

Why Call People by Name?

- Publius Cornelius Scipio is said to have known the names and faces of all citizens of ancient Rome.

- Themistocles knew the names of 30,000 Greek citizens.

- George Washington called every soldier in his army by name; Napoleon did, too.

- Andrew Carnegie, Charles de Gaulle, and Franklin D. Roosevelt are also acclaimed for their memory and for calling people by name.

These people were leaders. By using people's names, you can

- Win friends
- Motivate others to work with you
- Influence people (think of politicians!)
- Enjoy people more (a show of interest usually turns into the real thing)
- Save time (having made good personal contacts, you'll be able to rely on people more)
- Weaken resistance, soften opposition, and dilute antagonism

Above all, calling patients by name personalizes care.

The Name Game

Sometimes hospital personnel offend patients by addressing them in ways perceived to be inappropriate. In such cases, we don't mean to offend but unwittingly presume a too-familiar form of address. By following a few simple guidelines, you can avoid such situations.

The professional norm is to address an adult by last name, prefaced by Mr., Mrs, or Ms. Many people consider a stranger using their first name to be forward. Don't use a first name until invited to do so, and then take the invitation as a compliment.

Never use diminutives, like "honey" and "sweetheart." When addressing teenagers, avoid nicknames like "Katie" for Katherine or "Billy" for William, unless told to use these. When in doubt, ask what someone would like to be called.

In general, always address someone in the most respectful form. Some names might offend; others won't. Always choose the lowest-risk alternative.

What's in a name? It seems like such a little thing. But addressing someone in a way perceived to be offensive can be upsetting. And without much to do except lie in a hospital bed, people will often stew over the little upsets and become, without saying a word, angry and resentful. By applying the principle of lowest risk, you can play the name game and win.

Dos and Don'ts of Names

DO refer to people respectfully and in a professional manner.

DO call patients and visitors by last name until invited to do otherwise.

DON'T slip into calling patients "honey," "sweetheart," "dear," "doll," and so on. Be especially aware in your care of older people.

DO call people what they want to be called. To find out, start with "Mr." for men and "Ms." for women. That's what current standards of etiquette recommend. For women, start with "Is that Ms. Jones?" If she prefers something else, she's apt to tell you, and then you can respect her preference.

DON'T make assumptions about people's marital status.

What's Your Name Again?

Vivien Buchan of Toastmasters suggests four ways to do better remembering names:

1. Pay attention. Ask to have a name repeated. It will not offend people; it will impress them.

2. Concentrate. Look for characteristics that distinguish someone from others.

3. Associate. Relate a characteristic with the name.

4. Observe. Study people regularly to strengthen your ability to see characteristics and practice your imagination.

Clip 'n' Copy
Volume 1, Issue 1

How to Remember People's Names

Most of us realize how powerful and personal it is to call people by name, but we say, "I'm terrible at it. . . . I have a bad memory. . . . I just can't remember names!"

Not so! The ability to remember names is a skill you can learn. It's a matter of training your memory.

Rule 1: Start saying and thinking to yourself, "I have the hospital's best memory for names!"

Stop telling yourself, "I never remember names." Whatever you think about yourself will come true.

Rule 2: Be sure to hear the name.

The major reason why we don't remember a name is that we don't really listen for and hear the name in the first place. It's not a matter of forgetting. It's a matter of "not getting." If you don't hear the name, admit it and ask the person to repeat it. They won't mind. Say, "Would you pronounce your name again please?" or "How do you spell your name?" or "Am I pronouncing your name right?"

People find it flattering when you ask about and repeat their name.

And Research Says

Increasingly, people want their doctors to call them by first names only if they can do the same with their doctors.

Dr. Hans Mauksch, *Bulletin of the New York Academy of Medicine* 57 (no. 1, 1981).

Rule 3: Use the name immediately, and use it again during the initial conversation.

Right after you meet someone, repeat their name. "How long have you worked at Einstein, Michael?" Experiments show that people who repeat a name immediately after hearing it improve their ability to recall the name later by as much as 34 percent.

Then, during your conversation, use the name two or three times more and make a remark about it. "Is that an old family name?" Spell it to yourself or out loud. Through repetition, you will make the new name familiar.

Rule 4: Use the name when you part.

Always say, "Good-bye, Mrs. Jacob," not just "Good-bye," and "So long, Helen," not just "So long." People receive this kind of attention as a compliment.

Try these techniques for two weeks. The results will amaze you.

More on Remembering Names

(They might seem crazy, but they work!)

- Associate the name with something. For someone named Virginia, think of basking in the sun in beautiful Virginia Beach. For Mitch, think of Mitch Miller conducting sing-alongs. For Graham, think of graham crackers. For Hudson and Jordan, think of rivers.

- Create a silly or ridiculous picture in your mind that connects the name with the person. For someone named Mr. Chandler, for example, picture a chandelier hanging from his long nose. (Don't worry, you'll see this in your mind's eye; Mr. Chandler won't know!) Most people remember what they see more than what they hear. So create a picture for yourself. The more ridiculous the mental picture, the harder it is to forget. In fact, if you try to forget it, you'll remember it even better.

- Break the sound of the name down into similar sounds that mean something to you. For Blumenthal, think "bloomin' tall;" for Greenbaum, think "green bomb."

- At the end of the day or when you get back to your work area, write down all the new names you just learned.

Try these tricks. After all, Honey Hazelnut—I mean, Henry Hazlitt—said, "Our thoughts are so fleeting, no device for trapping them should ever be overlooked."

Skill Builder: Round-Robin Skill Practice

Use this skill builder to help people become more comfortable with their specific greeting protocols.

In a staff meeting or work team, divide staff into threes, with each trio designating a person A, person B, and person C. Then complete the following three steps:

1. Have person A be first. Person A explains who his/her customers are and sets the scene to practice the greeting protocols with the other two trio members. After person A tries out the greetings, the trio members give feedback on what was effective and on how the greetings could become more effective.
2. Then, persons B and C take turns, each practicing and getting feedback before moving on.
3. At the end, convene the group and invite people to talk about what was hard, what was easy, and what advice they gave to others. This will maximize everyone's effectiveness.

Troubleshoot with Staff

Some staff will complain that providing good greetings consistently is impossible because of situations that make it difficult. Give people a chance to voice these barriers to good greetings and engage your team in developing solutions.

Here's a skill builder to help you hold a troubleshooting discussion with staff. It will help to identify barriers to good greetings and develop solutions so staff don't let barriers give them excuses for noncompliance. Following are instructions for holding a staff meeting toward this purpose:

1. Ask for two volunteers—people who are willing to play devil's advocate. Good candidates for this are people who perhaps like to play a "yes, but . . ." role in groups or people who don't but wish they did.
2. With the devil's advocates standing aside, ask staff what makes effective greetings difficult. Push for situations where they've fallen down on the job and push for their excuses. List

these situations in the first column of a two-column flipchart page.

3. Ask coworkers to discuss further each barrier identified. Invite the devil's advocates to question every excuse people have for not greeting customers according to their protocols. Have some fun with it.

4. At the end, ask people to seriously look at every problem with greeting people well and to help identify solutions. How can people think differently about the problem so that they can greet their customers well anyway? What changes can the team make in the work environment in order to reduce the barriers?

5. In your closing remarks, be sure to include the following:
   —Agreements about how the barriers will be handled
   —A thank-you for staff commending their hard work and their effort to impress customers from the first interaction moment

 Tips

- Some people might think they don't need these skill builders and troubleshooting discussions, but these cement the protocols in people's minds and also raise people's awareness about what they're trying to accomplish in using a standardized, designed greeting more consistently.

- Don't feel compelled to facilitate these skill builders and team meetings yourself. You probably have a staff member who is respected by colleagues, who will be very good at it, and who will welcome this as a job enrichment activity.

Step 6: Do a Trial Run of the Protocols, Assess Their Effectiveness, and Improve Them Based on Feedback

 Key Actions

- Assess your greeting protocols.
- Provide resources for troubleshooting.

Now that everyone is familiar with the concept of improving greetings, and both managers and staff have been given orientation to the protocols, it's time for a trial run. Such a practice session will reveal unnoticed kinks in the process and allow you to make adjustments before the protocols are widespread.

 ## Assess Your Greeting Protocols

During the trial run of your new protocols, teams need to solicit feedback on protocol use and effectiveness. Options include check-in meetings with the steering committee, team leaders, and staff, as well as observations, simple customer surveys, and checklists.

The following four steps present a method for developing an observation:

1. Figure out who is in a position to watch a sample of greeting behavior by each staff member (a coworker, an invited observer, a supervisor).
2. Select an observation period (for example, 90 minutes at two different times during the week).
3. Use the observed person's protocol as a checklist.
4. Have the observer check off the elements of the protocol that they see the person do.

Afterward, someone in your service looks at "compliance" or "degree of implementation." Summarize the data to answer the question "To what extent are people implementing their protocols?" This is important because you need to know first if protocols are being followed. Then, and only then, can you find out how well customers like them.

Following is an example of a protocol made into an observation checklist.

Sample Protocol Observation Checklist

Escort's Protocol for Entering Patient Room: How Are We Doing?			
Observer: _____ Date: _____			
	Yes	No	Not Applicable
Knocked before entering a patient's room.			
Right away, smiled and made eye contact with the patient and anyone else there.			
Said "hi" to the patient first, addressing the patient by Mr., Mrs., Miss, or Ms. until invited to use a first name or nickname.			
Said "hi" to anyone else in the room.			
Introduced self and job to the patient first (unless they'd already met) and checked wristband for positive identification.			
Introduced self to anyone else in the room (unless they'd already met).			
Stated the purpose of the transport (for example, "I'm here to take you to ____").			
If they could, told visitors when the patient would be back.			

What else did the escort do to make a good impression?

What did this escort do especially well?

What problems did you see?

There are two methods to evaluate customers' reactions to the protocols: one is through staff discussion, the other through the use of checklists completed by an outside observer.

Staff Discussion Method

1. Ask "How did we do?" Encourage staff to tell stories of how they used the protocols and the reactions they got from customers.
2. Encourage staff to talk about how it feels to have a consistent approach to serving customers.
3. Find out changes they think need to be made to the protocols.
4. Describe methods under way to check progress. Explain tools that will be used, who will be collecting data, and so on.
5. Congratulate people on their good work during the trial run.

Checklist Method

Have someone from outside your service complete a checklist tailored to the protocols people are supposed to be using.

First Impressions Telephone Skills Survey

Date _____

Please tell us how we're doing! For one week, when you phone us, complete this short survey after each phone call. Please send your completed form to Team Leader, First Impressions Improvement Project. Thanks a lot for your help!

Did the staff member . . .

Call #	Date	Time	Number of times phone rang	Respond politely (relaxed, friendly)	Introduce self?	Announce department?	Offer help?
1				Y / N	Y / N	Y / N	Y / N
2				Y / N	Y / N	Y / N	Y / N
3				Y / N	Y / N	Y / N	Y / N
4				Y / N	Y / N	Y / N	Y / N
5				Y / N	Y / N	Y / N	Y / N

Provide Resources for Troubleshooting

Offering consultant teams and style clinics as resources for your staff are two great methods to help people as they begin working through the process of improving greetings.

Method: Offer a Consultant Team

Have your steering committee or special troubleshooters available to consult on problematic protocols or barriers preventing use of the protocols. Call this a help clinic on problem solving. Invite people to bring their evaluation results or any problems they're having with protocol use or effectiveness for help from available consultants.

Method: Offer a Style Clinic

Do individuals on your staff need or want to polish their personal style in meeting and greeting customers? In these powerful clinics, groups of five help each other polish their first impressions behavior.

Here's a model for a highly effective style clinic. You can adapt it if no video equipment is available.

1. In the group of five, each person's approach to meeting and greeting is videotaped.
2. In another room, with a private coach, each person looks at his or her tape and receives confidential feedback and suggestions. The coach should note and give advice on things such as what was effective (verbally and nonverbally), what got in the way (verbally and nonverbally), and whether the individual missed any key behavior.
3. Returning to the group of five, people then try out improvements, and the group points out their strengths.

These clinics are a safe place for personal insight, experimentation, and improvement. Clinics take about an hour for five people.

Step 7: Institute the Refined Protocols and Build New Habits

 ## Key Actions

- Equip personnel with job aids.
- Remind people daily to use their new protocols, since repetition is a habit builder.
- Recognize and reinforce people's efforts.

We recommend a 21-day habit-building period during which steering committee members, people you line up as mystery visitors, and coworkers observe people's greetings and remind each other to persist in using the recently upgraded versions.

 ## Equip Personnel with Job Aids

Don't forget at this point to make sure all staff have job aids, such as cards with their greeting protocols on them. Suggest ways people can access these easily. For instance, people who walk around with carts can attach them in plastic covers to their carts. Highly mobile people can carry them in acrylic card covers attached to their key ring. People who work at desks can place them on a stand or in a frame for easy reading.

 ## Remind People Daily to Use Their New Protocols Since Repetition Is a Habit Builder

Here's a chance for your steering committee to get creative. Ask them to think of a way to remind people every day to stick with their greeting protocols so that habits will develop. For instance, figure out 21 ways to mark the countdown of days of habit building. Have them think of a daily giveaway to keep people's awareness high, and use this to mark progress toward habit building. Or think of a paper campaign that cleverly calls attention to the greetings people are supposed to be using. For instance, "It's day two! Two-day is a good day two greet people with your new greeting pro-two-cols!" Give out a warm fuzzy one day, plastic "eyes" on another day, rose-colored glasses another day, a mirror for self-reflection another day, coffee and donuts or fruit with the quip

"Sweets to the Sweet! Keep our customers seeing our best selves." Or a foot with the quip, "Keep putting your best foot forward. It's day 12 and our habits are building!" A subcommittee or your steering committee can have some fun thinking of an awareness campaign with a positive boost during this period of first impressions "stick-to-itiveness."

Here is a game board graphic used by the Albert Einstein Healthcare Network to help teams chart progress through the 21-day habit-building period.

Building First Impressions Habits

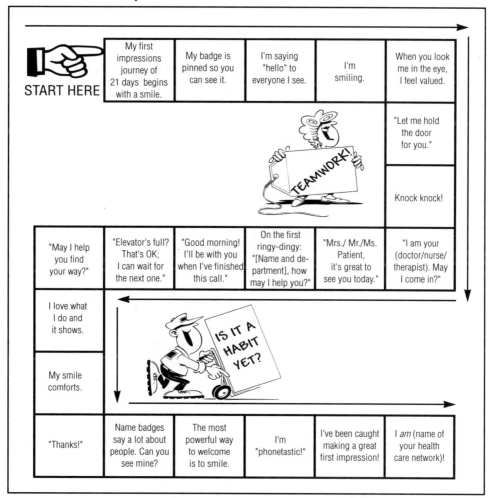

Reprinted, with permission, from the Albert Einstein Healthcare Network © 1996.

Recognize and Reinforce People's Efforts

Here too committee members can get creative. The idea is to think of ways to reinforce and recognize the individuals who are doing a great job of their greetings. One approach involves awarding caught-in-the-act coupons; another involves charting habit building.

Method: Awarding Caught-in-the-Act Coupons

These coupons enable all staff to recognize each other's efforts. Duplicate a batch of coupons like the ones reproduced below. Give some to every staff member to award to any employee during habit building.

First Impressions Last! Here's a pat on the back for a welcoming and polished greeting! **Living • Our • Values**	**First Impressions Last!** You are a *super* greeter! Here's a standing ovation. **Living • Our • Values**
First Impressions Last! I'm impressed with your friendly hello—and I appreciate you for it! **Living • Our • Values**	**First Impressions Last!** Your greeting is warm and welcoming—and I noticed! **Living • Our • Values**

Reprinted, with permission, from the Albert Einstein Healthcare Network © 1996.

Method: Charting Habit Building

Another approach is to chart progress through habit building by posting calendars and marking off days. Along the bottom of each week, mark the step you are currently in; for example, "Step 5: Assess/solve problems; make improvements," or "Step 6: 21-day habit building."

Tips

- The goal here is to remind people to try out their greeting protocols repetitively and eventually use them habitually. Anything your steering committee can do to remind people will help.
- This is a time for reminders, not evaluation. The message is "Do it, do it, and do it again until it's automatic."

Step 8: Check the Implementation and Effectiveness of the Protocols against Your Targets

Key Actions

- Check implementation.
- Check effectiveness using a service report card and protocol-specific devices.

Step 8 provides methods for staff and managers to get together and discuss how the implementation is going forward. This crucial step provides everyone with opportunities to learn from the experience of others in the organization.

Check Implementation

We repeat that it doesn't make sense to see how customers like the greetings they're getting unless you make sure first that staff are following their protocols. If you evaluate the results when staff aren't following their greeting protocols, you run the risk of mistakenly concluding that the protocols weren't effective. Instead, results were probably disappointing because the improvements were never implemented.

To check implementation, set up observations like you did during the trial run and habit-building periods. Repeat those methods here.

Check the Effectiveness of People's Greetings and Build in a System for Ongoing Monitoring

If you have a survey system for monitoring the satisfaction of patients and/or other customers, modify it to include from now on at least one item related to first impressions. For instance, add an item that reads "Staff made me feel welcome" or "Staff members made a good first impression on me."

Or if you have room for more specific items, consider the following:

- Staff members greeted me in a welcoming way.
- Staff members introduced themselves to me.
- Staff members called me by name.

Also, monitor the effectiveness of specific greeting protocols by readministering the surveys or the mystery guest techniques you used to monitor the effectiveness of greetings during step 6, the trial run. And regardless of which check-up methods you use, synthesize the results and convene staff to review them, since feedback will spur them on to make further refinements and also encourage them if the results look good.

Step 9: Share Experiences and Results—Learn from Each Other and Celebrate Successes

 ## Key Actions

- Help staff share their experiences and learning.
- Recognize teams for their contributions to improvement.
- Celebrate successes.

If teams did their homework, improved first impressions are now being made servicewide. Be sure to share and celebrate group and individual accomplishments. Celebrate with your team, encourage their participation in progress reporting, and also provide a short written story of your team's first impressions work and results.

 ## Help Staff Share Their Experiences and Learning

If you had many work teams following the same process to improve greeting customers, all the more reason to help them share their learning and results.

Here's a quick skill builder for a meeting on sharing about first impressions. It will help individuals and teams share their approaches and learning. This can be done in a separate meeting or during a celebration of the effort and can be accomplished with either written or display media.

Convene people from different work teams together. Pose a series of topics one at a time and invite people from the different work teams to share in response to the topic. Some topic ideas are as follows:

- A real highlight of our team's first impressions process . . .
- The most difficult challenge we faced and how we overcame it . . .
- What about the process helped us improve our greetings?
- What about the process was unnecessary or got in the way?
- The people who helped us and how they helped . . .
- Our greatest accomplishment . . .
- What we're most proud of in our work . . .

You can use these same topics to generate bulletin board displays or write-ups in your employee newspaper or special bulletins. Collect lots of entries in response to each topic and string them together to display the diverse experiences people and teams had throughout the first impressions process.

 ## Recognize Teams for Their Contributions to Improvement

Here's another opportunity for your steering committee to get creative. Some services hold recognition ceremonies at which they give out awards to teams for the "best greeting of patients," the "most consistent use of protocols," the "most thorough approach to specific customer groups," "the most upbeat greetings," and the highest satisfaction scores on surveys for first impressions. Other services develop certificates for teams. Steering committee members personalize letters to each team and send them a certificate of appreciation such as the one that follows.

Certificate of Recognition

for

Living Our Values Every Day

This certifies that

_____

has been observed meeting and greeting our customers in a style that is
polished, professional, welcoming, and helpful. The result:
More satisfied and cooperative customers and a good
reputation for our department and network.
Thank you from a grateful coworker.

Signed _____   Date _____

Reprinted, with permission, from the Albert Einstein Healthcare Network © 1996.

Celebrate Successes

As you know, it's essential to celebrate the hard work and accomplishment of *everyone*—emphasizing the fact that people worked hard together to improve service for the sake of customers. Have your steering committee figure out the best approach to doing this. Consider, for instance, convening everyone for coffee and donuts and hanging a banner that says "We make great first impressions!" Have the steering committee members there actively greeting everyone and introducing themselves to anyone they don't know. Once most people have convened, have members of the steering committee say a few words of appreciation to everyone and encourage people to keep the new habits alive and not let the improved greetings backslide. You might also include "toasts" that allow people to thank others who helped, inspired, or supported people during the process.

Step 10: Institute Ongoing Methods for Sustaining Top-Notch Greetings of Customers

 ### Key Actions

- Institute an ongoing way to monitor the effectiveness of greetings.
- Build into your hiring process a screening method that helps you hire people who make a good first impression and orient them to the appropriate greeting protocols.
- Add effectiveness at greeting customers to job descriptions and the performance review process.
- Keep awareness of the new protocols high.

When you finally reach this step, think "follow-through." Take steps to secure the gains and maintain the improvements people have made in first impressions behavior.

 ### Institute an Ongoing Way to Monitor the Effectiveness of Greetings

As described under step 8, include at least one question in your customer satisfaction survey that will allow you to collect feedback from customers about the perceptions of staff greeting behavior.

Also, institute a system of periodic spot checks so that slippage is noticed and someone carries the responsibility for initiating a reminder campaign. If you conduct focus groups periodically with customers, include questions that ask how your staff are doing in first impressions.

Focus Group Questions

- Think of the first moments when you meet our staff. What were your first impressions?
- What exactly did they do when they greeted you?
- How did you feel as a result: annoyed, ignored, satisfied, impressed?
- What advice would you offer us to improve the first impressions we make on our customers?

If you don't do periodic focus groups with customers, consider instituting such a system: It produces rich qualitative information about the quality of your services. Eventually, you'll be able to use such focus groups to learn more about the customer view of staff performance on every service dimension you pursue as a break-through objective. Because focus groups yield such rich information, the results will help you pinpoint important areas needing follow-up or reinforcement.

 ### Build into Your Hiring Process a Screening Method That Helps You Hire People Who Make a Good First Impression and Orient Them to the Appropriate Greeting Protocols

Because you'll be moving on to pursue another service objective and hopefully will never again need to give so much attention to first impressions, you'll need to build into your hiring process methods to ensure that you hire people who are already prone to creating good first impressions. Then, you'll need to orient them to the greeting protocols associated with their new jobs and customers.

Add screening methods to the hiring process. When people in your service interview applicants, have them observe each applicant's greeting approach, recording their findings on the form people use to rate applicants.

Interview Checklist

1. Does applicant:
   _____ Smile? _____ Make eye contact? _____ Say hello?
   _____ Introduce himself or herself? _____ Call interviewer by name?
   _____ Make a positive first impression?
2. During the interview, ask the applicant to show their way of greet-ing someone who approaches them on the job. Tailor the scenario to their new job if possible. For instance, "In your role as front desk receptionist, imagine that I walk up to you. Show me how you would greet me." Rate the candidate on instinctive behavior in this greet-ing situation.

 ### Add Effectiveness at Greeting Customers to Job Descriptions and the Performance Review Process

Make sure job descriptions include a statement that spells out that creating positive first impressions is a job expectation. Do this for all job descriptions, not just those for new employees. A good state-ment might be "Makes positive impressions on customers by behav-ing in ways that are warm, welcoming, professional, and helpful."

Reinforce this by including in your performance review an eval-uation of impressions made on customers. Add to every staff mem-ber's performance review such dimensions as "effectiveness in greeting customers."

 ### Keep Awareness of the New Protocols High

And finally, to build ongoing attention to first impressions into your service, have your steering committee plan some method of long-term reinforcement or reminders. Such a plan might include poster campaigns with reminders such as the following:

- First impressions last.
- A smile is the shortest distance between two people.
- Call people by name and make them feel special.
- Of all the things you wear, the most important is your expression.

   Other ideas:

- Have a monthly system of mystery visitors who monitor first impressions and provide feedback to staff.

- Focus on one customer group a month and raise staff awareness of what these customers appreciate in greeting behavior. Post customer quotes on bulletin boards, for instance.
- Create a wall for photographs of "The Great Greeter of the Month" and create a simple system for staff to use to nominate other staff as "Great Greeters."

 Tips

- Follow-through is not easy. Usually, steering committees feel "finished" after celebrating people and results and stop short of planning for follow-through. Needless to say, this ensures a downward slide and later disappointment when great greetings turn back into lackluster greetings. Early on, build into your planning process an explicit time to plan for follow-through and include some new people in this planning process to reenergize steering committee members whose energy might be fizzling.
- Announce to all staff your follow-through strategies. This will reassure people who think your strategy was a flash in the pan that it isn't. It will also let resistant people know that you remain serious about the standards you've established for improved greetings and that you intend to make these standards stick by holding people accountable for using them.

Possible Pitfalls and How to Address Them

Inevitably, especially with the first impressions objective, some staff members resist by such measures as minimizing the importance of the objective or by considering your effort a temporary fad. Here are comments you and other leaders of your strategy are likely to hear, with suggested responses.

Comment: "We are health care professionals. I can't believe we're working so hard on something as cosmetic as first impressions and how we greet people."

Response: "We wouldn't be working on this if we didn't have customers telling us that some of our staff fail to build their confidence in us. This starts with the way we welcome people into every interaction. This is something we have never paid attention to, and we think it's something we can fix easily. Also, know that the feelings we generate in the first few seconds of our interactions with customers create impressions of us, and most people don't change these impressions. We're trying to get all interactions off on the right foot."

Comment: "You are trying to routinize behavior that should be spontaneous and should allow for people's different styles. You're trying to make us robots."

Response: "Yes, we're trying to create routines—routines that reflect a very, very high standard. Right now, we have people who greet customers according to a normal curve of behavior. Some are awful. Most are pretty good. And some are terrific. By creating protocols (or routines), we define an effective greeting that brings everyone up to a top-notch level. Then, if we can make performance at that level 'routine,' we have everyone providing great greetings to our customers. In that sense, we are indeed trying to create new, better routines. Are we trying to make people into robots? No, not at all. Our greeting protocols include key elements that should be present in a good greeting, and some of these protocols include suggested language. The hope is that people will find their own best way to put this all together while including the elements that are known to reflect good greetings. There is certainly room for your own style to an extent, as long as the style meets the high standard we're setting."

Comment: "I can't believe you're expecting staff to follow these great greeting protocols, when managers here don't follow any such thing! In fact, some pass me by in the halls without even acknowledging me."

Response: "You're absolutely right that no one should be exempt from providing great greetings. The management team is going to discuss this, because every manager needs to be as attentive to their greeting behavior as everyone else. Thanks for speaking up."

Comment: "All this work to fix six seconds of an interaction??"

Response: "Yes. It takes a lot of coordination to help everyone in every work team to make similar improvements. It's up to you whether it requires a lot of work. If you and your coworkers sit down and fix your greeting approaches and agree to use them consistently, you are essentially done."

Conclusion

The goal is simple. Professionalize and warm up the first few seconds of every staff member's interactions with every customer. And this will set off a chain reaction of positive interactions, making customer satisfaction and appreciation more likely and reducing frustrations suffered by staff. If you can think of ways to simplify the approach—and you certainly can if you're in a small service like a medical practice—go for it. Really, all we're talking about is getting people to consult their customers to see what they want in the way of a greeting, design greetings with these features in mind, and use them regularly to make positive impressions on customers.

Other Helpful Resources

One Ringy Dingy, video with Lily Tomlin on telephone behavior, with a heavy emphasis on greetings. Mentor Media, 275 E. California Blvd., Pasadena, CA, 91106; 800-359-1935.

For many more devices for screening applicants for customer service excellence, read *Achieving Impressive Customer Service: 7 Strategies for the Health Care Manager* by Wendy Leebov, Gail Scott, and Lolma Olson (AHA Press, 1998; available by calling 800-242-2626).

Chapter 5

• • •

Do-It-Yourself Kit for Improving Explanations to Customers

A key dimension of excellent service involves the quality of information and explanations staff and the organization provide to customers. This do-it-yourself kit is designed to help you improve the quality and quantity of explanations staff give to customers, including patients, coworkers, managed care companies, and their other customers. The fact is, your team can provide better service and greater value to customers by giving appropriate, high-quality, understandable explanations.

Consider these important facts:

- The quality of explanations provided to patients has a very important influence on the satisfaction of patients and their families. Patients need and want to know what to expect and why, why they're kept waiting, what they're supposed to do, and much more. Also, good explanations are key to patients' knowing how to take their medications and take care of themselves.
- As health care professionals, our responsibility goes far beyond making an effort to communicate. We need to find ways to communicate effectively—ways that work for our patients and other customers. If we are not understood, no matter how hard we tried, we have failed in our communication and we won't get the results we want.

- We serve diverse patients, and we need to make sure our methods of explaining reach them all. We need to vary our methods, language, vocabulary, words versus pictures, and more—using multiple methods and checking back for understanding.
- We need to let people know what they can expect, as this is a key element of hospitality. Explaining things thoroughly and honestly is critical to showing responsiveness to our patients.
- We owe others in our organization explanations too, and this takes teamwork. Others need to know what they can expect, why we need what we're asking for, how they can access our services more easily, what we will do for them by when, and so on.
- With customers and coworkers alike, we promote trust through honest, complete and well-delivered explanations.

"Improving explanations" makes a great breakthrough objective because it gives teams, all of whom give explanations to customers, opportunities to work on a wide variety of important communication improvements, with help and resources readily available.

- You can improve all kinds of explanations: written, face-to-face, phone.
- You can improve instructions and layout on forms and signs, making them more understandable to the user.
- You can get help translating explanatory materials into other languages.
- You can develop and experiment with alternative methods for explaining key things well (for example, pictures, checklists, maps, words, and so on).
- You can increase the consistency of explanations among staff so that different people don't tell different customers different things.
- You can streamline the explanations given at various points in a service process.
- You can develop or improve tools for orienting and training new staff.

What Is a Great Explanation?

Here's a simple model for a great explanation. While explanations vary in structure and format according to their complexity, your customers, the environment, and other circumstances, a great explanation follows a cyclical process. To set a standard for effective explanations, we'll be building on the following model throughout this tool kit:

The Three Circles Explanations Process

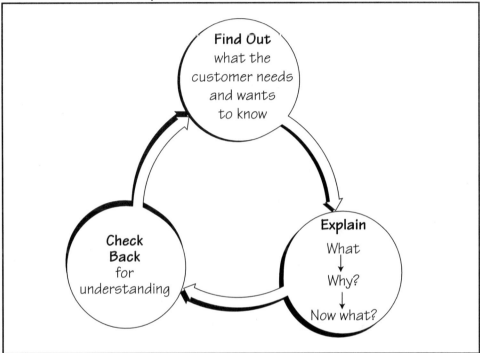

Find Out What the Customers Want and Need to Know

It's important to consciously ask what the customers or customer groups *want* to know and *need* to know. If you don't pinpoint customer needs before providing an explanation or designing one, you are very likely to omit important elements.

The assessment of explanation or information needs has two components:

• To show responsiveness and dedication to customer concerns and preferences, you need to ask customers what they *want to know*. In a face-to-face or phone situation, you can ask them directly. When you're preparing to write an explanation, you need to consult customers (for instance, in a focus group or interview) to find out what they would like to know if faced with the situation you're addressing.

- You also need to figure out, drawing on your experience and knowledge, what the customers *need* to know and whether they can articulate this need or not.

In addition to finding out what content the customer wants explained, it's also important to find out *how* they would like it explained: In writing? With a checklist? With a demonstration? To themselves and a family member? At a particular time of day when they are most attentive? With an interpreter?

Explain

While the structure of explanations will need to vary because of differing content, goals, and customer factors, most great explanations include these elements:

1. *What:* These are descriptive facts—the *beef* of the explanation.
2. *So what:* You need to tell or show the customer why you're telling them something—why it's important to them—to inspire them to listen to and absorb it. Also, if you cannot respond to an information need, you need to explain why not.
3. *Now what:* You need to be utterly clear on expectations and next steps. What are you expecting them to do? What will *you* do? What will happen next? What should they be watching for? Are deadlines involved?

Check Back for Understanding

Just because you've provided an explanation, it doesn't mean the customer heard it or understood it. That's why it's so important to find a tactful, respectful, and timely way to make sure that they did, like asking them to repeat their understanding of what they're supposed to do next. It's not enough to ask, "Any questions?" although that's better than nothing. When people don't understand something, many find it hard to form a question to find out what they haven't understood. Also, many people are reluctant to ask questions because they fear looking stupid. That's why you need to take the initiative and bear the burden of finding out what they've understood and what they have not. To do this in a way that's not insulting, tell them you want to know if *you* have been clear, not whether *they* have understood. For instance, "Would you mind repeating back to me what you understand to be the next steps? This is complicated and I'm afraid I might not have been clear."

Once you know what hasn't been understood, you're back at the beginning of our cyclical model and need to go around again.

The goal of producing consistently high-quality explanations is of course complicated, because communication itself is so complicated. There is fact and there is feeling. People vary in what they hear and perceive because of background, mind-set, language, and many other variables. Different customers have different information needs. There is so much to explain—a virtual mountain of information that people find relevant to their care and concerns. Meanwhile, information is changing daily, so it's very hard to stay up to date. *And,* there are many methods of communicating that require employees to vary their modes in hopes of matching the mode to the recipient of the communication. Because of the many variables involved, the pursuit of this objective must be grounded in the information needs and communication style preferences of *customers!* That's the challenge.

10 Steps to Improving Explanations: The Process in a Nutshell

You can use the same basic steps for improving explanations as you used to improve first impressions, just customized a bit to this new objective. Have your teams work together to identify explanations needing improvement, make improvements, test them, refine them, and build the improvements into their everyday routines and jobs. It's a straightforward process.

The 10-Step Process for Improving Explanations: Key Actions

Step 1: Focus people on the power of great explanations and on your plans. Build commitment.
—Orient your management team to your explanations objective and plans.

—Distribute a fact sheet to staff about the forthcoming explanations objective.

—Orient staff to the explanations objective and to the universal protocols.

—Generate enthusiasm for the objective with an energy-building activity.

Step 2: Assess people's current explanation approaches and set priorities and targets for improvement.

—Consult staff and customers to identify explanations needing development or improvement.

—Use a decision matrix to select "the vital few" manageable priorities for improvement.

—Assess the current level of quality and customer satisfaction with the explanations selected for improvement.

—Set targets for improvement.

Step 3: Attack your priorities. Design improved explanations.

—Develop clear roles and a clear work plan that shows which staff members will develop or improve which explanations, by which deadlines.

—Use universal explanation protocols, templates, and guidelines to develop and/or improve explanations to better meet specific customer needs and concerns.

—Offer just-in-time help to aid in design.

—Develop job aids to support use of the newly improved explanations.

Step 4: Communicate new explanations and expectations to staff.

—Plan your approach for communicating the new explanations as new job expectations.

—Reinforce these new expectations in a staff meeting.

Step 5: Equip staff with needed tools and skills, including job aids reminding them of their explanations and practice delivering the explanations effectively in appropriate situations.

—Prompt people in management roles to use and support great explanations.

—Offer a workshop for managers titled "The Manager as Explainer."

—Offer staff practice in providing good explanations.

Step 6: Do a trial run of the explanations, assess their effectiveness, and improve them based on feedback.
—Have staff try out the improvements with their customers and get feedback.
—Troubleshoot the problems. Make revisions.
—Help selected staff deliver face-to-face explanations more effectively.

Step 7: Institute the refined explanations and build new habits.
—Orchestrate people through the 21-day habit-building phase in which they are encouraged to use their newly improved explanations with their customers *consistently*.
—Provide everyday reminders.
—Recognize people for their persistence and effectiveness.

Step 8: Check the effectiveness of the newly improved explanations against your targets.
—Readminister your original measures of quality and customer satisfaction for the improved explanations and check progress.
—Provide feedback to staff.

Step 9: Share experiences and results. Learn from each other and celebrate successes.
—Help staff share their experience and learning.
—Celebrate successes.

Step 10: Institute ongoing methods for sustaining top-notch explanations to customers.
—Institute ongoing monitoring to hold the gains.
—Figure out a schedule and plan for periodically touching base with customers to find out their information needs.
—Build into supervisory agendas periodic observation and coaching of staff responsible for delivering face-to-face explanations.
—Build into your hiring process a screening method that helps you hire people good at explaining, and orient them to the explanations inherent in their jobs.
—Add to performance appraisal forms a dimension related to explanations.
—Develop a long-term plan for keeping awareness high.

Before starting up, make preliminary decisions. Form your steering committee and engage them in developing the best infrastructure for your strategy. Consider the guidelines discussed in chapter 2. Take care to include on your planning team people in both clinical and nonclinical roles so that the objective is seen from the start as powerfully applicable to people in both kinds of jobs. Engage your planning team in reviewing the details in this do-it-yourself kit and tailor it as needed to create the plan they think will work best for your team, structure, and service.

Step 1: Focus People on the Power of Great Explanations and on Your Plans

 ## Key Actions

- Orient your management team to your explanations objective and plans.
- Distribute a fact sheet to staff about the forthcoming explanations objective.
- Orient staff to the explanations objective and to the universal protocols.
- Generate enthusiasm for the objective with an energy-building activity.

Step 1 is your real kickoff to improving explanations. By taking this step you will orient both management and staff to the goal and protocols and stir up everyone's excitement for the project.

 ## Orient Your Management Team to Your Explanations Objective and Plans

If your management team is big enough to warrant a formal introduction to this new service objective, hold this meeting:

Management Team Orientation to the Great Explanations Objective

1. *Present the objective.* Explain the process for selecting explanations as your next service objective. Acknowledge everyone who was involved in selecting the objective and creating the plan.
2. *Ask people to brainstorm the many different situations when explanations are required or given.* Afterward, comment about the many types of explanations provided within people's jobs (for example, explanations on forms and patient education materials, care plans and instructions, medication explanations, descriptions of procedures and policies, signs, and so much more). Ask people to imagine the effects of improving the many explanations provided by your service and people.
3. *Ask people to trace the consequences of good explanations versus inadequate ones.* Form trios if you have more than 10 managers and supervisors or keep the group together if you have fewer. After they have had three or four minutes to do this, ask people to report and look for patterns. Summarize the payoffs of good explanations (for example, patient compliance leading to better outcomes, less work for staff because people have fewer questions and make fewer mistakes, more satisfied customers because people are upset with caregivers who keep them in the dark, and so on) and the costs of inadequate explanations (repeat questions, repeat visits, frustrated and angry customers, besieged staff, and so on).
4. *Explain the plans, schedule, and leadership structure for your explanations strategy.*
5. *Pinpoint the roles expected of managers:*
   —To articulate the importance of explanations work and devote personal energy and enthusiasm to support people's efforts to participate and contribute
   —To free people up to work on improving explanations that need to be developed or improved for their particular customers
   —To attend the briefing "Manager as Explainer" in which the management team will explore ways they as individuals can improve the quality of their explanations to employees, especially explanations about changes occurring in the organization. Announce the date for this.
   —Invite people to add other key roles
6. Invite questions and address them.

Distribute a Fact Sheet to Staff about the Forthcoming Explanations Objective

A fact sheet like this one is a quick and easy way to inform everybody about the goal you're about to undertake.

Great Explanations Fact Sheet for Staff

Why Focus on Great Explanations?

Great explanations is our next service objective. By improving the quality and quantity of explanations we provide to our customers, we can better demonstrate our commitment to communicating with them effectively and giving them a positive and helpful experience with our services and team.

- It turns out that research on patient satisfaction shows that excellent communication with patients and family (about what they can expect, about tests, how they take care of themselves, who will be doing what and when, why there are delays, and so on) is a *major satisfier.*
- Everyone can help meet this objective. The fact is, *everyone explains things to others,* even if you don't relate to patients. People communicate with other staff and other providers. Everybody has customers!

Think of all the situations when members of our staff explain things to customers. We explain instructions on forms. We explain directions on signs. We explain procedures in person and in written materials. We explain medication and when and how to take it. We explain diagnoses and what they mean to the patient and family. We explain things constantly to our customers. It is a central and critically important part of our services.

Our Approach to Improving Explanations

Our work on great explanations will be _____ months long, because there's so much involved and people have so many other priorities at the same time.

- Our first step will be to generate the many explanations we give or need to give to customers of our service. Then, we will select those that need the most work and have the biggest impact. And we'll focus on improving those.

- Then we'll organize ourselves with buddies or in teams to actually make the improvements in the explanations we decide to improve. I'm glad to say we have several tools that will help us do this efficiently and well.
- Then we'll try them out during a trial run and evaluate their effectiveness.
- Then we'll smooth them out and make them into standard materials or protocols.
- Then we'll start using them consistently, building new habits of using them during our 21-day habit-building period.
- To keep us focused, we'll have along the way some methods for keeping awareness high (like bulletin boards that feature people's improvements and whatever other creative methods our steering committee develops along the way).

Join in and help to improve our customers' experiences. If you have questions or want to volunteer to help, call our great explanations guru (name) at (number) today.

 ## Orient Staff to the Explanations Objective and to the Universal Protocols

Hold a staff/team meeting to orient all staff to this objective. Explain the rationale for adopting this objective. Discuss the benefits and opportunities that exist in pursuing this objective. Introduce the universal protocols and reasons for beginning to use them immediately. And clarify your plans for engaging everyone in improving the quality of explanations to customers so that everyone impresses customers in their efforts to satisfy customers' information needs and concerns. Here is a possible agenda for the staff orientation meeting and a list of universal protocols to be introduced at the meeting.

Staff Orientation to Great Explanations

1. Explain the purpose of the meeting to discuss the new service objective and approach.

2. Give an overview of the great explanations goal:
   "To continue our work to improve service, we're taking on another breakthrough objective—to improve the quality and quantity of explanations we give to our patients and other customers. We'll select explanations to work on that are most relevant to our team and customers. Options are:
   —Improving and polishing all kinds of explanations: written, face-to-face, phone
   —Improving instructions and layout of forms and signs, making them more understandable to the user
   —Translating explanatory materials into other languages
   —Developing and experimenting with alternative methods for explaining key things, for example, pictures, checklists, maps, words, and so on

3. Present the plan and discuss the key points of the process:
   —We'll identify key explanations we give in this service/team/department/program and work on improving each of them. We'll work on good ways to tell people what they can expect, to explain procedures, to be clear about plans, and more.
   —We know that customers need a variety of explanations from staff and that the explanations vary depending on who the customer is. So, in order to figure out which explanations need to be given to whom and the best way to do this, we need to first pinpoint all the explanations we give (or should give) to our various customer groups. Then we'll figure out which ones are priorities. Here's an example.
   —Show radiology flowchart. (See step 2.)
   —We'll ask ourselves which explanations need to be given at every step in our interactions with our customers. How do we give them now? How could we do better? Can we create tools to help us, like checklists, job aids, brochures?

4. Explain how we're going to do this.
   —Hand out the diagram of the three circles explanations process. Explain that this simple process can be applied to any explanation.

—Give an example from your own area or use this one:
  —A visitor looks confused in the lobby.
   Ask, "May I help you find something?"
   Explain the "what," "why," and "now what" of great explanations:
   • What? You're looking for Klein 100.
   • Why? That's where you go for preadmission testing.
   • Now what? Go straight down this hall to the end. Turn right at the glass doors and follow the hallway around to the left. Klein 100 will be just ahead.
  —Check back: Do you want to repeat that back to me to make sure I explained it well?
—Emphasize again that this model can be used for any explanations, with both internal and external customers.

5. Hand out universal protocols. (See following figure.)
   —Explain that these universal protocols cover many situations that most employees encounter in their work.
   —Note that everyone is expected to study the protocols and start using them now. Explain how they will also be used as guides to develop or improve specific explanations given to both internal and external customers.
   —Go through the universal protocols, answer any questions, and address concerns.

6. Clarify the next steps. Explain your preferred process for identifying priorities for job-specific explanations and proceeding to engage people in developing the improved explanations.

7. Invite reactions.

Great Explanations: Universal Protocols

Explaining Directions

1. Offer help to lost or confused people, for example, "Can I help you?"
2. Clarify where they're going.
3. When possible, take them there.
4. If it's easy to explain, give verbal directions.
5. If complicated, give directions to the nearest information desk or security officer, or take them halfway there and explain the remaining directions.
6. Invite questions.

Explaining Delays and/or Mistakes

1. Apologize for the situation, for example, "I'm really sorry this happened."
2. Show concern for the customer's feelings, for example, "I know you must be frustrated."
3. Explain what you can do to help without blaming others or saying "It's not my job."
4. Follow through.
5. If the delay continues, update the customer frequently.

Explaining a Handoff

1. Assure the customer that you will help, for example, "I'll be happy/glad to help you."
2. Ask questions to clarify what the customer needs.
3. Explain to the customer that you're going to refer them to someone else. Give the name or role of the person and how to reach them.
4. Invite questions and ask if there is anything else you can help with.
5. Follow through and make the contact for the person.

Explaining What People Can Expect

1. Acknowledge customer's purpose, for example, "I understand that you're here for _____."
2. Explain what the customer can expect or what will happen.
3. Explain who will be doing what, for example, "The technologist, Kim, will be doing the MRI, and I will talk to you when you are finished."
4. Give some idea of how long the test, procedure, or activity will take.
5. Invite questions.

Getting an Explanation You Need

1. Say what you need, for example, "I need to understand _____ because _____. Would you please explain that to me?"
2. Listen.
3. Ask person to clarify anything that's unclear.
4. Repeat back what you heard.
5. Thank the person.

Generate Enthusiasm for the Objective with an Energizing Activity

Here's another opportunity for your steering committee to get creative. To get them thinking, see if they can adapt the "Great Explanations Riddle Runaround" developed by the Albert Einstein Healthcare Network to the size and scope of your service. This activity invites people to voluntarily form *teams* that will compete with one another to solve weekly riddles and perform required tasks.

The Riddle Runaround's purposes are to rally people around the great explanations goal; to build enthusiasm and excitement; to create an upbeat beginning to a process that involves lots of people's energy, initiative, and hard work; to get people thinking about what enters into top-notch explanations.

Welcome to the Great Explanations Riddle Runaround!

✍ If you choose to participate, each week you'll get an assignment (or two) that has some connection to the theme of great explanations. (Sometimes you will need to stretch to see the connection!)

✍ Complete the assignments over the next five weeks and send your stuff to the steering committee head by (deadline).

✍ A panel of judges will review all completed assignments and award points based on three criteria: creativity, clarity, and accuracy. Each criterion is worth 10 points.

✍ You may want to use the great explanations universal protocols and the three circles explanations process (find out, explain, check back) as guides to creating great explanations.

✍ Winners will be announced (date)

Riddle Runaround Assignments

Week 1: November 14–November 18

Assignment #1:
On the poster board provided, draw a map of our health care facility that is easy to read and helps visitors find their way from place to place. Be sure to include all buildings. You can use our current map as a reference to help you get started.

Assignment #2:
In writing, explain the following for your facility:
1. How an inpatient gets television service
2. How an inpatient uses the telephone
3. What a patient must do on his or her day of discharge

Clue for Week 2
On 11/21 or 11/22 between 12 and 1
Search through a tunnel and have some fun
Look for your assignment, we'll tell you what to do
No more info right now, this is just a clue!

Week 2: November 21–November 25

Assignment #1:
Record on an audiotape an explanation of a clinical diagnostic test (for example, upper GI, cardiac catheterization, IUP) without using any clinical words.

Assignment #2:
Create a T-shirt explaining one of your team members' jobs. The T-shirt must be created by your team members. Turn in the shirt with the rest of your items.

Clue for Week 3
Between 8 and 5 on 11/28 and 11/29
Dial 456-KXXX and find out what to do!
The assignment is relevant to this week's special day
So don't miss out or you won't know what to say!

Week 3: November 28–December 2

Assignment #1:

- Videotape and write up a favorite recipe for "stuffing."
- Next, tell us your favorite remedies for overeating!

Assignment #2:

Write a model explanation to apologize to a patient for a delay.

Clue for Week 4

This week's assignment will be found
In a place where subacute care is all around
Between 2 and 4 (on 12/5 and 12/6)
go to the information desk and get ready for kicks!

Week 4: December 5–December 9

Assignment #1:

Explain in writing how to do the Electric Slide!

Assignment #2:

Change the lyrics to the song "Locomotion" using the theme of "great explanations." Sing on a cassette tape. You must do the whole song with at least three of your team members singing.

Clue for Week 5

You're at the end; this is the last clue
We've really enjoyed telling you what to do
To get your assignment and be complete
Go to the place that has something to eat.
Go there on 12/12 or 12/13 between 2 and 4
We'll be there, just outside the door.

Week 5: December 12–December 16

Assignment #1:

Explain how to get from the parking garage to our building for someone in a wheelchair. Write these instructions and record on your cassette from week 2.

Turn in all completed assignments by (date) to (person).

Tips

- It is critical to stick with this first step until everyone has had a chance to be introduced to your objective and voice any concerns they have about it. Take the time you need to build enthusiasm in everyone, adding a time period for getting input into your plan if people are inclined to give it.
- Be sure to include both clinical and nonclinical people as presenters in the briefings for your management team and staff so that people in both types of jobs support the objective from the start.

Step 2: Assess People's Current Explanation Approaches and Set Priorities and Targets for Improvement

Key Actions

- Consult staff and customers to identify explanations needing development or improvement.
- Use a decision matrix to select "the vital few" manageable priorities for improvement.
- Assess the current level of quality and customer satisfaction with the explanations needing improvement.
- Set targets for improvement.

Teams need to identify—for each customer group—a manageable number of top-priority explanations most needing improvement. The Pareto principle states that 20 percent of your efforts produce 80 percent of your impact. Applied here, the Pareto principle says that 20 percent of the explanations customers need produce 80 percent of the results important for your service. The workload might be too great if teams try to devote time to improving *every* explanation they give to anyone. The challenge is to identify the explanations most worth improving. Perhaps there are a select few things that need to be explained repeatedly to customer after customer. Or, there may be a select few things that are essential for customers to understand, where a lack of understanding would have the most dire consequences.

Teams need to ask, "Which explanations, if handled *expertly,* will create the greatest positive impact for customers?" If they target these vital few to improve, their work will be manageable. Then, teams need to make sure they select some explanations that affect people *in each position,* so that everyone participates in the process and everyone makes improvements.

Consult Staff and Customers to Identify Explanations Needing Development or Improvement

We provide four options which teams can select among or combine.

- Option 1: Map the service process to pinpoint improvement priorities.
- Option 2: Ask customers their priorities.
- Option 3: Involve staff to identify improvement priorities.
- Option 4: Solicit advice from other work teams that have a perspective on your customers' needs.

Option 1: Map the Service Process to Pinpoint Improvement Priorities

This approach is ideal for departments, programs, or interdisciplinary teams responsible for a process. For example, in a hospital, Admissions could map the admissions process. The stroke program could map the typical patient's process and explanation points along the way. The various people in Preadmission and Outpatient Testing could work together to map the typical patient pathway through these processes. People across divisional lines who are involved in a joint replacement clinical pathway could identify the explanation requirements and methods at each step in that pathway. A breast surgeon in a cancer center could map the patients' pathway through their treatment process and identify explanation needs at each step, and so on. Here's how to do this:

1. Start by creating a flowchart of the process.
2. For each step in the process/pathway, identify explanation points that patients/customers need at that step (clinical and procedural). Talk with patients/staff about the information needs at each step and what they think would work best.

Sample Patient Pathway: Radiology Outpatient Service

Patient Pathway	Explanation Points
Receptionist greets patient	• Receptionist asks name • Indicates his or her department/service
Receptionist registers patient	• Receptionist tells patient what information he or she needs and why • Shows patient how to fill out form
Receptionist seats patient to wait	• Receptionist shows patient where to sit • Indicates length of wait • Explains what will happen next
Receptionist hands patient to technician	• Receptionist introduces technician
Technician shows patient changing room	• Technician tells patient what to take off • What to do with clothes/purse • What to do when ready
Technician takes patient to test room	• Technician explains where patient is going
Technician readies patient for test	• Technician describes the test • Tells purpose of test • Indicates how patient should be positioned, what to do, and so on
Technician returns patient to changing area	• Technician tells patient to change now or wait for quality check on picture • Informs patient if picture is okay or needs to be retaken • Explains what to do after changing; where to go
Patient returns to front desk	• Receptionist explains next steps
Receptionist takes paperwork and says good-bye	• Gives directions to patient if needed

Option 2: Ask Customers Their Priorities

Teams can consult their customers to find out what the customers most want and need to know and *how* they want to learn this. Specifically, identify each key customer group in your service. Select a method for consulting representatives of each group about explanations they most want or need. Use interviews or convene several customers at once to conduct a discussion with members of each customer group.

Customer Questionnaire

Customers, Please Help!

We're working on improving the quality and quantity of explanations we give to our customers. You are one of our customers. We'd like to know from you what you want or need us to explain well to you (whether we do that in writing or in person).

- In your experience with us, which explanations were/are most important to you? What do you most want to know? When? How?
- When have you felt frustrated with our service or people? Is there something we could have explained in order to reduce that frustration?
- What explanations did you receive from us? About what? And how did we explain those things (for example, in writing, face-to-face, on the phone)? How could we improve those explanations?
- Since we can't improve all explanations at once, if we were to focus ourselves on making the most important improvements in our explanations, which explanations do you think we should work on improving?

Option 3: Involve Staff to Identify Improvement Priorities

Convene staff in each position and ask them to brainstorm every explanation they give to customers. To help them cover the subject, probe for more ideas by giving them categories to respond to: explanations we give to patients, to family members, to employees who call, to physicians, to coworkers, to managed care companies; explanations we give on the phone, in writing, face-to-face; explanations of problems, inconveniences, procedures, and plans. Also, ask staff to identify important explanations by analyzing customer complaints, confusion, and questions. Many complaints happen because something wasn't explained—a plan, a delay, what people could expect. By analyzing repeated complaints, you can identify opportunities for improving explanations. Ask staff to brainstorm complaints they hear over and over. Then, ask yourselves which complaints could have been prevented by a *well-designed* explanation.

Another option is to ask staff to inventory the explanations they individually give on a particular day. Have them track and jot down every explanation they find themselves giving to anyone— whether on the phone, in person, or in writing. To make it easy and clear, give people the following form to fill out. Then, sort the forms by "customer group." Compile all explanations given to, for instance, "patients" or "family members" or "physicians" or "fiscal" or "employees."

Explanations Inventory

This inventory should be completed by individual staff members:

My name _____

Position _____

Explanation to whom (patient, family, physician, employee)	About what? Content of explanation	How is the explanation accomplished? (face-to-face/by telephone/written)

Which three explanations do you think are most important to improve?

1.

2.

3.

Option 4: Solicit Advice from Other Work Teams That Have a Perspective on Your Customers' Needs

The opinions of members of other work teams can be invaluable in helping you to refine your protocols for explanations. Surveys and memos that can be anonymous, like the following, often result in the best responses.

For the Sake of Great Explanations: Give a Helping Hand

Suggest to another department/team an explanation you think they need to improve.

Dear _____:

The following explanation needs improvement:

As far as I know, this explanation is now:

- Not done at all
- On a handout, brochure, or fact sheet
- On a sign
- Done verbally by staff in person
- On a form
- Done on the phone by staff

Here are some ideas about how to improve this explanation:

Signed (optional): _____

 Use a Decision Matrix to Select the "Vital Few" Manageable Priorities for Improvement

Once teams have many ideas about which explanations need improvement, they'll need to narrow them down to a manageable and important few. To pick the vital few, screen them against criteria.

For instance, have a group of staff complete these steps for your service/team.

1. Make a chart for each customer group. (For example, secretaries might have a chart for "internal staff," "patients who call," "people who call from other services.")
2. List the explanations that are given or need to be given to each customer group.
3. Then, copy and complete the chart that follows for each customer group, making sure some explanations are included relevant to each position:
   —Write in the position of the people who give the explanation.

—In the left-hand column, make a long list of the explanations that are given or need to be given. Don't select, just brainstorm with staff every explanation that typically needs to be given to that customer group.

—Rate each explanation on three criteria, using a three-point scale. The criteria:

–Frequency: "How often do we need to explain this to this customer group?" (1 = rarely; 2 = medium; 3 = often/repeatedly)

–Importance to customer: "How important is it that our customers understand this? How serious are the consequences if we're ineffective with this explanation?" (1 = not very important; 2 = somewhat important; 3 = very important)

–Importance to staff: "How important is it to staff that the customer understand the information conveyed? (Does misunderstanding create problems for staff in this or another team/service?)" (1 = not very important; 2 = somewhat important; 3 = very important)

–Weakness: "How weak do we think this explanation is now? Is this one we know needs improvement?" (1 = strong; 2 = somewhat weak; 3 = very weak)

—After filling it out for every explanation, add the numbers across to get a "total" for each explanation situation.

—Examine the results. The explanations with the highest scores are in greatest need of improvement. If the team focuses there, their efforts will have the greatest payoffs. Select the top-priority explanations for each customer group, making sure that some are included that affect people in each position.

—Note: Ask yourself if any of your top priorities might also be explanations that are given by many people in other areas of your services as well, for example, informed consent, billing information, discharge instructions, explanations of tests, and so on. If yes, avoid a duplication of effort. Form interservice teams to standardize protocols for explaining those things well and consistently.

Decision Matrix for Selecting the Vital Few Explanations for Improvement

Customer Group _____					
What needs explaning?	Frequency	Importance to Customers	Importance to Staff	Weakness now	Total

 ### Assess the Current Level of Quality and Customer Satisfaction with the Explanations Selected for Improvement

Options for this step include asking staff, asking customers, asking a colleague, and using a focus group.

Option 1: Ask Staff
Having chosen high-priority explanations for improvement, engage staff in taking stock of whether and how these explanations currently happen by consulting customers and staff to assess your methods and their effectiveness.

For each explanation that you identified as a priority:

- Find out exactly how staff explain this now. (What methods or tools do you use? Is there a protocol or checklist to help? Does everyone explain this the same way? Is there any planned approach to training staff on this?)
- Assess how well current methods are working. To find this out, consult your customers (patients, family members, coworkers, and so on). Try interviews, focus groups, or a short survey.

Option 2: Ask Customers

Asking customers for their opinions on the quality of the explanations they have received is an obvious option. Use a form that's simple and won't take much time to fill out, like the following one:

Sample Customer Assessment: How Well Do We Explain . . . ?

You received an explanation of _____

We're asking you, if you don't mind, to take a minute to tell us how well we explained this.

1. Do you recall receiving this explanation?   Yes ___ No ___

2. How was this explained? (Check all that apply)
   ___ In person   ___ On the phone
   ___ In writing   ___ Other? Please tell how_____

3. Was the explanation given at the right time?
   ___ Too soon   ___ At the right time   ___ Too late

4. Did you *ask* for the explanation or did someone explain this without you asking?
   ___ I asked for it   ___ Explanation was given without my asking

5. How clear was it?
   ___ Very confusing   ___ Somewhat confusing
   ___ Somewhat clear   ___ Very clear

6. Was it made clear to you how you could get more information if you had questions later?   ___ Yes ___ No

7. To you, how important or necessary was this explanation?
   ___ Very important/necessary   ___ So-so
   ___ Unimportant/unnecessary

8. Comments?

Thank you!

Option 3: Ask a Colleague or Associate's Opinion

Ask colleagues, people from other services, or even friends or family to help evaluate your top-priority explanations. Give them an explanatory memo, the written explanation in question, and an evaluation form to complete.

Sample Colleague Opinion Memo

To:

From:

Subject: We're asking your help.

We're working on improving the quality of the explanations we give to our patients and other customers. We're working to improve the explanations communicated on memos, forms, signs, checklists, brochures, bills, and more. Will you please help us by evaluating the attached explanation? I've attached an evaluation form you can use to tell us your impressions and suggestions. Or, you can write your comments in any way you want or call me at _____ with your comments. Thank you very much for your help. Our patients will be better served because of it.

Form for Evaluation of Written Explanation

Written explanation attached

Please return completed form by _____ to
_____.

Please rate the following from 1 to 4, with 1 being "strongly agree" and 4 being "strongly disagree."

Content/Substance

The purpose of this written explanation is clear.   1   2   3   4

The explanation seems to include all important
information.   1   2   3   4

Quality of the Writing

The writer avoids technical terms and uses simple language that a customer can understand.	1	2	3	4
The structure (including length of sentences and syntax) makes it easy to understand.	1	2	3	4
The tone is respectful.	1	2	3	4

Format

The layout is organized.	1	2	3	4
The format is welcoming.	1	2	3	4
The presentation is polished and neat.	1	2	3	4
The print quality is good and easy to read.	1	2	3	4
Overall, this is a great written explanation	1	2	3	4

Your advice, suggestions, questions? (Please don't hold back. The more specific, the better!) Thank you!

Option 4: Focus Group Checkup

Invite people who are not involved in health care and who can therefore look at your patient-, family-, or community-oriented explanations with fresh eyes. Such people might include the following:

- A few of your customers or ex-customers
- A group of consumers, if the explanations are for patients
- A few staff members in very different jobs or fields

Focus Group Invitation

We are working on improving the effectiveness of explanations we give to our patients, customers, and others. To help us evaluate our written explanations, we're inviting a small group of people to sit down with us, look at our materials, and give us advice. Will you please join us? We would really appreciate it.

Date:_____Time:_____Place: _____

RSVP by calling: _____ We'll provide (lunch, dinner, etc.).

Focus Group Discussion Format

- Welcome people and have people introduce themselves. Express your gratitude to people for coming to help.
- Restate the purpose (the explanations goal and your desire to improve the written explanations given to people on forms, check-lists, signs, handouts, and so on).
- Describe how the group will work: You'll show people one written explanation at a time and invite people to react to what it says, anything unclear, ease of reading for people of varying reading ability, attitude conveyed, and so on.
- Proceed to show explanations and invite reactions. Don't react or defend. Listen, listen, listen! Ask clarifying questions. Ask if others agree with points made by one group member. Listen, listen, listen. To help you probe for details, end the examination of each piece by asking: "So what is your main advice?"
- Thank people for their help. Express your gratitude for people's time and thoughtfulness. If people are customers, send a thank-you note as well.

 Set Targets for Improvement

Convene people who play a role in the explanations about which information has been collected. Analyze the information, identifying strengths, weaknesses, and suggestions. Based on this analysis, set specific goals for improvement. If quantitative information was available, set quantitative targets for improvement as well. For instance, "Let's move to 95 percent positive ratings of the quality of our explanations of follow-up care. Also, let's aim for a shift from good to excellent such that at least half of our positive ratings are 'excellent,' not 'good.'"

 Tips

- Intuition counts here. People need to select explanations that they believe need work. Still, because there are so many possibil-ities, it is important to cast a wide net to solicit customer opin-ions and consider explanations team members might not have thought of before honing in on those to improve.

• During this step, make sure people set specific goals about the nature of the improvements they want to make. Is the writing poor? Does the explanation need graphics? What needs to be done to it to ensure improvement and greater customer satisfaction? By articulating the specific current problems with each explanation, teams provide those participating in explanation redesign with targets or specifications to meet.

Step 3: Attack Your Priorities and Design Improved Explanations

 ### Key Actions

• Develop clear roles and a clear work plan that shows which staff members will develop or improve which explanations by which deadlines.
• Use universal explanation protocols, templates, and guidelines to develop and/or improve explanations to better meet specific customer needs and concerns.
• Offer just-in-time help to aid in design.
• Develop job aids to support the newly improved explanations.

Now that everyone has been oriented to the goal of improving explanations and your research into current explanation needs is complete, it's time to design the effort. The tools we present will help you stay organized and on track as you plan how to move forward.

 ### Develop Clear Roles and a Clear Work Plan That Shows Which Staff Members Will Develop or Improve Which Explanations by Which Deadlines

What seems to work best is to develop specialty duos or small teams each responsible for one type of explanation (for instance, "patient education materials," "signs," "instructions on forms") or to team people up by target customer group (one team works on all explanations for doctors, another for elderly patients, another for internal customers, and so on) Then, to prevent these duos from getting stuck, assign each a buddy with knowledge of the available resources—someone who touches base with them periodically to make sure they're on track. They can also call this buddy any time for help, advice, access to experts, and the like. Connect these buddies to a pool of experts on such things as language translation, editing, explanations, formatting, and style practice. Also, recommend that design teams get feedback on their improvements throughout the design process.

 ## Use Universal Explanation Protocols, Templates, and Guidelines to Develop and/or Improve Explanations to Better Meet Specific Customer Needs and Concerns

By using these design aids individually or in teams, staff can make their improvements meet a higher standard because of not having to start from scratch to figure out how to organize the explanations or what to include as key components. Some design aids follow:

- Anatomy of a Great Written Explanation
- Patient Education Protocols
- Anatomy of a Great Phone Explanation
- Anatomy of a Great Face-to-Face Explanation
- Language Tips
- 10-Step Approach to Explaining Tasks/Projects to Coworkers/Staff
- Job Aid for Writing Good Memos

Anatomy of a Great Written Explanation

Follow this format to improve explanations on forms, procedures, tests, discharge instructions, fact sheets, brochures, letters, memos, and checklists.

Plan It before You Write It

1. Clarify who the readers will be and what they want to and need to know. What might they wonder about? What might they worry about?
2. Pinpoint your purpose, ideally in terms of benefits for the reader. (For example, "I want to help you . . .")
3. Note the main points you want to cover—the pieces of information you need to convey.
4. Sequence these pieces of information so that they make sense.

5. Pinpoint follow-up needed or wanted.
    —What will you or others do? What can the reader expect?
    —Specifically, what are you asking the reader to do? (What? When? How?)
6. Decide how to open the door to further communication: If the reader has questions or concerns later, who can they contact and how?

Write It

1. Start by stating your purpose and what you're asking the reader to do.
2. Provide any background needed to explain the situation
3. Give the information in a logical sequence.
4. Get specific about follow-up
    —What will you or others do? What can the reader expect?
    —Specifically, what are you asking the reader to do? (What? When? How?)
5. Open the door to further communication: If the reader has questions or concerns later, who can they contact and how?
6. Show you care. (For example, "Thank you. I appreciate your time.")

Brochure/Fact Sheet/Checklist

1. Give the item a clear title—one that makes its purpose clear
2. State your purpose, its benefits to the reader, and an overview of the content.
3. Note the main points you want to cover—the pieces of information you need to convey.
4. Sequence these pieces of information so that they make sense.
5. Pinpoint follow-up needed or wanted.
    —What will you or others do? What can the reader expect?
    —Specifically, what are you asking the reader to do? (What? When? How?)
6. Decide how to open the door to further communication: If the reader has questions or concerns later, who can they contact and how?

Tips

- When possible, use personal pronouns like "I, you, we." These keep readers more interested and make it easier for them to understand.
- Use active, not passive verbs to make clear who is doing what. Examples include "I will send you the pamphlet" instead of "The

pamphlet will be sent" and "The scheduling coordinator will schedule you" instead of "You'll be scheduled . . ."

- To make it understandable to the widest range of people, use short words and sentences. And avoid jargon and initials—some people might not understand them.
- If both males and females will read this, don't use gender-specific words. Instead of "he," use "he or she" or make everything plural.

Patient Education Protocols

Purpose: Ensure that the right information is provided by the right people, at the right points in the patient's care, and in ways that are understood and retained by the patients and their families.

Step 1: Identify a key patient population.

Step 2: Create a simple chronological flowchart of the main points in the patient's experience with your service or procedure. For instance, patient arrives on unit, has history and physical, has preprocedure prep, has procedure, has postprocedure routines, receives report, prepares for discharge, and receives instructions for postdischarge care.

Step 3: Identify for this patient population what needs to be explained at each point.

Step 4: Identify available resources (checklists, pamphlets, pictures, message points for face-to-face explanations, and so on).

Step 5: Create a patient teaching plan that clarifies who, what, when, how the explanation should be given, and builds in how to check for understanding.

Step 6: Try the plan and evaluate its effectiveness with patients.

Step 7: Revise and crystallize the plan into a protocol that's easy to follow and easy to verify completion of (such as a checklist).

Step 8: Communicate the protocol and its details to staff and coach them on its effective use, the location of materials related to it, and any documentation requirements.

Step 9: Orient all new staff to this protocol so that they follow this standardized approach.

Anatomy of a Great Phone or Face-to-Face Explanation

1. Greet the caller professionally by identifying yourself, your department, and your function (to establish your credibility at the start so your information can be trusted).

2. Find out *specifically* what the caller needs to know and why; also find out what they already know.

3. If the explanation the customer needs is simple and short, tell them what they need to know. If a longer or more complex explanation is required, first give an overview if it. Tell them that the full explanation you are about to give is complex, so they can get set for it. Then give them the details.
   —For phone explanations, does it make sense to suggest that the person take notes? If so, say: "You may want to write this down. Would you like me to wait while you get a pencil?" (Or, if you're discussing this face-to-face, "Would you like a pencil?")
   —For face-to-face explanations, can you provide a fact sheet with the main points listed?

4. Check back for understanding. With a complex explanation, check back with the customer periodically throughout the explanation to make sure they are understanding you. Don't wait until the end. Find out what's unclear, making it easy for people to ask questions. For example, "I realize this can be a lot to grasp at once. Is there any way I've confused you?" Or, "I deal with this all the time. I know it's complex and I'm not always as clear as I'd like to be. Do you have questions?" For long explanations, do this along the way; don't wait until the end of the explanation.

5. Recap the main points. Discuss "Now what?" Emphasize next steps: what they can expect, what you'll do, what others will do, what they need to do, and when all of the preceding will occur.

6. Consider follow-up. Will it help to provide written information to back up the explanation (appointment card, check sheet, pamphlet, map, video, directions)? If so, tell caller how you'll follow up, and get their address and phone number. Then follow up as promised.

7. Open a door to further contact in case the customer has questions later; encourage them to contact you or another appropriate person and tell them how they can *easily* do so.

8. Show you care. The following examples communicate caring:
   —"Hope your surgery goes well."
   —"Hope this isn't too much trouble. I really appreciate your getting me this information."
   —"It was good to see you/talk to you (again)."
   —"Good luck to your mother/wife/etc."
   —"I'll see you/talk to you soon."
   —"Thank you."

Language Tips

1. Always explain why you're there or why you're calling.
   —"I'm _____. I'm here/I'm calling to _____."
2. State your purpose in terms of benefits for customer (if possible).
   —Not so good: "I'm Jim and I'm here to make sure you don't have any illegal software on your computer." Better: "I'm Jim and I'm here to check the software on your computer to make sure you won't be in any trouble if the copyrights are checked."
   —Not so good: "I'm Donna and I'm here to change the linen." Better: "I'm Donna and I'm here to make sure you have nice fresh sheets."
3. Respect people's time.
   —Give people a time estimate: "This will take about _____ minutes/hours/days."
   —Ask if it's a good time.
4. How to say "no" when you must:
   —Say what you *can* do before saying what you *can't*.
     –"I can call security for you, but I can't give parking passes to anyone who is not a Premier Years member."
     –"I can send you resource materials, but we can't do special training for your team."
   —Explain why you can't do it in a way that will build, not kill, the customer's confidence. Then show you care to make the customer feel good.
     –Not good: "I'm sorry you had to wait, but we're short staffed." Better: "I'm sorry we've been keeping you waiting. We can't always tell how long our patients will need, and our patients this morning needed more time than we thought. It looks like your doctor will be ready for you in about 10 minutes."

—Not good: "Sorry it took me so long; this place is a zoo." Better: "I'm sorry it took me so long to call back. It took several steps to get what you needed, and I wanted to get it right."

—Not good: "I'm sorry we can't reduce your hospital bill. That's just what it costs!" Better: "I'm sorry we can't reduce your hospital bill. What we can do is help you arrange a payment plan that's easier for you."

5. Tell people what's next—what they can expect.
   —"I'll be back/call again _____ (when).
   —"I'll do _____. You'll do _____."
6. Invite questions and further contact. Make it easy for people to admit something is unclear.
   —This can be confusing. "Is there anything you're not clear about _____?"
   —"If you need anything in the meantime, _____."

10-Step Approach to Explaining Tasks/Projects to Coworkers/Staff

1. Explain the purpose of the task or project: Why is this to be done? What is its value for the organization? What will be done with the results?
2. If you want things done in a certain way, detail the steps to be taken.
3. Provide a time frame: When is the task/project or parts of it expected to be done?
4. Define success and failure and quality criteria or standards, so that people working on this know when to stop—and when not to.
5. Clarify available resources and how to gain access to them.
6. Clarify what to do if a person hits a snag or problem.
7. Check back for understanding; for example, "So, what's your understanding of the purpose? The task/project? The key steps? Quality criteria/standards? The deadline? The resources? What to do if you hit a snag or problem?"
8. Clarify as needed.
9. Encourage questions.
10. Express confidence in the person's ability to meet your expectations.

Job Aid for Writing Good Memos

> Most memos are explanations. To help you write a good one, take a quick look at this job aid.
>
> **Good Memos Have:**
>
> • Clear purpose up front
> • Short words and sentences
> • Active, not passive voice
> • No jargon
> • No padding or fluff
> • Bullets, subtitles, and **bold**
> • Contractions (for example, "don't," not "do not")
> • Clear actions you want from reader
> • Way to make it easy to respond, if needed
>
> And when in doubt, try it out (on a pal)!

 Tips

• These tools can save your team loads of time because they provide a structure for developing explanations.
• Make sure your resource people are familiar with these tools and that they have them on hand when they're consulting with people in the process of developing their explanations.

 Offer Just-in-Time Help to Aid in Design

Offer "office hours" on specific topics when skilled people will be available at a central location to provide help. Some services or organizations poll talent internally and make staff with needed skills available during these office hours. Other organizations hire experts (writers, layout experts, graphic artists, and so on) for a day each and offer design teams a chance to make appointments for consultation (and in some cases follow-up production work). Here are a few ideas for help clinics, but better yet, examine your improvement priorities and develop the right help clinics to support your priorities:

• Help clinic on writing effective patient education materials: Have good writers and organizers and marketing people available to help individuals or teams figure out their overall approach to materials they want to develop, especially a customer-friendly outline and approach.

- Writing clearly so people can understand: Have an editor or two available in person and/or via fax/mail to review drafts of explanations and edit them. And/or hold a workshop on how to check for readability and clarity, how to write in the active voice, how to write simply, and how to use personal words to increase people's reading comprehension.

- Explaining through alternative methods: Offer a work session in which people can help each other develop pictures, graphics, drawings, and metaphors to help make explanations clearer than words can do alone.

- Making forms user-friendly: Have a small team of people review drafts of forms and debug them for user-friendliness.

- Developing phone explanations that work: Have open phone hours when people drafting phone explanations try them out on staff (playing customers) by phone and get feedback.

- Editing and formatting help for written explanations (signs, pamphlets, checklists, newsletters, forms, and so on): Find people good at desktop publishing to volunteer to lay out newly improved explanations in ways pleasing to the eye. This can include written explanations and also *job aids* for staff describing their job-specific explanation protocols. This service is a *big* hit, and the people who volunteer love it too!

- Help on evaluation: Have a colleague with evaluation savvy on hand to help teams develop or polish the methods they'll use to check up on explanation use and effectiveness. They can help develop mini-surveys, checklists, or whatever will work best for the explanation being developed and its target customers. Remind people to bring along the explanations needing evaluation.

- Arrange for resource people on developing culturally appropriate explanations; find interpreters and identify people who can translate explanations into other languages.

 ## Develop Job Aids to Support the Newly Improved Explanations

Do you need to design and provide instructions for a new filing system through which staff have access to new written explanations?

Do you need a card that shows the steps to follow to access computer files for new explanations, so that staff can print out the appropriate ones when working with patients? Do you need a laminated explanations sheet that includes mini-explanations needed to handle the top 10 most typical questions asked by callers?

The task here is to figure out what props you can provide to staff so that they have easy, at-your-fingertips access to the new explanations, since this will make them infinitely more likely to use them.

Step 4: Communicate New Explanations and Expectations to Staff

 ### Key Actions

- Plan your approach for communicating the new explanations as new job expectations.
- Reinforce these new expectations in a staff meeting.

At this point in the process, all staff members must be informed of the explanation protocols that have been developed and which ones they are expected to use with customers. The following sections discuss various strategies for bringing everyone up to speed on the planned changes.

 ### Plan Your Approach for Communicating the New Explanations as New Job Expectations

Once you have customer-specific and job-specific explanations, all employees must be alerted that they are from now on supposed to use them in their everyday work. There are several straightforward ways to communicate this to staff. Each supervisor can talk with each of his/her direct reports individually, the supervisor could meet with the entire group of people who have the same position, the leader can hold a staff meeting to talk with everyone on the team at once, or the leaders of teams that developed the job-specific explanations can meet with the subgroups of staff to whom these apply. In every case, the following seven components of the presentation should be sufficient to establish new expectations and clear up any confusion associated with them:

1. Thank people for their input and help in developing the job-specific explanations.

2. Distribute them in the form of polished job aids for easy reference.

3. Go over each one, and answer questions. Ideally, feature a few face-to-face explanations by having someone on the development team demonstrate them.

4. Talk about the next challenge, which is to start using them routinely on the job—to replace any previously used materials or face-to-face explanations with these new and improved ones.

5. Describe the remaining steps in the process (trial run, revision, habit building, celebrating success), and the support available during these steps when problems arise.

6. Invite questions.

7. Thank people for going through the awkwardness of changing their ways for the sake of their customers.

 ## Reinforce These New Expectations in a Staff Meeting

Holding a general staff meeting is the best way to ensure that everyone receives the same information about the new expectations and has an opportunity to air concerns and ask questions. Here is a possible format for such a staff meeting.

Communicating Expectations in a Staff Meeting

1. Clarify the overall goal of improving explanations. Review with staff the effects of better explanations on patient outcomes and customer satisfaction.

2. Review the universal protocols, making sure everyone received these as job aids. Invite and address questions.

3. Congratulate the design teams and resource people who worked to develop or improve the explanations selected as top priority. Give everyone an overview of the improvements and show off the job aids that describe them.

4. Make it clear that people are expected to use and distribute these new explanations in the appropriate situations and that this is now expected of everyone as part of their jobs.

5. Invite reactions and questions.

6. Describe next steps in the strategy to improve explanations.
   —Describe how the trial run will work.
   —Describe the schedule and approach for making these behaviors reality, including the trial run, reassessment, and habit-building and follow-through strategies designed to hold the gains.

Tips

- Present the universal and job-specific explanations to staff, including why they're important and how they were developed. Make it very clear that performance in accord with these is a job requirement. In short, the people who communicate expectations in this step need to mean it.
- It helps also to communicate the expectations in writing in the form of a reminder memo. There is no such thing as too many ways to reinforce this point: From now on, everyone needs to use the improved explanations.

Step 5: Equip Staff with Needed Tools and Skills, Including Job Aids Reminding Them of Their Explanations, and Practice Delivering the Explanations Effectively in Appropriate Situations

 Key Actions

- Prompt people in management roles to use and support great explanations.
- Offer a workshop for your management team titled "The Manager as Explainer."
- Offer staff practice in providing good explanations.

 Prompt People in Management Roles to Use and Support Great Explanations

Provide managers and supervisors with a list of actions that will strengthen their role as explainers and supporters of the great explanations process.

Management Prompt: Support Great Explanations in Six Simple Steps

Managers,

All eyes are upon us. Staff commitment to pursuing our great explanations objective will mirror our commitment. If we don't show seriousness about this work, staff will understandably cite this as evidence that it is really not a priority or is at worst a double standard. How can you show your commitment?

1. Ask staff for feedback about explanations you've provided to them lately.
2. Participate actively in assessing explanations and identifying priorities for improvement. Make suggestions. Offer to help.
3. Express interest. Ask people about the explanations they are developing. Look them over. Appreciate people's work. Give specific feedback when you like what you see and when you don't.
4. Select some explanations to improve for your customers. Tell everyone that you are engaged in improving these explanations and invite staff feedback once you have drafts to show people. Consider their suggestions and make improvements.
5. Do all you can to free up staff so they can work on explanations, Provide phone coverage and backup, allocating funds for this when justifiable. Support staff initiatives like sponsorship of customer focus groups and printing of evaluation forms.
6. Be a role model, a booster, and a supporter. And allocate resources to support your rhetoric about the importance of this objective.

 ### Offer a Workshop for Managers Titled "The Manager as Explainer"

If your organization is large enough to have several people in management or supervisory roles, hold a workshop in which you (or a facilitator of your choice) examine every manager's special responsibility to improve the quality of explanations he or she gives to staff. When staff see that their managers are working on making improvements themselves, they will be that much more inclined to take the objective seriously. The skill builder outlined here helps managers strengthen their own explanation skills when explaining organizational changes, the "big picture," and job expectations.

Skill Builder to Reinforce the Manager's Role as Explainer

1. Ask managers and supervisors to brainstorm everything they explained to members of their staff this past week. Comment that they are explaining all the time because of their powerful role as communicators and interpreters of events, tasks, and needs.

2. Explain the purpose of this skill builder: "We as leaders are supposed to be looking at our own explaining behavior, because this is
   key to our effectiveness with staff. This session is a chance for
   all of us to build our own skills as explainers, so we become more
   effective in our powerful role as communicators and so that we
   show we know we are not exempt from needing to improve our own
   explanations."
3. Review the explanations process (three circles) on an overhead
   transparency and on a poster.
4. Explain changes, policies, procedures, and other things in a way
   that helps people accept them: "Frequent changes hit all of us in
   health care today. It's difficult for staff who want a safe and
   secure work setting to deal with all that's going on. The leader's job
   is to explain changes and events in such a way that it is easier for
   people to accept the information and know what to do with it in
   their own work and lives. Let's explore the kinds of changes happening here." Follow the steps provided here to learn how to generate
   such explanations.
   —Jot down things that you think you need to explain to your staff,
     particularly those that will have an *impact* on them. These can be
     large and small, within your team, your entity, the whole system,
     and so on. (Allow 3 minutes.)
   —Ask "What did you identify?" (Record responses; save for future
     use.)
   —Say "Now, let's pick one change many of us need to explain to
     staff, a change that we expect people to resist or have negative
     feelings about. Divide up into trios and—following the first circle
     in the model (finding out what the customer needs/wants)—
     answer the following questions:

Questions That Help You Design Your Explanation

- What outcomes/improvements do we expect as a result of
  what's happening?
- What exactly will happen?
- Specifically, how will people be affected by this?
- What questions/objections might people have?
- How will you answer those questions/objections?

5. Allow 10 minutes for trios to use planning questions. Call the group back together.

—Ask for feedback about planning questions.

—Say, "By answering these questions before you begin your explanation and by keeping these dos and don'ts in mind, you are better prepared to go on to the second circle (explaining *what, why,* and *now what*). Well-planned, well-done explanations will prevent or head off a lot of resistance if you have anticipated it and addressed it in your designed explanations. This is why we should be *planning* explanations of tough things, instead of shooting from the hip and then dealing with the fallout. Good explanations prevent some resistance; people might not always *like* the news you are explaining, but with a good explanation, they may have an easier time accepting it.

6. We're providing you with a model for explaining nearly anything to your staff, including positive and negative changes. I've already presented a set of questions that can help you prepare to explain. Now, here's a model to use to actually design your explanation.

Manager's Model for Great Explanations

- Describe *what* we're doing, what's happening, and so on.
- Describe *why* we're doing whatever we're doing and why it's needed—outcome/purpose/results.
- *Check back for understanding* and ask for reactions.
- *Clear up any misunderstandings* or questions and acknowledge any objections.
- Ask for ideas on how to make what we're doing go as smoothly as possible.
- Describe what will be happening next (*now what*).
- Ask for support and commitment.

7. Provide scenarios for practice by selecting other critical issues from the initial brainstorm. In trios, practice explaining selected issues (assign one to each group). Here are examples of issues appropriate for this exercise:

—Although we can't tell people whether or not there will be more layoffs and whether or not their own particular job is secure, we do need to explain the turbulent economic times and how we are responding to these times within the organization.

—Is there a strategy going on to increase productivity or reengineer services? If so, explain why productivity or reengineering is happening in your organization and the benefits that will come if people can achieve improvements.

—You've heard lots of rumblings about physician behavior interfering with staff morale and patient satisfaction. You want to explain the situation.

—Explain why employees need to be flexible and open to change—organizationally, departmentally, and in their own jobs (for example, why they may need to accept additional responsibilities even though not previously part of their jobs, or cross-train to learn new things).

8. Call the group back together and ask each group to share their explanation with the larger group.

 ## Offer Staff Practice in Providing Good Explanations

In role-play situations, have staff try out a new and improved explanation on each other.

Staff Skill Builder #1

1. Have people work in groups of three. One person is an explainer, one is a customer, and one is an observer. Set the scene so that the customer and observer know who the customer is, the circumstances that call for a good explanation, and the nature of the explanation needed.
2. Have explainer and customer interact, with the observer watching.
3. Afterward, have customer give feedback on what went well and what didn't, and offer advice to make it better.
4. Then, have the observer do the same.
5. Improve the explanation protocol based on this exercise.

Or, have people try out the explanations on people in other teams/departments—people completely unfamiliar with the content—and invite their feedback. And finally, test your improved explanations on customers. Ask them to complete the evaluation form, or interview them using the same questions.

Staff Skill Builder #2

1. Have staff think of a policy or practice involved in their job—a policy or practice that customers question them about. Write down the questions that customers raise about it or the way the customers complain about it.
2. Form trios. Focusing on one person at a time, have the person whose turn it is go through the following process:
   —Explain the customer's question/concern.
   —Respond as he or she would to the customer.
   —Receive feedback from the others in the trio about the effectiveness of the explanation and about how to make it more effective.
   —Then do a replay using the feedback to make improvements.
3. Afterward, their trio partners give them feedback, responding to the question, "What worked better this time?"
4. After one person gets a turn to try out a response, receive feedback, do an improved replay, and receive feedback again, the next person gets a turn to go through the entire process with the customer concern he or she noted.

Tips

- Good written explanations and good explanation protocols don't mean good delivery of explanations. If you bypass the step involving staff skill building and practice, you run the risk of having a file cabinet chock full of great explanations that never reach the customers' eyes and ears. Give staff the time and guidance needed to deliver the improved explanations they design.
- Recognize that staff skills vary and that you already have people great at giving explanations. These people are likely to be your best teachers. Harness them to help facilitate the practice sessions so that their feedback is readily available to others.

Step 6: Do a Trial Run of the Explanations, Assess Their Effectiveness, and Improve Them Based on Feedback

 ## Key Actions

- Have staff try out the improvements with their customers and get feedback.
- Troubleshoot the problems. Make revisions.
- Help selected staff deliver face-to-face explanations more effectively.

Step 6 is your opportunity to test the protocols and practices you've developed and fine-tune them before full-scale implementation. The following subsections offer step-by-step guidance on how to accomplish this trial run and gather feedback effectively.

Have Staff Try Out the Improvements with Their Customers and Get Feedback

Here are tools teams can use to assess improvements during the trial run. Feedback using these tools helps people make course corrections that make the ultimate explanations markedly better. Options include focused mini-surveys, observations as a way to check progress, and staff evaluation meetings.

Option 1: Focused Mini-Surveys
These surveys evaluate specific explanations developed by staff. See the tool presented in step 2 as an example. Use these surveys to get feedback on the clarity, appropriateness, understandability, and format of each specific explanation.

Option 2: Observations as a Way to Check Progress

- Figure out who is in a position to watch explanations going on by each staff member (a coworker, an invited observer, a supervisor).
- Select an observation period (for example, 90 minutes at two different times during the week).
- Use the observed person's explanation protocol as a checklist.

- The observer checks off the elements of the protocol that they see the person do.
- Afterward, examine compliance or degree of implementation. Summarize the data to answer the question, "To what extent are people implementing their improved explanations?"

Sample Explanation Observation Checklist

Observer:		Date:	
	Yes	No	Not Needed
Did staff find out specifically what the customer needed/wanted to know?			
In the explanation given, did the staff member explain the information?			
Did the staff member explain *why* the information was important?			
Did the staff member clarify *next steps*—what the staff member would do and what the customer needed to do?			
Did the staff member check back for understanding?			
Did the staff member show patience?			
Was staff member attentive to the customer?			

What was particularly good about the explanation?
What would make it better?

Option 3: Staff Evaluation Discussions

- Ask "How did we do?" Encourage staff to tell stories of how they used their improved explanations and what they felt customer reactions were.
- Encourage staff to talk about their own perceptions of strengths and weaknesses, and how to make even more improvements.
- Find out changes they think need to be made to protocols.

 ### Troubleshoot the Problems and Make Revisions

Revise the explanation protocols to make them more effective. Iron out the kinks. How? With feedback from the previous assessment in hand, hold work sessions—times when people needing to revise explanations can get together in one room and do their work, inviting help from others as needed. This reserves special time for the work to get done while providing a productive, supportive atmosphere that makes the work more manageable for people who are not professional writers or communicators. Ideally, have people there who can help polish the writing, improve formatting, and so on.

 ### Help Selected Staff Deliver Face-to-Face Explanations More Effectively

Frequently, evaluations of the improvements reveal that some staff are ineffective in delivering what appear on paper to be high-quality explanations. Offer a style clinic on explanations for selected staff who need personal coaching to improve their delivery of explanations.

Explanation Style Clinic for People Who Deliver Face-to-Face Explanations

For this objective, have people who deliver explanations face-to-face come together to try *delivering* their newly improved explanations in an effective manner. Use a round-robin approach or a video for which each person tries out an explanation, receives feedback, and redelivers the explanation by drawing on the feedback to make immediate improvements.

Tips

- Do the trial run quickly, perhaps within one week's time, so that efforts are concentrated, not drawn out. Intense energy spent on assessing the explanations and making the improvements keeps up the pace and moves people to the important step of instituting changes and building new habits.
- Create an atmosphere of open learning so that people who developed explanations don't get defensive in the face of feedback from coworkers or customers. Ask what people are learning. Encourage people to focus on making the explanations great for the sake of customers.

Step 7: Institute the Refined Explanations and Build New Habits

 ### Key Actions

- Orchestrate people through the 21-day habit-building phase in which they are encouraged to use their newly improved explanations with their customers *consistently*.
- Provide everyday reminders.
- Recognize people for their persistence and effectiveness.

Since habit-change experts suggest that people need three weeks of intense practice to change a habit (for example, eating by a diet or quitting smoking), we use that period as the length of the habit-building period we suggest for step 7. These will be 21 days of hard work; every staff member must keep the refined explanations in mind and consciously remember the new protocols. The following sections offer advice and tools to keep the goal foremost during this crucial period.

 ### Orchestrate People through the 21-Day Habit-Building Phase in Which They Are Encouraged to Use Their Newly Improved Explanations with Their Customers Consistently

One great method for accomplishing this is self-monitoring using a chart that measures stick-to-itiveness. The purpose of such a chart is to keep staff conscious of the explanations they are supposed to be delivering to customers.

Equip people with a chart for monitoring themselves that focuses on one explanation a day. The idea is to fill in the first two columns with the customer (target audience) for a specific explanation and the nature of the explanation. Then, for one customer after another, staff enter a check mark in the "Remembered" or "Forgot" column to record whether they remembered to provide the newly improved explanation. At the end of the day, have staff figure out their implementation success rate or stick-to-itiveness. Create a place for posting the rates.

Stick-to-itiveness Chart

Customer	Explanation needed	Remembered?	Forgot?	Comments/ Suggestions

Today, I remembered to deliver the new explanation to _____ customers, but not to _____ customers. That gives me an implementation rate of _____ percent.

 ### Provide Everyday Reminders

Use ticklers to provide everyday reminders about the objective. Post or send out a daily memo with a whimsical, eye-catching character and a reminder about which day it is in the habit-building period. Perhaps your committee or a special creative committee can develop a quip a day to go along with it.

Explanation Tickler

In a good explanation

1. You tell them what you're gonna tell them.

2. Then, you tell them.

3. Then, you tell them what you told them.

Today is day 3. We're one-seventh of the way to a habit!

 ### Recognize People for Their Persistence and Effectiveness

If your steering committee can develop a clever approach here, all the better. Or, consider using "gotcha explaining" coupons.

Gotcha explaining!

Congrats on keeping our customers informed.

Reprinted, with permission, from the Albert Einstein Healthcare Network © 1996.

Give all staff a stack of "gotcha explaining" coupons to give to each other when they witness a carefully delivered, focused explanation. Before giving a coupon, the grantor needs to jot down the name of the recipient and the explanation being given. The grantor should also sign the coupon. Halfway through your habit-building period, give everyone who earned a coupon a free frozen yogurt or other goodie. And at that time, promise that people who end up with five more "gotcha" coupons will get a better prize after the 21 days are over (and think of a good goodie so you can keep that promise).

A variation is to give customers some of these coupons, too, and ask the customers to give them to staff who do a great job of explaining.

Gotcha for giving me a very good explanation.

Thank you!

Tips

- The idea here is to remind people to use their improved explanations and to keep their attention on this. Otherwise they fall back into old habits. This is not the time to focus on giving evaluative feedback. Fine-tuning can be done after the next assessment period or by convening staff to discuss how their new explanations are going.
- Look for staff with whimsy and creativity and graphics capability to develop jazzy reminder campaigns and recognition methods during this period. They're on your staff somewhere.

Step 8: Check Effectiveness of the Newly Improved Explanations against Your Targets

Key Actions

- Readminister quality and customer satisfaction measures for the improved explanations and check progress.
- Provide feedback to staff.

Now it's time to step back and take a careful look at what has been accomplished up to this point. Step 8 involves effectively re-administering the surveys and other evaluation instruments that helped you gauge what was lacking in your explanations in the first place, then communicating the feedback to staff.

Readminister Your Original Measures of Quality and Customer Satisfaction for the Improved Explanations and Check Progress

Revisit the targets or specifications you set for improving each particular explanation and see how you did by readministering the survey instruments you used in step 2.

Provide Feedback to Staff

Hold a meeting in which people review the results of their efforts, including an examination of the evaluation results. Ask the following questions:

- Where did we begin? Where are we now?
- What more do we need to do to finalize the explanations we targeted for improvement?
- How are we going to do it?

In addition, communicate ongoing need for improvement. Note that there is more distance to travel in meeting customer needs to an impressive extent and that from here on, this needs to be an ongoing process—perhaps less intensive but still ongoing. Ask people to begin thinking about next steps, which will be discussed at the next meeting.

 ### Tips

- Some people bypass this step because they feel finished now that they have instituted improved explanations. This is a problem because people run the risk of considering explanations finished when they are still not meeting quality or customer satisfaction targets. This is a time to use self-discipline to stop and ask, "Have we reached our goals with this explanation?" and "Are we ready to make these standard practice or do they need more work?"
- Typically at this stage, explanations need minor revision at worst and can be accomplished by individuals with minimal if any team involvement.

Step 9: Share Experiences and Results—Learn from Each Other and Celebrate Successes

 ### Key Actions

- Help staff share their experience and learning.
- Celebrate successes.

Step 9 is the point at which people in various departments or work teams meet to discuss and analyze their experience with improving explanations so far. The following sections offer some tips on how this staff collaboration can best be accomplished.

 ## Help Staff Share Their Experience and Learning

Help teams and individuals compare notes about the process and show off their improved explanations. Two ways to do this are the sharing of great explanations stories and bulletin boards.

Method: Sharing Great Explanations Stories
Invite teams to report on their great explanations work and then engage your steering committee in deciding on an event and other ways to share people's stories and feature teams.

Format for Great Explanations Stories

1. Team/service/department
2. Team leader and members
3. Before and after:
   —Our explanations (if any) before we made the improvements
   —Our improved or new explanations (examples of your improvements—actual written explanations and protocols for face-to-face or phone explanations)
4. Main problems encountered during the process and actions taken
5. How we evaluated the effectiveness of our improved explanations
6. A summary of our results
7. Noteworthy contributors: People whom you would like recognized for their contributions, along with a short description of what they did that deserves recognition
8. Future plans to maintain high standards of explanations and make continuous improvements

Method: Bulletin Board Sharing
Many of the explanations people will improve are likely to be written explanations. And even those that are not will be summarized into protocols for delivery to customers in face-to-face interactions. Because of this, you'll have loads of material you can display on bulletin boards as a way to show people the many improvements made

and also to recognize the many people who contributed to the process. Make a gigantic "Before and After" bulletin board on which you display the explanations before the improvement process alongside the improved explanations. The contrast is dramatic and gratifying, because you'll probably see barely legible, shoddy explanations on the "Before" side of the bulletin board and polished, user-friendly counterparts on the "After" side.

Also, especially if your organization is large, people will have improved literally hundreds of explanations. Post a comprehensive list of the titles of all improved explanations. People will be excited at the thought that all of these explanations were improved in the concentrated period of time you devoted to this objective. The list itself is inspiring. Also, use the list like an inventory of available explanations: People can be invited to request or order improved explanations, since often an explanation improved for one part of your services can help another team as well. For instance, an ortho-pedic team in one rehabilitation hospital developed a fact sheet titled "How to Use a Walker" for hip replacement patients and later found that the people in the medical surgical area of the acute care hospital sibling could make great use of this explanation as well. If one service creates a wonderful map that directs patients to find the service, that same explanation, with very minor modification, could help other services direct their patients to their sites as well. The spillover from area to area can be astounding when you advertise the list of explanations that exist and make it easy for people in one service to order explanations created by another service.

 ## Celebrate Successes

From this sharing of stories and accomplishments, your steering committee will learn about individuals and teams that made great contributions to the process and outcomes. Recognize and feature staff for creating improvements and also for leading or helping each other through the process.

Method: Certificate Recognition
Certificates like the following offer tangible reminders to people of what they've accomplished so far and provide them a sense of their value to the process.

Certificate of Recognition

for

Service Effectiveness

This certifies that

_____

*has been observed providing great explanations to customers
in a style that is polished, responsive, patient, professional,
and helpful. The result: More satisfied and cooperative
customers and an excellent reputation for our services.
Thank you from a grateful coworker.*

Signed _____   Date _____

Method: Reward Explanations

If you developed a bulletin board for sharing results, consider giving blue ribbons and prizes for great explanations. Bring in a small group of customers to be the blue ribbon panel of judges to evaluate the new explanations on the basis of clarity, user-friendliness, and readability.

Tips

- Usually, you find that a few individuals did much of the developmental work of improving explanations because they had skills in identifying customer needs, writing, formatting, and the like. Make sure they are recognized for their efforts. At the same time, you'll find that some people were particularly helpful as process leaders, coaches, organizers of the effort, and energy boosters. And you'll also know of people who didn't help in development of the new explanations (because that might not be their strong suit), but who learned the new explanations that fell within their jobs and incorporated them into their everyday mode of operating. Be sure that your recognition methods reach all contributors, whatever their contributions.
- Also be sure to recognize both teams and individuals. In a bigger organization, it becomes clear that some work teams embrace the great explanations objective and take on ambitious numbers of explanations to improve. They knock themselves out because they see this process as a great opportunity to make improvements important to their customers. Other teams do the minimum. Be sure you fuss over the teams that gave this their all.

Step 10: Institute Ongoing Methods for Sustaining Top-Notch Explanations to Customers

 Key Actions

- Institute ongoing monitoring to hold the gains.
- Figure out a schedule and plan for periodically touching base with customers to find out their information needs.
- Build into supervisory agendas periodic observation and coaching of staff responsible for delivering face-to-face explanations.
- Build into your hiring process a screening method that helps you hire people good at explaining, and orient them to the explanations inherent in their jobs.
- Add to performance appraisal forms a dimension related to explanations.
- Develop long-term plans for keeping awareness high.

This final step in the process is in many ways the most important one. Without incentives and reminders, the success of any effort can be forgotten in the rush of daily work. This is the point at which you must find ways to ensure that the improved explanations you and your staff have been working on for so long now become the standard for everyone.

 ## Institute Ongoing Monitoring to Hold the Gains

Have work teams develop a plan for spot-checking explanation use and effectiveness using the same evaluation devices they used during the trial run and progress-checking steps.

 ## Figure Out a Schedule and Plan for Periodically Touching Base with Customers to Find Out Their Information Needs

Invite discussion of how teams can continue to pay attention to improving explanations. Ask "What is a process we can set up so that we continue to identify specific explanation needs and continue to work on making explanations better?" Discuss what people consider to be reasonable expectations. Discuss options like forming an explanations subcommittee that identifies needs and locates people to address them, with an expectation of some number of fixed explanations per year.

Consider instituting a system of periodic focus groups held by each service individually in which they pump current or former customers for an evaluation of their explanatory information and style. Invite reactions to specific explanations that are on the priority list for improvement or have been newly developed. Consumers can make great suggestions leading to the setting of new improvement priorities. Focus groups like these trigger *continuous* improvement in a very natural way because caregivers who hear consumers' perceptions and needs *want* to do better in meeting those needs.

Focus Group Guide

1. Invite customers to discuss their memories and perceptions of explanations received during their experience with your service:
   —At what points in your experience with us did you receive explanations or information from staff?
   —Thinking about those times, how would you evaluate the explanations or quality of information your received from our staff during your experience with us?
   —Specifically, when did you feel a need to understand something better?
   —What could we have done to help you at that point?
3. Now, we'd like to show you some explanations we currently use and ask you how we can improve them. Take a look. What do you think?
4. Now, here are drafts of *new* explanations we would like you to comment on before we produce them for everyday use. What do you think?

 ### Build into Supervisory Agendas Periodic Observation and Coaching of Staff Responsible for Delivering Face-to-Face Explanations

The quality of staff delivery of face-to-face explanations needs ongoing attention. Inevitably, this needs to be on the supervisor's plate of responsibilities. Have the steering committee send a set of monthly "tickler" memos to supervisors reminding them to do a spot check of people delivering explanations.

Sample Tickler Memo

To: Supervisors

From: Steering Committee

Subject: Great Explanations

What's happening to the quality of staff explanations to their customers? Get a glimpse. Make it your business to observe one or two explanations per staff member in this next week. Here are some quality criteria—in the form of a checklist—to guide you:

____ Provides the appropriate information to fit the customer's need at the time.

____ Maintains eye contact.

____ Communicates clearly, in step-by-step fashion.

____ Checks back for understanding in ways that are more effective than "Do you understand?"

____ Provides written reinforcement when information is dense, complex, or involves many steps.

____ Makes it easy for customer to ask questions (doesn't make them feel stupid or slow).

____ Shows patience in answering questions and reexplaining if necessary.

____ Gives consumer a way to make contact later if questions arise later.

 Build into Your Hiring Process a Screening Method That Helps You Hire People Good at Explaining, and Orient Them to the Explanations Inherent in Their Jobs

To screen job applicants on their ability to explain, select among the following questions those most appropriate to the position you're interviewing the applicant for and build these questions into the interview process.

Interview Questions

1. Can you think of a procedure you followed in your last job, one with several steps in it? Please explain it to me in detail. What was its purpose and what were the steps involved?
   Listen for:
   —Clear purpose
   —Clear, sequenced explanation
   —Avoidance of unexplained jargon or abbreviations
   —Interest or effort to check to see if you understood

2. Sometimes a customer needs something for their own comfort that we can't provide, or they ask us to do something that we aren't permitted to do. Can you think of a time that happened? Tell me about it in detail.
   —Who was the customer?
   —What did the customer want that you could not provide?
   —Why couldn't you provide it?
   —What did you say to the customer?
   —What was the result?
   Listen for
   —Tactful approach to saying no
   —Clear explanation that goes beyond "I can't, I'm not allowed to . . ."
   —Realization of consequences of saying no
   —Empathy with customer's feelings

3. Give applicant something to read about a service provided by your organization. Ask them to read it and then to explain it to you in their own words.
   Listen for:
   —Clear explanation
   —Avoidance of jargon
   —An invitation to check your understanding or ask questions

4. Describe a time you had to explain something to someone who had difficulty understanding what you were talking about.
   —What was it?
   —Why was it hard for them to understand?
   —What did you do about it?
   Listen for
   —Awareness of why someone had trouble understanding
   —Understanding and respect for diverse communication needs/ styles

—Ability to find another way to explain what was hard to understand

—Effort/initiative to explain it differently in hopes of getting message across

5. Describe a time you kept a customer waiting.

—When you arrived, what happened?

—What did the customer say?

—What did you say?

Listen for:

—Apology

—Clear explanation of delay

—Taking personal responsibility; not blaming someone else

About orienting the new employees: Once you have selected new people and they begin their jobs, identify a person to serve as buddy or coach—someone who can orient the new employees to the explanation protocols inherent in their jobs and appropriate to their customers. Make this aspect of orienting the new employees someone's clear responsibility.

Add to Performance Appraisal Forms a Dimension Related to Explanations

Build into all employees' performance review/appraisal forms at least one dimension related to providing quality explanations, such as "Provides high-quality explanations in accord with explanation protocols associated with service to customers; also provides clear, understandable explanations in response to customer questions; checks back for understanding and encourages customers to ask questions."

Develop a Long-Term Plan for Keeping Awareness High

Without a plan for keeping the objective fresh in people's minds, your improvement process may lag. Try forming a great explanations squad, holding monthly explanations work sessions, and offering your staff explanations skill builders.

Method: Form a Great Explanations Squad

Now that the tools are in place and people have experience making improvements, create a system that promotes continuous reexamination of explanations in need of improvement and harnesses people's energies to make these improvements. Form a squad that has ongoing responsibility for identifying explanations in need of improvement and organizing people to do the work. Build into their work process a quarterly treasure hunt open to all staff in which the great explanations squad solicits ideas about explanations needing development or improvement. Also have them design a simple display device (such as a bulletin board) and a simple award system (such as certificates) for recognition of people and teams who produce improved explanations over time.

Method: Hold a Monthly Explanations Work Session

Reserve a time and place, get people good at writing and formatting, and hold an open work session in which people from work teams can convene and help each other make improvements in explanations. Promote this as a reminder to people to pick explanations needing improvement and assign someone to do the work.

Work Teams: It's That Time Again!

Pick an explanation needing improvement for your customers' sake. Encourage someone to step forward to do the work in a supportive atmosphere where help is available.

Attend this month's great explanations work session:

Date _____ Time _____ Place _____

Resource People available _____

This is an opportunity for strides forward in customer satisfaction. Don't miss it!

Method: Develop Skill Builders for Explanations

Build into staff meetings short skill-building briefings on one sub-skill at a time that contributes to improving explanations. For instance, spend 20 minutes a month working on a single, definable, manageable skill. Skills might include:

- Finding out information needs
- Tactful language for checking understanding
- Explaining delays

The idea is to identify subskills that will help staff become increasingly effective communicators of information and build these skills one at a time. To get you started, here are short outlines for approaches you can use for each subskill cited in the previous paragraph. After you run out, invite staff to identify other skills and find a volunteer to handle a quick skill builder on each.

Skill Builder on Finding Out a Customer's Information Needs

1. Overview: "Since we repeat the same processes for customer after customer, we know many of their information needs and have built into our processes and services ways to meet those needs. But we can't think of everything! This skill builder is a chance to generate ways to find out more about what customers want and need to know. Sometimes, we rely too much on saying things like, 'Do you understand?'—to which customers respond 'yes.' Then we move on. This doesn't help them say what they do or don't understand or want to know. The challenge for us is to find the right words and open-ended questions that will help the customer reveal their information needs. Finding the right words is not always easy, so we're going to spend a few minutes on it."

2. Ask people to think of a group of customers who come to them for a complex set of services. Invite examples from group.

3. Pick one customer group from the list—preferably a group that everyone has some exposure to. Ask "When they come to us for service, what questions could we ask them at the beginning, middle, and end of the service to find out what they want and need to know at each point?"

   —Let's start with *before the service begins.* What could we ask them so we're clear on the information they already know they want?

   —Invite brainstorming of questions, listing all contributions on a flipchart page. (For example, "You're here for _____. Before we begin, are there questions you have? What do you want to know as we go through this process, so I can be sure to address this?")

—What about *during the service?* What could you ask the customers during the service itself to extract from them their information needs? (For example, "At this point, is there anything unclear to you? Has what just happened left you wondering about anything?") Brainstorm questions.

—What could we say *at the end of the service?* (For example, "That brings us to the end of the procedure you came for. At this point, do you have any questions about what happened here today? Is there anything you're wondering now? Now, let's look ahead. What's your guess about any questions you might have tomorrow after you're gone from here? And next week? Do you wonder anything about what you're supposed to do next or how you need to follow up?"

4. Now, give out a worksheet to everyone and ask them to pull from the brainstormed lists two questions that would be good prompts for them to use with their specific customers. Write these into the appropriate section of the worksheet.

Good questions for (customer group)

Before

1.

2.

During

1.

2.

After

1.

2.

---

5. Suggest that people take this sheet back to their work area and use it as a prompt or protocol when they next deal with their customers.

Skill Builder on Tactful Language for Checking Understanding

1. Start with the game "What is wrong with this picture?" Pose a series of statements such as the following to staff and ask them to critique them:

   —Imagine that I have just explained a procedure to a patient and I want to know if the customer understands. What do you think of these ways of finding out?

   –What is wrong with this one? "That's a lot I just told you. Do you understand?" (The problem here is that people say "yes" even when they don't understand, because they're embarrassed to admit that they don't.)

   –What is wrong with this one? "I *told* you that, but I'm not sure how well you absorbed what I said." (This is insulting and implies that the customer didn't pay attention or is stupid.)

2. Invite staff to suggest other problematic ways to check back for understanding and invite the group to analyze the problems with each.

3. Draw conclusions. A key skill in making sure explanations are effective involves "checking back that you have been understood." It doesn't work to ask "Do you understand?" because people tend to say "yes" even when they don't. The effective explainer needs to find *tactful* ways to check the customer's understanding without implying that the customer is slow or stupid or wasn't listening.

4. Engage staff in a quick brainstorm of ways to check a customer's understanding without reflecting on the customer's intelligence at all. Supply examples if people have trouble with this, such as: "This is complicated and I'm not sure I did a very good job of explaining it. Would you mind telling me your understanding of what I said?"

5. Pass out 3 x 5 cards and ask staff to select one of the tactful alternatives generated—one that they like—and write it on their card as a prompt to take back to their work site and use with their next customers to check for understanding.

Skill Builder on Explaining Delays

1. Introduce "delays" as a situation that plagues customers, whether internal customers or external customers. Describe the purpose of this skill builder as helping each other get better at explaining delays.
2. Ask people to pinpoint a customer group that repeatedly experiences delays in your services. Pull out the universal protocol on explaining delays and have trios write out the exact language they recommend when explaining this delay to distraught customers.

Universal Protocol: Explaining Delays and/or Mistakes

- Apologize for the situation—for example, "I'm really sorry this happened."
- Show concern for the customer's feelings—for example, "I know you must be frustrated.
- Explain what you can do to help without blaming others or saying "It's not my job."
- Follow through.
- If the delay continues update the customer frequently.

3. Share the results with the whole group, listening for variety of language and also adherence to the main elements of the universal protocol on explaining delays.

P.S. For more skill builders, use this same structure to create skill builders on *each* universal explanations protocol discussed in this chapter (explaining directions, explaining a handoff, explaining what people can expect, and getting an explanation you need).

Tip
Because communication needs of customers are nearly endless, great explanations can't be allowed to die. That's why these methods for ongoing work on improving explanations merit considerable attention. Don't let people stop short of making long-term plans just because some fatigue might have set in from working intensely in the short run to improve specific explanations.

Possible Pitfalls and How to Address Them

What can you expect in the way of staff resistance to great explanations? Not much. Clinical and nonclinical people alike tend to see the value in this objective.

They do, however, express three main concerns. One centers on—you guessed it—the shortage of time. Many people assert that they are just too busy with their everyday responsibilities to devote time to the design or redesign of explanations or educational materials or pamphlets or fact sheets or any other explanatory device. They say they don't have time to systematically test their explanation devices, nor do they have time to make revisions. When people cite time limitations as being the only constraint on working on explanations, it becomes all that much more important to prioritize and select the vital few explanations needing improvement and use that precious time to create the biggest impact. Also, it is extremely helpful to identify resources beyond your staff for writing, polishing, formatting, and even testing explanations.

But our experience tells us that much of the insistence that "we don't have time" is attributable not to time scarcity, but instead to feelings of inadequacy staff members have when asked to design or redesign communications. Many staff want to improve explanations, but when they look at the ones they're using, they don't know where to begin. They feel at a loss. They don't know how to make the needed changes.

For people who are not professional communicators, it is indeed difficult to stare at a pool of information (often existing only inside their heads, not on paper) and figure out how to organize it: what to say first, second, and third, and how to communicate it in an understandable, accessible way—especially in writing. People feel at a loss.

This is why the protocols and tools provided under step 3 are so important. They provide guidelines to people who are inexperienced at writing, inexperienced at structuring communication, and insecure about their ability to create from scratch. Emphasize to staff that they have the most important resources they need—knowledge of customers and their information needs, and knowledge of the technical information that needs to be communicated at various steps in the customer's pathway through their services. With this in hand, it is a matter of finding ways to communicate. The tools offered here provide templates that make the job much easier. Have these tools available and help direct staff to tools that can help them so that there is less chasing of tails, less reinventing of wheels, and less fuel for people's feelings of inadequacy during the design process. Also, make every effort to line up additional resource people who do have special expertise in communications to help along the way—college interns in journalism, desktop publishers willing to do some pro bono work for a good cause, retired writers—anyone who can help to ease staff anxiety about writing and producing communications products that go beyond their comfort zones.

The third expression of staff resistance to great explanations relates to the pressure to assess at several points in the process. Many people feel resistant to systematically monitoring implementation or effectiveness. They are relieved to have what they perceive as improved explanations and impatient to implement them and consider them done. The challenge here is to maintain an experimental mind-set and insist that you don't know whether the new approaches are improvements or not until you test them. It does take time to evaluate, but you will end up with much better products as a result.

Consider raising these three predictable forms of staff resistance up front with staff and discussing them fully in the hopes of preventing resistance from inhibiting people's energies and efforts—and limiting your results.

Helpful Resources

The possibilities are endless. Encourage people to keep their eyes open for and refer coworkers to good resources, including the following:

- Books on communicating aloud and in writing
- Workshops on writing and public speaking
- Internet resources

Please let us know about your pursuit of great explanations. What worked? What didn't? What advice do you have for others who pursue great explanations in their health care organizations? Call or write the authors with your results, so your cohorts from other health care organizations can learn from your efforts.

Chapter 6

• • •

Do-It-Yourself Kit for Improving Service Recovery

Service recovery is about handling customer complaints effectively. Service recovery is a terrific breakthrough objective for *all* staff for the following reasons:

• Complaints are inevitable.
• Customers, both internal and external, complain to people who provide services to them.
• That means that all staff members have their customers complaining to them some of the time.

So, everyone in your service, no matter what his or her job, has opportunities to handle complaints, and everyone needs to be able to field complaints in a way that reflects positively on your team, your service, and your organization.

Some health care customers are dissatisfied no matter how good your service is. People's past health care experiences vary, as do their expectations, their anxiety levels, and their concerns. While managers and clinicians share responsibility for instituting effective service processes that produce consistent quality and customer satisfaction, dissatisfaction still occurs. Even if the quality of your service remains absolutely constant at a high level (which is no easy matter), people's perceptions and evaluations of it may still vary dramatically.

All of this makes customer complaints inevitable. And because they are, we need to do all we can to unearth them and resolve them. The fact is, people who go away mad usually tend to go away. If they have a choice, and most do, they go to another provider next time. Complaints are therefore a gift, because they provide us with a second chance to make things right.

If you're thinking "But we hear very few complaints!" consider this: No news is *not* good news! Patients who don't complain aren't necessarily happy with your service. Thirty percent of dissatisfied customers never complain to the service organization that wronged them. Instead, they resentfully spread the word to their network of family and friends and take their business elsewhere when they get the chance. On the other hand, when a person is satisfied with a health care service, he or she tells an average of five family members and friends about it. If people are dissatisfied, they tend to tell twenty people; that's four times as many. That means you have to satisfy four for every one you disappoint, just to stay even in terms of your reputation. If you can convince people to complain, you have a chance to turn a dissatisfied customer into a satisfied customer— with big positive effects on the grapevine.

As much as it goes against the grain of managers and staff, we should literally be *begging* patients and other customers to complain about our services. Consider this chain-of-events model that shows how expressed and resolved complaints are an investment in your service's future.

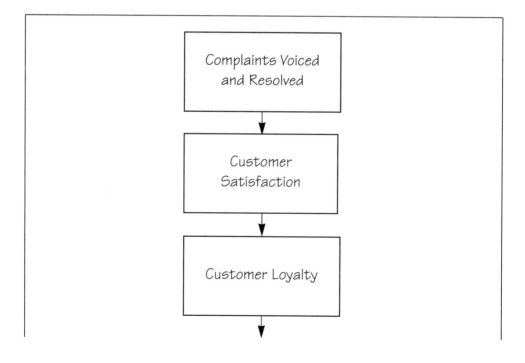

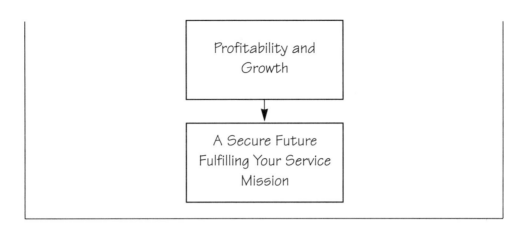

One more thing: Accrediting agencies care about your service's systems for handling complaints. For one, the Joint Commission on the Accreditation of Healthcare Organizations' *Comprehensive Accreditation Manual for Hospitals* now includes specific guidelines for complaint management:

- A mechanism must exist for receiving and responding to patients' and families' complaints concerning quality of care.
- Patients and families must be informed of their right to present complaints and the process by which they can present complaints.
- The organization must analyze the complaint and, when suggested, take appropriate corrective action.
- Each patient or family member making a significant complaint must receive a response from the organization that substantively addresses the complaint.
- The presentation of a complaint must not in itself serve to compromise any patient's future access to care.[1]

Health care organizations should provide a system for receiving and responding to customers' complaints. They should keep clear and accurate records of complaints and, whenever possible, take action to correct any problems that their built-in service experts—their customers—raise. By involving everyone in service recovery, you will more than satisfy accreditation agency reviewers. You will impress them.

Service Recovery: Turning Lemons into Lemonade

In the service sector, the process of making things right in the face of customer dissatisfaction is called service "recovery." It means simply doing all you can to correct a wrong perceived by the customer—and doing it in such a way that the customers' interests are protected and their emotions calmed. In the face of complaints, customers are impressed when you apologize, acknowledge their inconvenience or discomfort, take ownership, provide alternatives, keep your promises, and do so in a timely and courteous fashion.

Whose Job Is Service Recovery?

Everybody's! According to John Goodman, president of the Technical Assistance Research Programs (the national expert on complaint research), well over half of complaining customers complain to frontline staff. They don't seek out a complaint department or customer/member/patient services representative. If frontline people think it isn't their job to hear out customers and handle their complaints, you build one more frustration into your customers' experience. Now they have to find the "right person" to complain to and voice their complaint again. And finding the right person might not be easy.

Imagine if every person in your service saw themselves as a patient/member relations rep—an ambassador of goodwill—and welcomed and handled complaints effectively. These people would nip complaints in the bud. Not only would this stem the tide of customers' frustration, but it would impress them, because few expect staff to handle their complaints in a responsive and immediate way. More customers would walk away from the service thinking, "They frustrated me, but when I told them, their response was impressive. They cared, they gave me alternatives, they acted, and they kept their promises. What more can I expect?"

"Do We Have To?"

The fact is, many employees resist the responsibility of hearing and handling complaints—for some very understandable reasons:

• Some balk at what they perceive as customers' unrealistically high expectations. They think, "If only they knew how short staffed we are or how hard I work, they would know to expect less."

- Some don't know grace under pressure, so they back away from hearing complaints, especially heated complaints.
- Some want desperately to make things right, but feel oppressed by dysfunctional work processes or systems that caused the complaint in the first place. They resent management for putting them in the position of needing to apologize for problems that were not their fault.
- Others want to make things right for customers, but can't do it alone. They must rely on others to come through for them, and they feel powerless to do so.
- And still others want to make things right, but are repelled by red tape that blocks them from meeting customer needs in difficult situations. They see bureaucracy, authority lines, and resource constraints as killing their initiative.
- Some bristle at the thought that the complaining customer might expect an apology. They think an apology is an admission of guilt. They think that "I'm sorry" means "I'm wrong" instead of "I regret that you've been inconvenienced or uncomfortable."

Five Components of Effective Service Recovery

For your team to excel at service recovery, you need to have a *system* in place for service recovery—a system that reaches beyond the scope of any individual.

There are five key components to such a system. All five components must be present and effective for your service to handle customer complaints in a way that impresses one customer after another. The five components are as follows:

1. Effective systems for inviting/encouraging customers to complain.
2. Guidelines for staff and latitude to act and atone.
3. Documentation and a feedback loop that channels problems revealed through service recovery into an improvement or problem elimination process.
4. Clear protocols for handling customer complaints effectively.
5. Staff skilled in service recovery—aware of protocols, and able to listen nondefensively, empathize, handle emotion, solve problems, and follow through to closure.

Effective Systems for Inviting/Encouraging Customers to Complain

You need regular, reliable ways to encourage customers to complain, since their silence doesn't mean they're happy with your service. Surveys, suggestion boxes, follow-up interviews, and staff who ask, "So, how is everything?" are all vehicles for encouraging customers to speak up about any problems.

Guidelines for Staff and Latitude to Act and Atone

For fear of using a much overused word, staff need to be *empowered*. They need to have the authority to make decisions about and handle most customer complaints autonomously so that they can take responsibility and initiative and act on customer complaints without feeling "my hands are tied." To accomplish this, you need the following:

- Clarity about the extent of their authority to act on complaints without getting approval from higher-ups.
- Defined courses of action related to the most frequent complaints.
- Minimal red tape and minimal need to gain authorization for every action.
- A clear system of resource people, clear authority lines, and backup systems, so staff have easy access to appropriate people when dealing with difficult complaints or those with financial, legal or ethical implications.

Documentation to Channel Problems Effectively

You need to be able to identify patterns of complaints so you can proactively intervene to prevent these recurrent complaints in the future. To track patterns, you need documentation of problems discovered through service recovery. Otherwise, you have no evidence of recurrent patterns. Without this feedback loop, the process of problem elimination or improvement is halted.

Clear Protocols for Handling Customer Complaints Effectively

At any moment, a customer might complain to any member of your staff. People complain to whomever is nearby, whomever they can access easily. Because of that, unless you want your customers to see your staff pass the buck, every staff member needs to be able to handle complaints themselves. And to achieve any consistency in the way they handle complaints, you need to establish protocols for handling complaints—protocols that spell out the elements of effective complaint handling and also protocols for handling specific kinds of predictable complaints.

Staff Skilled in Service Recovery

Assuming staff have protocols and guidelines in hand, they also need the communication skills prerequisite to handling complaining customers effectively. They need to be able to listen without being defensive. They need to be able to empathize with customer concerns and frustrations. They need to be able to solve problems. And they need to have the persistence, patience, and resourcefulness to follow through to the point where the customer is satisfied or recognizes that all that can be done has been done.

What It Takes for Individuals to Be Good at Service Recovery

Because strategies to pursue breakthrough service objectives are designed to engage every staff member in the process, we developed, with standardization in mind, a model that staff members can use to upgrade their approach to handling customer complaints so that their behavior in response to complaints is skillful, respectful, and effective. You'll see this model, which comprises the following tasks, built into several strategy steps.

Model: 10 Steps to Service Recovery

Step 1: *Listen patiently without interrupting. Don't argue or get defensive. Put aside whatever you're doing and focus your complete attention on the customer. If the customer is within hearing distance of others, suggest moving to a private area where you can both hear well and communicate confidentially. Listen attentively, encouraging the person with direct eye contact and nodding until the person seems finished. Don't disagree, agree, argue, or fight back.*

Step 2: *Apologize. On behalf of the organization, say, "I'm really sorry about this" even if it was not your fault. Show that you, as a representative of your service, are not happy that anything about your service frustrated or disappointed your customer.*

Step 3: *Use a "glad but sad" statement.* Show appreciation that the customer spoke up and empathy for his or her viewpoint and feelings. Consider how you would feel if you were in the customer's shoes. Show an open-minded attitude. Tell the person you're glad they spoke up by saying something such as "I'm very glad you mentioned this to me, since this gives us a chance to do something about it for you." Go on to show you recognize and care about their feelings (whether frustration, anger, anxiety, stress, or worry). Use such statements as "I can imagine how frustrating that must have been for you," or "I understand how upsetting this is."

Step 4: *Ask questions to fully understand what the problem is and what it is that the customer wants. And check your understanding.* Don't jump to conclusions about how the problem should be resolved. After people have expressed their emotion, they can get clearer on the problem, and so can you. You don't know what a customer needs in order to feel better without asking. Ask them. People at this stage will usually recognize when it's too late to fix the problem, and they'll admit that they will be happy if you at least pass along their concerns to the appropriate parties. Summarize the facts as you understand them so far. Put into your own words what you think the customer said. Then, ask questions to fill in the exact details. Repeat this back to the customer to make sure you have it right.

Step 5: *Fully discuss options.* Explain clearly what you can and cannot do. Discuss all possible courses of action that you think could address the problem, and ask the customer to choose. Give the customer that power. Tell the customer what you have the power to do and what you don't have the power to do *before* you make any promises to them. If the customer wants something beyond your power, offer to locate the right person and represent the customer to that person.

Step 6: *Reach a decision and discuss the details of what the customer can expect.* Don't leave the person hanging. If you can't resolve the problem yourself, find the person who can, and tell the customer you'll get back to them. Arrange a time and method for communicating the results. If you can reach a conclusion, discuss what, how, by whom, and when.

Step 7: *Genuinely thank the person for speaking up.* "It gives us a chance to make things right," or "Your feedback helps us to improve our service," or "We want to do right by you, and you've given us a second chance" are appropriate statements here.

Step 8: *Follow through. Do what you say you'll do when you say you'll do it.* Act promptly and keep your promises. Update your customer regularly about your progress and explain any necessary changes in plans. Check back with the customer to make sure no stone has been left unturned.

Step 9: *Document the complaint according to guidelines.* This makes it possible to identify patterns that call for *preventive efforts.*

Step 10: *Do all of the above with an attitude that shows care, professionalism, and respect.* Even if you handle all of the steps above perfectly, you will fail to satisfy the customer if you show the slightest bit of displeasure, impatience, exasperation, or condescension.

10 Steps to Improving Service Recovery: The Process in a Nutshell

This do-it-yourself kit presents a 10-step improvement process parallel to that used in the previous two kits. The improvement process addresses both the need to modify your systems to ensure that all five components of an effective service recovery system are in place and, at the same time, to ensure that every individual on your team is equipped to handle complaint interactions effectively.

The 10-Step Process for Improving Service Recovery

Step 1: Focus people on your service recovery objective.
— Orient your management team to your service recovery objective.
— Announce the objective to staff using a "staff alert."
— Orient staff to your service recovery objective and plan.
— Generate enthusiasm for the objective with an energy-building activity.

Step 2: Take stock of current performance and set priorities and targets.
—Examine existing complaint data.
—Assess gaps in current system of service recovery.
—Engage staff in setting priorities.
—Select priorities for improvement.

Step 3: Attack priorities and design improvements.
—Institute systems for inviting/encouraging customers to complain.
—Define the limits and ground rules for staff authority.
—Agree on a format/protocol for documenting complaints and channeling the results into a problem elimination process.
—Develop specific complaint protocols for handling unpreventable complaints.

Step 4: Communicate improvements and new expectations to all staff.
—Hold a meeting to communicate service recovery expectations to staff.
—Provide service recovery protocols in the form of job aids.

Step 5: Equip staff with needed tools and skills.
—Help managers be effective with service recovery.
—Build staff skills in service recovery through training.
—Provide written skill builders to reinforce skills.
—Provide practice in handling difficult complaints and difficult people.

Step 6: Do a trial run, assess performance, and make improvements based on feedback.
—Provide people with a self-assessment device.
—Institute a method for collecting and recording difficult situations so you can address them with staff and fine-tune people's approaches.
—Solicit customer feedback.
—Make improvements in protocols and practices.

Step 7: Institute improvements and build new habits.
—Provide daily reminders to use service recovery protocols.
—Reward successes.

Step 8: Check performance against targets.

—Examine evidence of overall satisfaction with your services.

—Readminister any measures you have of complaining customers' satisfaction.

—Engage staff in evaluating the success of complaint-specific protocols.

Step 9: Share experience and results; learn from each other and celebrate successes.

—Help staff share service recovery successes.

—Celebrate improvements in customers' overall satisfaction.

Step 10: Institute ongoing methods for sustaining top-notch performance.

—Institute a system for ongoing feedback.

—Build into hiring process screening methods for service recovery skills.

—Add service recovery responsibilities to job descriptions and the performance appraisal process.

—Provide periodic education and reminders.

The following sections present each step and key action in detail and offer tools for successful completion of each segment of the process as well as methods for tailoring tools to your specific needs.

Step 1: Focus People on Your Service Recovery Objective

 Key Actions

- Orient your management team to your service recovery objective.
- Announce the objective to staff using a "staff alert."
- Orient staff to your service recovery objective and plan.
- Generate enthusiasm for the objective with an energy-building activity.

Your first step toward the goal of improving service recovery involves two crucial activities: uniting all involved people—management as well as staff—in awareness of the objective and creating excitement for the objective. The following sections address these two processes.

Orient Your Management Team to Your Service Recovery Objective

There are certain processes and ground rules that need to be clear and in place before you engage all staff in taking a more active and effective role in service recovery with their customers. Convene managers and/or your service recovery steering committee to assess the extent to which these processes and ground rules are in place in your organization and figure out how to deploy resources to build or improve any that are not currently effective. Use this session to orient managers to your new objective.

Leaders' Orientation to Service Recovery Objective

1. Announce or review the fact that improving service recovery is your service's next breakthrough objective. Define "service recovery" and review the reasons for selecting it as the next service objective.
2. Introduce the meeting's purpose.
3. Help managers identify and articulate the benefits of effective service recovery. Pair people up and ask them to work together to complete this worksheet on the benefits of service recovery.

Main Benefits of Service Recovery

For Customers:

_____

_____

_____

_____

For Staff:

_____

_____

_____

_____

For Our Organization:

_____

_____

_____

_____

Invite people to share their responses with everyone.

4. Summarize the benefits: Describe the research on the benefits of service recovery as well as the main benefits people described.

—Give an overview of the elements that need to be addressed in order to do a thorough servicewide approach to improving service recovery. (See notes on the "Five Components.")

—Invite people to comment and add to the list any elements they think need to be present that you have not discussed.

5. Describe plans for prerequisite work involving an assessment of current practices in relation to the above list of elements key to a thorough servicewide approach, identification of needs that must be filled before going public with staff, and planning for effective staff involvement. Clarify the following:

—Who will spearhead the effort?

—Will this leaders' group be the planning team, or will you form a committee of key stakeholders and/or enthusiasts?

—What will be the planning process? And what is the timing projected for startup?

—What can this group expect in the way of communication about the status of the strategy?

6. Invite questions and concerns. Address them together.

 Announce the Objective to Staff Using a "Staff Alert"

A memo or "staff alert," like the following one, that is sent to the entire staff, is a great way to provide a "buzz" about the forthcoming project.

Staff Alert to Service Recovery Objective

To: Staff

Subject: Our Next Service Objective—Turning Wrongs into Rights with Service Recovery

Wouldn't it be great to work in a place where every customer is totally satisfied with your services, and therefore they never complain about anything?

That sounds nice but it isn't realistic. The fact is, no matter how well organized, efficient, and customer friendly our services and people are, some of our patients and other customers will still complain to us. And people will complain to *all* of us, not just to people who have the handling of complaints as their specific job responsibility.

When people complain, they see the person hearing the complaint—at that moment—as the representative of our whole service. They want to be heard. They want to be understood. And they want the person hearing their complaint to respond with sensitivity and preferably with some action that will make things right. While sometimes it's necessary to refer people with complaints to others, the customer gets more annoyed as each new complaint handler gets into the fray.

Imagine how impressed our customers would be if the first person they complain to hears them out, thanks them for speaking up, and then goes a long way to fixing the problem. This would enable us to turn annoyed customers into impressed customers.

As we pursue our next service objective, we're going to work together to do exactly that! We're going to build the effectiveness of every one of us as complaint handlers so that every one of us has the skills to hear and understand customers' complaints, calm them down, and take steps to make things right.

The Name for It—"Service Recovery"

In the last few years, the art and science of handling complaints effectively has been named *service recovery*. Service recovery means doing all you can to correct a wrong perceived by a customer so that the customer's interests are protected and his or her emotions calmed. Some people think of this as turning lemons into lemonade!

The term *recovery* is used to reflect the need to help the customer recover—to restore them from a state of frustration or disappointment to a state of satisfaction. We're going to call our service objective *service recovery*, and after building our service recovery skills and systems together, we'll make service recovery everyone's job throughout our services.

How We'll Proceed

Team(s) will be developing protocols for service recovery, some for all of us to use and some more suited to people in specific jobs. Then, we'll all have a chance to sharpen and practice our service recovery skills in a service recovery workshop. We'll also look at our systems for inviting complaints and make sure customers feel welcome to express themselves. And we'll figure out how to track complaints and evaluate our methods and their results, as all members of our team play an increasingly active role in inviting and handling complaints.

_____ will serve as project leader for our service recovery objective. So, contact him/her if you have suggestions or want to serve on the steering committee. Otherwise, watch for the details and join in.

 ## Orient Staff to Your Service Recovery Objective and Plan

After the brief, introductory message, it's time for everyone to have a more detailed initiation into the specifics of your service recovery objective. Hold an orientation session, either as part of a regular staff meeting or as a meeting on its own, and follow an agenda like this one.

Introducing the Service Recovery Objective

1. To introduce the objective, the facilitator shares personal commitment to the new service goal of improving service recovery. The facilitator might make a speech like the following, for instance:

   We're meeting today because I want to involve you in the first steps toward pursuing our new service objective, which has to do with better managing *complaints* throughout our organization and in our service in particular. Service recovery is what we're calling our new service objective, because, when we manage complaints well, customers *recover* from being upset with us! I'm really glad to be talking with you about our new service goal because I think it's a powerfully important goal and one to which we *all* can successfully contribute—to our customers' benefit.

   Effective service recovery doesn't happen by accident. It happens by design. That's why we're designing and instituting a strategy that builds our consciousness about the importance of all of us handling complaints effectively, that equips each of us with the skills to do it, and helps us track complaints so we can learn from them. Then we can make improvements in services that prevent complaints that we hear repeatedly. Today, I'll describe how we'll approach service recovery in our team and get your ideas about how we can do a better job of it for our customers. To get us focused, we'll talk about the benefits of improving service recovery for our customers, our organization, our team, and ourselves as individuals. We'll take stock of what we do in the way of service recovery now and how we do it now. And we'll discuss steps in our service recovery improvement strategy.

2. The facilitator should now introduce staff to what effective service recovery is, perhaps through an exercise such as the following:

> To begin thinking about effective service recovery, I want everybody to think of a place (a store, a business, a beauty shop, a restaurant, hotel, and so on) where you feel you have seen people handle your complaints really, really well. Take a few minutes to see that place in your mind and relive the experience of complaining and seeing a real pro handle your complaint effectively.

> Now, turn to someone sitting nearby and describe this place and the specific behaviors of the people there that made you feel they handled your complaint so well.

—The facilitator should now call people back together and ask a few volunteers to talk about the places that came to mind and the specific behaviors that constituted effective complaint handling there. If someone says "The people were good," the facilitator should push for specifics (for example, "What exactly did they do that made you think they were effective in handling your complaint?").

—After hearing several responses, the facilitator should emphasize the importance of the goal by saying, "While most of the behaviors you described apply to many complaint situations, we work in health care where customers are more often sick, worried, and frightened. So we have an even greater challenge to help people feel understood and helped!"

—The facilitator should summarize and review the benefits of handling complaints well for customers, for the organization, for the work team/service/department, and for the individual staff member.

3. The facilitator should ask employees to brainstorm the benefits of great service recovery for each of several constituencies. Their responses should be recorded on flipchart paper, a chalkboard, or a whiteboard.

Benefits of Excellent Service Recovery

For Customers:

_____
_____
_____
_____

For Organization:

_____
_____
_____
_____

For Our Team:

_____
_____
_____
_____

For Ourselves:

_____
_____
_____
_____

Note: Be sure they cover economics, competition for customers, relieving stress of already hardworking or overworked staff, inevitability of complaints so that skill in handling them well should be a staple skill, effect of customer dissatisfaction on public image, service recovery as a way to turn a disaffected customer into an impressed one, and so on.

—Summarize and make a strong personal statement about the importance of excellent service recovery in your service and by everybody.

4. The facilitator should engage staff in complaint analysis with the following steps:
   —Engage staff in talking about who their customers are and what they complain about.
   —Ask people to brainstorm who their customer groups are (for example, physicians, coworkers from the Billing Department, outpatients, and so on).

—Make the point that each customer group has different needs from your service and that these needs translate into different kinds of complaints because people complain when their needs aren't being met from their viewpoint.

5. Divide group into smaller groups of three.
—Ask groups to fill out the form "Who Are Our Customers and What Are Their Most Typical Complaints?"

Who Are Our Customers and What Are Their Most Typical Complaints?	
Customer Group	Typical Complaints
Patients	• Slow service • Hard-to-read instructions • Difficulty getting an appointment • Runaround about insurance

—Convene whole group and compile list of most typical complaints of each customer group.

6. The facilitator should assess current practices by asking the following questions. Once they are answered, the facilitator will lead a discussion of the strengths and areas that need improvement (being sure to remain nondefensive).
—Which customer complaints do we handle well? Which customer complaints are difficult for us?
—Toward which customers do we need to improve our complaint-handling practices and behavior?
—Where should our priorities be in improving service recovery by our team?

7. The facilitator should now give an overview of the servicewide strategy to improve service recovery.
—The facilitator should tell staff that excellent service recovery involves more than having skilled staff and that the strategy will address all of these key components:
–Component 1: Effective methods for inviting and encouraging customers to complain.
–Component 2: Guidelines for staff so they know what latitude they have to act to turn the customer's dissatisfaction into satisfaction. Staff will know whether they can compensate customers, give money back, or offer them some special convenience. They'll need to

feel empowered to make decisions about and handle most customer complaints autonomously so that they can take initiative
and act on customer complaints without feeling that their hands
are tied. To accomplish this, staff need:

–Clarity about the extent of their authority to act on complaints without getting approval from someone else.

–Defined courses of action related to the customers' most frequent complaints.

–Minimal red tape or barriers to doing what they want to do for
the customers.

–A clear network of resource people, authority lines, and backup
systems, so staff have easy access to appropriate people when
they need them—for dealing with more difficult complaints, for
spending money to solve a problem, or to do the right thing when
they think there are legal issues involved.

–Component 3: Some kind of documentation and a feedback loop
that channels problems revealed by complaining customers into
an improvement or problem elimination process.

–Component 4: Clear protocols for handling typical customer
complaints effectively.

–Component 5: Staff skilled in service recovery—aware of protocols and able to listen nondefensively, empathize, handle emotion, solve problems, and follow through to closure.

—The facilitator should now describe whichever strategy components
your service decides to include. For instance, will there be an over-
haul of methods for inviting complaints so customers feel that
people want to hear their concerns? Will every employee be trained
and then expected to handle complaints in their own roles, cutting
way down on referring complaints to others? Will there be any dif-
ferences in the documentation of complaints to allow people to
identify patterns of recurrent complaints that should trigger
process improvements? Will there be development of service recovery protocols, standards, and job aids to help staff handle the
really frequent, inevitable complaints that occur within their jobs?

8. The facilitator should now invite staff reactions to the plans so far
and also other approaches they suggest to strengthen your strategy.

9. Restate your personal enthusiasm about the service recovery
objective and your personal commitment to making significant
improvements as a result—for the benefit of customers, staff, and
the organization.

Tips

- Some people divide the staff orientation meeting into two sections to reduce the time demands. In two sections, each part can easily be completed in 45 minutes. Otherwise, it tends to take 90 minutes or a few minutes more.

- This awareness-raising and motivational step relies on effective facilitation. The facilitator needs to be a true believer because many staff don't want to hear that they're going to need to focus on handling complaints more effectively, that they are going to be seen as responsible for taking action to satisfy customers who are distraught by issues that might be far afield from their jobs. Is there someone in your service who characteristically handles the tough complaints, someone knowledgeable about the range of complaints customers voice and the range of possible ways to respond—a patient relations expert, maybe a customer service or member services representative, or a manager who finds him- or herself handling the complex complaints that no one knows how to handle? These people, because of their immersion in handling complaints, might be excellent facilitators of the activities at this first step.

Generate Enthusiasm for the Objective with an Energy-Building Activity

Engage your steering committee in creative thinking here. See if they can generate a *fun* activity that will focus attention on complaints. For example, create a "moans and groans" or "gripes and snipes" contest. Invite all staff to submit "moans and groans" or "gripes and snipes," namely complaints from customers. For each, they are required to write out three responses along a continuum: a horrendous response, a response of "so-so" or mediocre quality, and one that is wonderful and would bring honor to your services and people. Encourage people to submit these in a creative form—on paper, as a comic strip, on video, or any other medium of their choice. Hold a refreshment break during which the steering committee says they want to kick off the next service objective with some fun, even though complaints are not fun and are to be taken seriously. Award prizes and announce the forthcoming staff workshop on the new objective of service recovery. Offer prizes for the following contributions:

- The worst response
- The best response
- The widest range of responses
- The most dreaded complaint
- The most painful complaint
- Any others you can think of

Prizes can be crying towels, handkerchiefs, sob stories, groan sticks available at novelty stores (a hollow plastic wand that, when turned, creates a groaning noise), or other creative or symbolic options.

Tips

- Some people see complaints as intrusions, interruptions, and nuisances. Take adequate time at this first awareness-raising step in the improvement process to ensure that you help people shift their mind-sets about the value of complaints and see the benefits of welcoming them and handling them well. Don't scrimp on time here.
- Typically, staff welcome a service recovery objective because most people find complaints disarming or unsettling, and they welcome both clarity about their role and skills for more effectiveness. Managers might not feel the same way. Some fear that staff will "overstep" their bounds. Be sure to invite managers to voice their concerns and spend the time needed to address them. If you don't, these people will be ineffective in communicating the new mind-set to their teams.

Step 2: Take Stock of Current Performance and Set Priorities and Targets

Key Actions

- Examine existing complaint data.
- Assess gaps in current system of service recovery.
- Engage staff in setting priorities.
- Select priorities for improvement.

Because everyone on your staff probably has experience with complaining customers, many people can help with this step. The following sections outline a plan for examining the current complaint process in your organization and determining what it lacks.

Examine Existing Complaint Data

Does your service have data about the frequency and nature of complaints overall? Or do individual work teams have such data? Look for every source of data (satisfaction surveys, suggestion boxes, risk management files, and so on), and include anecdotal data from people. Examine it to identify patterns of complaints.

 ### Assess Gaps in Current System of Service Recovery

Convene managers and/or your steering committee of representative staff to audit your current approaches to service recovery and identify gaps in your system that need to be addressed in order to have an effective process. One method is to hold an assessment meeting to identify gaps in your service recovery system.

1. Remind people of the five components that comprise an effective system of service recovery.
2. Engage people in assessing your current practices. Have people interview each other in pairs using these questions:

What Is Our Organization's Service Recovery System?

1. How does our service invite customers to complain?
2. Are there employees specially equipped to hear and respond to customer complaints, like a customer service, member services, or patient relations department? If so, does every employee know how they can refer customers to them or call them when they've heard a complaint and need help?
3. To what extent does every employee feel responsible for handling customer complaints?
4. Is there a time frame within which staff are supposed to respond to a complaint?
5. Are there guidelines for how to respond to complaints, such as who to call, letters to use, and so on?
6. Are staff members required to document complaints they hear or make others aware that they've heard them?
7. Does our service have a way of analyzing complaints to determine recurrent complaints that ideally should be relieved by process improvement?

8. Is it clear to staff members who they can and should contact when they're stumped about what to do with a particular complaint?
9. Is there a particular model for handling a complaint that we are supposed to use? If so, how well does it work?

3. Now, drawing on this information, see which of the five components key to an effective service recovery system are present or absent and which need to be strengthened. A simple discussion can be effective here. Ask the following questions:
   —What do we have in place that serves the function of the first component?
   —How adequate is it in its current form?
   —What might we do to build or improve it so staff can be much more effective in their service recovery roles?
   —Repeat the questions for the other components.
4. Decide what to improve, by whom, and by when with these questions:
   —How do we fill every gap we've identified in a timely fashion?
   —Who will do this by when so that we can move on to engage all staff in our service recovery objective?
5. Clarify your improvement process from then on with these questions:
   —What exactly will need to happen before going public with the objective?
   —Who will carry forward the planning process and map out the remaining steps in the service recovery strategy?
   —What are the plans for involving staff? How and when will we do this?
   —What can this group expect in the way of communication about the status of the strategy?
6. Invite questions and suggestions.

 Engage Staff in Setting Priorities

In a staff meeting, or within each work team, ask staff to list the 10 most common complaints that come from each customer group in their service. Encourage people to consult whatever customer satisfaction data, survey data, or complaint documentation mechanisms they have to provide relevant information that helps here, and have everyone collaborate to list items on a form like the following:

What Upsets Our Customers?

Customer Group (Internal and External)	Common Complaints	Ideas about How to Prevent Them?	Ideas about How to Respond or to Ease Them?

Have teams then sort their lists into two columns as follows and also designate two priorities in each column:

Complaint Assessment

Complaints We Must and Can Prevent	Complaints We Can't Prevent but Can Handle Better
Things We Can Fix Right Away:	Things We Can Change, but Will Take Time and Money:
•	•
•	•
•	•

Teams then should turn in their lists to the steering committee.

 ### Select Priorities for Improvement

Have your steering committee examine the results of the key actions preceding and select priorities for improvement using the following four questions:

1. Which systems must you invent because they reflect gaps in your current systems?
2. Where are staff strong versus weak, and what skills do you need to build in them?

3. Which complaints on our team lists need to be prevented through some kind of bold initiative?

4. Which complaints on our team lists are unpreventable and therefore merit development of a protocol for consistently handling this type of complaint well?

The answers to these questions provide priorities for improvement on service recovery.

Tips

- There's no need to make this step complicated. The important thing is to consult whatever data exists about complaints and decide on a select few initiatives likely to prevent preventable complaints.
- Also, make it a priority to identify unpreventable complaints for which there need to be protocols that help staff be optimally effective when the complaints occurr.
- And finally, during this step, identify from a macro perspective any missing or faulty systems from among the five components that prevent service recovery from occurring regularly and well.
- To check your priorities, ask yourselves, "If we work on these priorities, will everyone have a role to play?

Step 3: Attack Priorities and Design Improvements

Key Actions

- Institute systems for inviting/encouraging customers to complain.
- Define the limits and ground rules for staff authority.
- Agree on a format or protocol for documenting complaints and channeling the results into a problem elimination process.
- Develop specific complaint protocols for handling unpreventable complaints.

Now that you've determined your priorities, it's time to begin designing the tools that will help your staff fulfill the service recovery objective. Because complaint handling is in many ways a sensitive issue for your staff, the development of protocols for a variety of complaints and the definition of staff responsibility and author-ity can give everyone the firm footing they need to begin making the needed changes.

Institute Systems for Inviting/Encouraging Customers to Complain

If your audit of your complaint systems revealed that complaints emerge despite no systems for inviting them, decide on and install a system that in effect encourages customers to complain. Options include:

- Mini-surveys inviting complaints located in public areas
- Suggestion boxes with forms that specifically invite complaints and remedies
- Phone follow-up calls to customers asking them to cite any problems they had with your people or services

Plan for processing the results and channeling them into a prob-lem elimination or service improvement process.

Define the Limits and Ground Rules for Staff Authority

The more freedom and power each individual worker has in han-dling complaints, the more efficient complaint management becomes for your service. There must be decisions staff can make and actions they can take without needing to ask permission. Their ability to act independently speeds the resolution process and lessens customer impatience and resentment. It also shows the cus-tomer that you have trust and confidence in your team's ability to make responsible and effective decisions.

Clarify what staff can and cannot do without permission, so they know the latitude they have to act on the customer's behalf. To what extent can they bend rules to satisfy a customer? Also, clarify what they should do if they're not sure they have the latitude to do what they think needs to be done.

One good method involves recognizing that people in positions of authority need to make these decisions, drawing on staff input if the decisions are negotiable. Address these questions and inform staff of the answers:

- How much freedom do staff have to bend rules to satisfy a complaining customer? Under what circumstances is it okay for them to act without permission?
- How should they respond when money or special resources are needed in order to satisfy the customer? Suppose a patient prefers a certain type of pillow for sleeping and we don't have it. Can they go out and buy one and be reimbursed? If so, what permission do they need to do such a thing? What are the limits on such actions?
- Suppose the cooperation of other people or teams is required to solve a problem. What channels do they need to go through to get that cooperation? Assuming they want to follow through quickly for the sake of the customer, at what point is the solution out of their realm?

    —Whom do they go to when they don't know what to do about a complaint? Who is the correct person to contact to get the answers they need as quickly as possible?

    —Under what circumstances are they required to tell their supervisor about a problem or complaint? Only when they can't solve it alone?

    —When are they expected to document a complaint? Is there a special procedure for this?

    —When is a written response to a complaint appropriate? Who actually writes the response, and what should such a response look like?

    —When they hear the same complaints over and over from many people and the problem is beyond their ability or authority to solve or prevent, where can they take this problem so that they, coworkers, and management can fix it at its root and prevent future dissatisfaction?

 ## Agree on a Format/Protocol for Documenting Complaints and Channeling the Results into a Problem Elimination Process

Your service/organization needs to keep track of complaints received from customers not only because the accrediting agencies that oversee your facility may require it, but also because your service needs to identify *repeated* complaints—patterns that deserve attention and prevention-oriented problem solving. If you aren't aware of how your organization tracks customer complaints, ask your supervisor. If he or she doesn't know either, use the sample format provided below and channel the results to the people or team responsible for setting improvement priorities and finding the people to tackle them.

Method: Suggested Protocol/Format for Documenting Complaints
Check on your service's formal process for recording patients' clinical complaints. There are guidelines for documenting these complaints that your manager can provide.

If you have no system of documentation or if the complaints fall beyond the documentation parameters, here's a simple format for documentation.

Format for Documenting Complaints

- The customer's name
- How to contact them (address, room number, phone number)
- Background on the situation (time, place, people involved, event)
- How the customer defined the problems
- How you responded; options you described
- What you promised or agreed to do
- Any suggestions you have regarding the solution
- How you can be reached for questions or a report on results (your name, position, phone number, address)

Method: Complaint Clearinghouse for Prioritizing and Coordinating Prevention Initiatives
Once you have a documentation system in place, data from it need to filter into a team that will review them and make decisions about what to do. One approach is a complaint clearinghouse—a team of people (membership can be rotating) responsible for reviewing complaint data and identifying improvement priorities and figuring out who in your organization can appropriately handle the prevention initiative suggested by the clearinghouse. Such complaint clearinghouses can serve an important function by meeting bimonthly.

Develop Specific Complaint Protocols for Handling Unpreventable Complaints

In this section we suggest two ways to develop protocols specific to certain kinds of complaints:

- Use universal protocols as guides to developing complaint-specific protocols.
- Hold meetings to develop complaint-specific protocols.

Use Universal Protocols as a Guide to Developing Complaint-Specific Protocols

One facet of your activity will be to develop protocols for staff on how to respond to unpreventable but recurrent complaints. Use the following universal protocols as templates to help people design protocols for dealing with specific complaints:

Universal Protocol: 10 Steps to Service Recovery

1. Listen patiently without interrupting. Don't argue or get defensive.
2. Apologize.
3. Use a "glad but sad" statement. Show appreciation that the customer spoke up and empathy with the customer's viewpoint and feelings.
4. Ask questions to fully understand the problem and what the customer wants. And check your understanding.
5. Fully discuss options. Explain clearly what you can and cannot do.
6. Reach a decision and discuss the details of what the customer can expect.
7. Genuinely thank the person for speaking up.
8. Follow through.
9. Document the complaint according to guidelines.
10. Do all of the above with an attitude that shows care, professionalism, and respect.

Method: Hold Meetings to Develop Complaint-Specific Protocols

Members of each work team need to develop specific protocols for everyone on their team to use to handle the recurrent unpreventable complaints they identified earlier as priorities. Use the following guides to help you develop specific protocols:

How to Develop a Complaint-Specific Protocol

1. Focus on the complaint. Define it.
2. Think it through from the customer's viewpoint.
   —Identify the reasons the customer is upset. Does the customer feel disrespected, ignored, mistreated, or what?
   —Typically, what do customers with this complaint want? (There might be several possibilities here.)
3. Identify the reasons why this complaint occurs. What is unpreventable about it?
4. Generate alternative ways to talk with the customer.
   —Specifically, what can staff say to acknowledge the customer's feelings?
   —Specifically, what can staff say to explain why the situation was unpreventable?
5. Select the appropriate universal protocol as a template and apply it to producing a specific protocol for handling this complaint. Include examples of the language people can use to communicate at each step.
6. Try it out and get feedback.
   —Try it aloud on group members.
   —Try it out on coworkers outside of the group. Invite their feedback.
7. Revise the protocol based on the feedback.
8. Produce on paper a job aid people can keep on hand to help them remember the key elements of an effective response.

The following protocol is useful for handling any complaint transmitted over the phone:

Universal Protocol for Handling Complaints on the Phone

- Give the caller your undivided attention and express your sincere concern.
- Allow the speaker to have his or her say. Don't interrupt.
- Write down all important details, including short phrases and major facts. Don't be afraid to ask questions so that you have the information correct.

- Repeat these facts back to the caller to be sure you have recorded them accurately.
- Be sympathetic, not defensive. It helps to calm the caller.
- Maintain a pleasant and even tone of voice. Don't lose your cool!
- Tell the caller exactly what you intend to do about the complaint you've received, to whose attention you will bring it, and when a response can be expected.
- Apologize to the caller for the inconvenience or difficulty *even when it's not your fault or the fault of the organization.* This is an important gesture of goodwill toward the public. A phrase such as "I'm really sorry you've been inconvenienced" is appropriate.
- Thank the caller for bringing the difficulty to your attention and giving the organization an opportunity to make it right.
- Be sure to follow through with whatever action you promise

Sometimes, staff members will find that they cannot help a customer, either because they are not familiar with the situation prompting the customer's complaint or because the nature of the complaint requires the involvement of someone at a higher level of authority or in a different role. Here is a protocol for referring complaints.

Universal Protocol for Referring Complaints to Someone Else

When you don't have the authority or knowledge to resolve a complaint, you might need to involve someone else. Before you refer a complaint to someone else, consider who would be the best person to help or, if you're not sure, ask your supervisor.

So customers don't see this as passing the buck or brushing them off, watch your words! Use sentences such as "I want to make sure we do all we can to respond to your concern and because of that, I want to involve (name). She/he is our (position) and is in a good position to help."

Suggested Complaint Handoff Process:

- Have all the facts about the problem on hand. Be sure you have confirmed all information with your customer and have recorded the relevant details.
- Have a clear idea of what the customer wants you or your organization to do about the problem.

- Relate your interaction with the customer to the appropriate person. Explain the alternatives you offered and the benefits and drawbacks you discussed. Be accurate and honest. It won't help the situation if you are more concerned with looking good than with resolving the customer's problems.
- If you made any promises to the customer, tell your colleague about them. Since you heard the customer's compliant directly, offer your recommendations as to what might be done.
- When you turn your information over to your colleague, make sure you agree on what role, if any, you will continue to plan in the resolution of the problem or in keeping the customer informed. Ask to be informed of progress so you can be sure that the complaint was eventually resolved and the customer told the result.

The following two examples of complaint-specific protocols are from *Resolving Patient Complaints: A Step-by-Step Guide to Effective Service Recovery.*[2]

Medical Receptionist: Wait Time for a Specialty Appointment

I. Patient/Customer Contact
  A. Listen. Focus on the patient/customer with attentive body language (if in person) and voice inflections (over the telephone or in person).
  B. Empathize; validate the patient/customer's perspective.
    1. "I'm glad you let me/us know that this is not a good time for you."
    2. "I understand you are frustrated by this."
    3. "It sounds like you're really worried about these symptoms."
  C. Clarify expectation for resolution.
    1. "When did you want to be seen?"
    2. "When are you available—are there any times you cannot come for an appointment?"

II. Acknowledge
  A. Apologize without assigning blame or guilt.
    1. "I'm sorry this isn't a convenient time for you."
    2. "I'm sorry (specialty/department) didn't offer you an earlier appointment."

    B. Verify the facts: "Let me make sure I understand what you've told me."

    C. Explain what you can do; provide general overview of the process you will follow to resolve the concern: "I'm going to talk to _____, Dr. _____'s nurse about your concerns and ask her/him to call you back. (S/he may want to pull your chart and review it with Dr. _____ first."

    D. Agree on next contact: I'm going to ask (nurse) to call you back today. If you don't hear from her/him by (time frame), please call me. Where can he/she reach you? Is there any time you won't be at that number?"

III. Respond/Refer

    A. Consult with others. Contact nurse to transfer complaint to him or her.

      1. Contact the resource person and relay all the pertinent information and facts about the problem.

      2. Negotiate with the resource person to assume responsibility for investigating, reviewing, and/or resolving the problem, including who will notify the patient/customer with the final resolution.

      3. Advise the patient/customer of the next step, including who the resource person is and how to reach him or her.

      4. Document in writing the pertinent facts and the plan for resolution, and send a copy to the resource person.

IV. Follow up

    A. Thank patient/customer: "Thank you for letting me help you with this."

    B. Share your organization's service recovery standards, if appropriate.

      1. You strive to recognize the patient/customer as an individual.

      2. You strive to provide the patient/customer with an easy, obvious process for sharing concerns.

      3. You strive to provide the patient/customer with a key contact person.

      4. You strive for a fair resolution.

      5. You strive for a fast resolution.

      6. You strive to provide consistent, clear, and accurate information.

C. Write follow-up letter.
1. Summarize patient/customer's request, the actions you took, and the resolution agreed on.
2. Apologize for the patient/customer's feelings of dissatisfaction or inconvenience.
3. Report any system changes that have occurred as a result of this complaint.
4. Offer to assist in the future if needed.
D. Document complaint and distribute, if appropriate.

Reprinted, with permission, from Liz Osborne, *Resolving Patient Complaints: A Step-by-Step Guide to Effective Service Recovery,* © 1995 Aspen Publishers, pp. 115–16.

Medical Receptionist: Staff Attitude and Customer Service

I. Patient/Customer Contact
   A. Listen. Focus on the patient/customer with attentive body language (if in person) and voice inflections (over the telephone and in person).
   B. Ask open-ended questions.
      1. "Who said this to you? When?"
      2. "What specifically did he/she say?"
      3. "Can you describe the encounter/situation in more detail for me?"
   C. Empathize; validate the patient/customer's perspective: "It sounds like that was a difficult/awkward/ frustrating situation for you."

II. Acknowledge
   A. Apologize without assigning blame or guilt.
      1. "I'm sorry you felt _____."
      2. "I'm sure it wasn't their intent to _____."
   B. Verify the facts: "Let me make sure I understand what you've told me."
   C. Explain what you can do; provide general overview of the process you will follow to resolve the concern: "I will document your complaint and share it with our patient representative. He/she will follow up from there."

D. Clarify expectation for resolution: "Is there anything else you would like done?"

   1. If they want to change their primary care physician, transfer them to physician selection office/department.

   2. If they want to make a second opinion appointment, make the appointment within the office or transfer the caller to the appropriate section/office for appointment scheduling. (Give other receptionist some background as to what patient/customer needs so patient/customer does not have to repeat story or get caught in bureaucracy.)

   3. If they have other expectations for resolution, refer them to a patient representative.

      a. Contact the patient representative and relay all the pertinent information and facts about the problem.

      b. Negotiate with the patient representative to assume responsibility for investigating, reviewing, and/or resolving the problem, including who will notify the patient/customer with the final resolution.

      c. Advise the patient/customer of the next step, including who the patient representative is and how to reach him or her.

      d. Document in writing the pertinent facts and the plan for resolution, and send a copy to the patient representative.

      e. If the requested resolution is refund of copayment, then office/department/division should have developed a process for doing this efficiently.

      f. If requested resolution is payment of bill for nonplan services, then request copy of bills (itemized with procedure codes) and nonplan records.

E. Agree on next contact.

   1. "I'm going to document this and send it to our patient representative. Would you like to talk to her/him too? When can you be reached? Where?"

   2. "I'm going to transfer you to physician selection/the department/office to change physicians/schedule an appointment."

III. Follow up
A. Bring closure to complaint by summarizing the patient/customer's request, the actions you took, and the resolution agreed on.
B. Thank patient/customer.
C. Share your organization's service recovery standards, if appropriate.
    1. You strive to recognize the patient/customer as an individual.
    2. You strive to provide the patient/customer with an easy, obvious process for sharing concerns.
    3. You strive to provide the patient/customer with a key contact person.
    4. You strive for a fair resolution.
    5. You strive for a fast resolution.
    6. You strive to provide consistent, clear, and accurate information.
D. Write follow-up letter.
    1. Summarize patient/customer's request, the actions you took, and the resolution agreed on.
    2. Apologize for the patient/customer's feelings of dissatisfaction or inconvenience.
    3. Report any system changes that have occurred as a result of this complaint.
    4. Offer to assist in the future, if needed.
E. Document complaint and distribute as appropriate.

Reprinted, with permission, from Liz Osborne, *Resolving Patient Complaints: A Step-by-Step Guide to Effective Service Recovery,* © 1995 Aspen Publishers, pp. 116–18.

 Tips

- The design step takes a tremendous amount of work to do well. You will get the most mileage from your efforts if you emphasize and support development of complaint-specific protocols, even though these are tedious to develop. For many more examples, see Liz Osborne's book *Resolving Patient Complaints,* referenced at the end of this chapter.
- Because development of complaint-specific protocols is inevitably tedious, make sure people pick "the vital few" to develop—those that upset customers the most, are least preventable, and if handled well, will have the greatest positive impact on satisfaction.

Step 4: Communicate Improvements and New Expectations to All Staff

 Key Actions

- Hold a meeting to communicate service recovery expectations to staff.
- Provide service recovery protocols in the form of job aids.

Step 4 comprises two important activities: Holding a meeting to introduce everyone to their new expectations regarding complaint handling and translating the protocols you developed in step 3 into job aids. The following sections offer concrete advice that help you move easily to the next step.

 Hold a Meeting to Communicate Service Recovery Expectations to Staff

The following detailed meeting plan shows how to inform staff of service recovery expectations.

Communicate Expectations to Staff: Learn "10 Steps to Service Recovery"

1. Introduction: Remind people of your service recovery objective. Then, explain that you'll clarify expectations of staff in this meeting and also introduce the step-by-step model for service recovery that this service is adopting as standard practice.
2. Clarify expectations of staff: Communicate expectation that every employee is supposed to handle people's complaints. Walk through the service philosophy.

> **Our Philosophy:**
> - If the customer complains to you, you are the right person to take charge of handling it. Our customers should only have to complain one time to one person. People hate it when staff "pass the buck." If you don't have the authority to act on a complaint, don't send the customer to someone else; find someone who can act on it and make the connection. Draw in others as needed.

- If you hear a complaint, at that moment, you are our organization, the goodwill ambassador who can make or break our reputation. Here, it is everybody's job to be a customer service rep. The buck stops with every one of us.

3. Invite reactions and concerns. And respond to them. Typical concerns are:
   —"What if I'm not the person involved, but the customer complains to me?" You are their first line of contact. Hear them out completely. Do all of the process steps right up until discussing the alternatives. Then, explain that you will need to contact (name the person) to see what the alternatives are, because that person (explain their more relevant role). Offer two alternatives: "I'll be glad to try and reach them right now while you wait, or if you would prefer I'll contact them and get back to you with what they see as the alternatives, or have them call you directly to discuss them. Which would you prefer?" Then, proceed with the rest of the process.
   —"What if I don't have time to handle the person or the complaint right then?" Somehow you need to find a way to listen. You might say, "I really want to hear your concern, but I've got to find someone to take over for me for a few minutes. Would you mind waiting just until I find someone to take over for me?" Then, look hard and fast! If you're dealing with another customer, find someone to complete the interaction with them and apologize for needing to depart for a few minutes. If you can't find someone to take over for you while interacting with another customer, say to the other complaining customer, "I really want to hear your concern, the minute I finish with my customer here. I'll be quick and I hope you don't mind waiting. It will take about _____ minutes."
   —"What if I don't know what to do about the complaint?" Go through as many process steps as you can and when you need to generate alternatives, admit that you're not clear on what the alternatives are and would like to take a few minutes to talk with whoever it is to get some information about the possibilities.
   —"What if there is nothing anyone can do about the complaint? Say, "I'm so sorry this happened, and I wish we could have prevented it." Then, proceed through the other steps, focusing on the options, if any, that exist now for minimizing the problems already created.

—"I was hired to do a job, and I'm too busy with that job to spend time dealing with complaints." We have to find a way to handle complaints. It is a lot less costly to handle them here and now than to not do this and see the customer go away mad and contribute to us losing business in the future.

—Brainstorm with people other issues that stand in the way of using the service recovery model effectively and engage the team's help in generating alternative ways to address them.

4. Introduce this meeting as a chance to examine and practice the step-by-step approach for handling a customer complaint that you want to establish as everyone's standard practice.

—"Sell" the idea of all adopting one tried-and-true step-by-step approach and then helping each other get better and better at it.

—Introduce the 10-step universal protocol for service recovery. Reproduce it as a handout. Assert that this model has been carefully developed so that it includes every element important to customers. If you leave out even one step, customers are less than satisfied with your performance in reaction to their complaint.

—Have people refer to their handout as you explain each step.

5. Walk the whole group through one example, with the facilitator playing the customer.

—Post the service recovery steps on the wall.

—Explain that you will play a customer with a complaint and voice that complaint to the group.

—Ask someone in the group to lead the discussion, guiding the group to use each step in the step-by-step service recovery process. By having a volunteer facilitate the group, the leader can role-play the customer.

Facilitator: Learn this situation so you can complain about it to the group, who together will play the supervisor and respond to your complaint using the step-by-step model.

The Situation

You arrived on time for a 10 A.M. outpatient appointment. You made the appointment four weeks ago. You had to arrange child care and take a bus so you could get to this appointment. You are paying hourly for the child care, and your baby-sitter said she needed you to be back by noon.

The receptionist took your name and asked you to sit down in the wait-ing area. You waited for 15 minutes and heard nothing. You went up to the desk to ask how much longer you would need to wait and the recep-tionist said the doctors were backed up and she couldn't predict. You sat down and waited another 15 minutes, getting more and more aggra-vated with no word of when you would be taken. You go again to the receptionist and ask when you'll be taken. She says she still doesn't know. You explain that you have a baby-sitter deadline and need to get home by then. The receptionist says she can't promise that you'll make it and asks if you would like another appointment.

You are upset and you show it. You remind her that you waited four weeks for this appointment, that you're paying a baby-sitter, and that you spend money and time on the bus getting here and that you do not want another appointment. You want to be taken in time to get home by noon. She apologizes for your inconvenience and repeats that she doesn't have the power to ensure that. You ask her to go find out when the doctor might take you and she says she can't because she has to stay by the phones. You decide to wait until 11:30 and go home if you haven't been taken by then.

It turns out that you are finally taken at 11:15 and you do get out by 11:30, but you are still angry. And, you have a follow-up appointment and are concerned that the same thing is going to happen again.

You go home and decide to call the supervisor of that service and complain.

The person who volunteered to guide the group says, "The scene starts with the supervisor picking up the phone and _____ making their complaint. Following the 10 Steps to Service Recovery:

- Patient expresses complaint. Group listens, listens, listens (step 1).
- Discussion leader asks group to suggest alternative responses in accord with step 2 and asks the customer to respond.
- Discussion leader asks group to suggest what to say next (in accord with next step of model).
- And so on through all steps of the model. So, in summary, the leader plays the customer all through this role play, and the group suggests and tries out alternative ways to follow the service recov-ery model in responding to the customer.

- At the end, the customer becomes the facilitator again and asks people's reactions to what they saw and heard.
  —What worked?
  —What didn't?
  —What questions do you have about using the model?

6. Next Steps and Future Plans for Service Recovery skill building
   —Encourage people to invite complaints from their customers by saying, "So, we served you today. What about our service to you did you like? What do you suggest we do differently?" so they can try out the service recovery process. Also, encourage people to listen for complaints and take charge once they hear them, again using the service recovery process.
   —Announce three-pronged follow-up.
   —At a forthcoming staff meeting (or workshop), everyone will have a chance to try out the model for service recovery—because it is not easy!
   —Workshop two weeks later on the finer points of using the process, particularly more skills for how to handle difficult emotion.
   —Biweekly one-hour skill builders on service recovery and chances to get help with tough customers and tough complaints.

Provide Service Recovery Protocols in the Form of Job Aids

Make sure every individual has job aids (posters, file cards, or other forms) that have on them the key elements they are supposed to include in their process of handling likely complaints. Chapters 4 and 5 offer examples of job aids that can easily be altered to suit the activities of service recovery.

Tips

- The key expectation that must be communicated here is that everyone, not just people in professional complaint-handling roles, is responsible for inviting, listening well to, and responding well to customer complaints.
- Make sure everyone in supervisory roles has a chance to voice any resistance they have to this and also has a chance to discuss the issues related to staff's latitude to act. This will help them communicate clear expectations in an unequivocal manner.

Step 5: Equip Staff with Needed Tools and Skills

 ## Key Actions

- Help managers be effective with service recovery.
- Build staff skills in service recovery through training.
- Provide written skill builders to reinforce skills.
- Provide practice in handling difficult complaints and difficult people.

The key actions of step 5 involve helping people learn new skills and, sometimes, examine their existing attitudes toward complaint handling. The greater variety of learning tools you can use during this step, the better. The sections that follow will start you on your way.

 ## Help Managers Be Effective with Service Recovery

Here is a skill-building workshop for your management team. Provide them with the following very ambitious list of roles managers and supervisors need to play in order to model service recovery, to coach staff through your service recovery strategy, and to support staff in their key and expanding roles in service recovery. Then, hold an open, frank discussion of where people have trouble with this list and identify what they need in order to fulfill their roles.

Every Manager's Role in Service Recovery

1. Articulate a welcoming, positive attitude toward complaints. Help your staff see complaints as a golden opportunity to turn potentially lost customers into loyal customers.
2. Institute methods for inviting complaints, instead of only relying on customers to speak up when they're disgruntled. Short written surveys, suggestion boxes, and staff questioning of patients (for example, "Are you satisfied with your visit today?") are helpful approaches.
3. Sell your staff on service recovery.
4. Help staff understand and accept complaints.
   —Help them believe that problems exist when customers say they do—anytime customers feel disappointed, dismayed, angry, or upset.
   —Emphasize that customers don't expect perfection, just concern and responsiveness.

5. Model excellent handling of complaints. Teach by your own example. Show staff that dissatisfied customers can end up grateful to you for your effort to please them and meet their needs.

6. Equip your staff with the skills they need to handle complaints effectively. Teach them the model for service recovery. Coach them. Provide practice on typical complaints and on-the-spot help.

7. Make sure employees have latitude to act. Set parameters within which employees may act to resolve complaints. Define the latitude they have to solve the problem or atone for a wrong. For instance, how much money can a solution cost without the employee having to get permission? Should the employee rule out any solutions that cost more, or should they consult a supervisor if the preferred solution costs more than their spending limit?

8. Prevent complaints by improving service processes. Figure out a simple way to log complaints, even those that are resolved, so that you can identify "here we go again" problems. Then, do preventive work.

9. Validate the time spent on service recovery. Make it clear to staff that it's not only okay, but important to spend extra time with an upset customer. Help staff figure out how to do this without abandoning their work and frustrating even more customers in the process. Discuss backup and coverage and buddy systems so that staff have alternatives when they need to spend time with a customer in order to right a wrong.

10. Designate a chief problem solver or adviser. Staff members need to know who to go to when they aren't sure what to do or have an idea but lack the authority to do it without permission. This person can be a manager, a supervisor, or a peer with more experience, system's thinking, and scope.

11. Create ongoing opportunities for employees to share successful solutions, whether these are in an employee newsletter or some other method of sharing solutions.

 Build Staff Skills in Service Recovery through Training

Here are several skill builders that you or a selected facilitator can conduct in staff meetings or in specially scheduled training or skill-building sessions.

Skill Builder #1: Using the Service Recovery Model

1. Divide the group into threes and ask people to pick a complaint typical of their customers at work. Have them flesh out the typical situation that gives rise to the complaint. Then, have one person in the trio play the customer and another play the staff member to whom the customer complains. The third person is the observer and coach.

2. The task is to try following the model as you hear and respond to the customer's complaint.

3. In each group, after one person has a turn handling the complaint, rotate and have someone else play the customer voicing a different complaint, so at least two people have a turn to try their hand at it. Afterward, ask people to discuss what happened.
    —How did it work?
    —What was hard?
    —What was easy?
    —What tips do they have for each other?

Skill Builder #2: Handling Emotions

This skill builder is neither quick nor easy. Find someone to serve as facilitator who is skilled at group process and also at handling people's feelings.

1. Explain that the purpose is to build skills related to one of the two key aspects of service recovery—handling emotion.

2. Provide a context for emphasizing the importance of handling emotion effectively by explaining the concept of right-brain and left-brain thinking and the implications for service recovery.

Some people who complain are "right brain" while others are "left brain," meaning that one side of their brain is dominant and leads to a particular style of behaving and responding in complaint situations. "Right-brain" people appreciate people who understand their feelings and might say things like "Do you know how aggravated I am?" "Left-brain" people, on the other hand, are more concerned with solving their problems and might say things like "I want to know how you are going to resolve this!"

The fact that complaining people vary in these ways is complicated by the fact that we as problem handlers have similar characteristics. Those of us with right-brain dominance are comfortable with emotion and expert in dealing with emotional people, while those of us with left-brain dominance prefer analytical thinking and see finding solutions to difficult problems a welcome challenge.

The challenge to us in service recovery is to deal effectively with both types of people. Since we are never certain which type of person we are dealing with, we need to resolve complaints by making certain that we attend to both styles and preferences. For some of us, it means learning how to deal with other people's emotions. Others will need to learn how to think through and resolve problems.

3. Explain that at several points in the service recovery process, we need to listen, listen, listen and show empathy and understanding—thereby handling emotion effectively.
4. Do role play: Have someone draw from their experience with patients or as a patient and share for 15 seconds the "rantings" of someone who has had a terrible experience with your services. They might include the following complaints:
   —Rude treatment by staff
   —Long delays
   —High cost
   —Dissatisfaction with the environment (too hot, too cold, and so on)
   —Having tests done more than once
   —Getting mailed the wrong information
   As this person rants, the facilitator should demonstrate poor listening—interrupt, be distracted. The facilitator should then invite another person to rant, and this time the facilitator should listen with eye contact and demonstrate good listening.
5. Listening traps: Refer participants to what they just witnessed and ask them to answer the questions listed in the following questionnaire. Review the main point—that listening is a very difficult skill because many distractions and habits interfere with it.

Listening Traps

Listening Traps	Yes	No
Does your mind tend to wander when you are supposedly listening to another?		
Do you tune the other person out in order to prepare your response?		
Are you often so wrapped up in your own feelings that it's impossible to really listen to another?		
Do you tend to jump ahead of the speaker and reach conclusions before you have heard the speaker out?		
Do you often figure you know what the other person is going to say before he/she has finished saying it?		
Are you anxious to contribute your ideas to the conversation or relate your experiences when another is trying to talk?		
Do you have a tendency to finish sentences or supply words for the other person?		
Do you get caught up with insignificant facts and details and miss the emotional tone of the conversation?		
Do you listen with half your attention tuned toward giving advice, solving the problem, or figuring out what to say to make the other person feel better?		
Are you human?		

6. Teach the first of two listening skills: paraphrasing.
   —Explain that paraphrasing is putting into your own words the content of what the other person has said, and repeating it back to the other person. This allows the listener to confirm that what she/he has heard is what the other person really meant.

This is very useful when the speaker is confused or not sure what they want. Paraphrasing helps clarify the communication.

—Ask for four volunteers. Give them a topic and ask them to discuss it, but tell them they must follow one rule: that each person must paraphrase what the person before them said before they say something of their own. Topic options: "What frustrates patients most?" or "What color should we paint the room?"

—One person states an opinion. The next person must paraphrase what the first person said before stating their own opinion. Keep going. Each person paraphrases the person before them until everyone has had at least one chance to paraphrase and speak.

7. Teach the second of the two listening skills: empathy.

—Explain that empathy is listening for how the person is *feeling* and reflecting back the feelings to them with words. Identify the feeling and then say to the person: "It sounds as if you're very angry (or upset, or frustrated)." This is very important and helpful when people are upset, angry, disappointed, frustrated, and the like. This technique lets them know you really listened and understood how they felt.

—Explain the power of empathy to defuse hostility and show the tremendous effect that employee behavior can have on a "hot" situation. When people complain, the best thing you can do for them is to hear them out without being defensive.

—Ask staff to name things that make patients and visitors angry. Comment that as staff members, we are often on the receiving end of angry, upset, and sometimes very demanding people. Many times it's a problem that has escalated somewhere else, but then people vent on us even when it's not our fault. The tendency is to defend ourselves or the organization. So, in a heated situation we may find ourselves saying things like:

 –"Wait a minute now, don't yell at me. I wasn't even here yesterday."

 –"Listen, I don't make the policies around here!"

—It's a natural tendency to want to defend or reason or set people straight. However, this is the very thing that further inflames

people, causing the situation to get more and more heated until it ends up out of control. The result: No one wins.
—Draw on a flipchart or whiteboard two curves and explain them: the hostility curve and the problem-solving curve.

The Hostility Curve

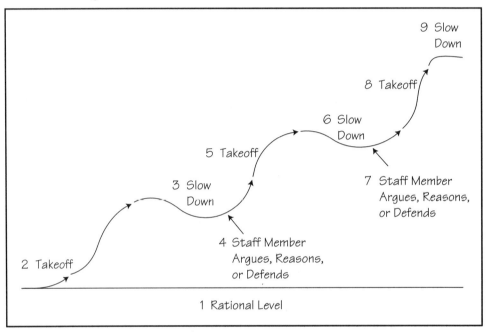

—Hostility curve: Usually a hostile, angry complaint follows a certain pattern which is shown in the hostility curve.
 –Most people are reasonable a good deal of the time. They function at a rational level. At this level, you can talk with them about things reasonably.
 –When something provokes a person, he or she may "take off," letting off a lot of steam, possibly becoming abusive to you or whomever is around, and in general expressing hostility. It may seem to go on quite a while. Once the person leaves the rational level, there is no use trying to get the person to be "reasonable."
 –But this blowup doesn't last forever. The hostile person eventually runs out of steam and begins to slow down if not provoked by anyone further.
 –As you see on the curve, if you argue or try to reason with someone (#4) at the slow-down point, you trigger another

"takeoff" or eruption of negative emotion, and this can go on and on. You've seen it happen in huge blowups, where one person keeps setting off the other. So, that's what *not* to do!

The Problem-Solving Curve

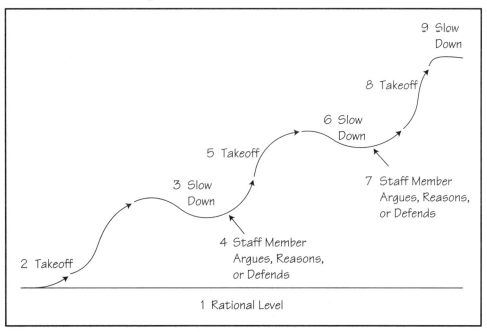

9 Slow
Down

8 Takeoff

6 Slow
Down

5 Takeoff

3 Slow
Down

7 Staff Member
Argues, Reasons,
or Defends

4 Staff Member
Argues, Reasons,
or Defends

2 Takeoff

1 Rational Level

—Problem-solving curve: Let's look at what we *can* do to bring the hostile situation under control.

–When the complainer is at the hostile takeoff stage, you can say something to defuse the anger. What you say makes a big difference. If you say something supportive, like "This can be awfully frustrating when you're under so much pressure" or "I know this has been a very upsetting experience for you," you can be very helpful to that person. In addition, you need to be supportive in your nonverbal behavior. Being supportive does not necessarily mean agreeing, but it does mean letting the other person know that you understand his or her feelings.

–If you do say something supportive, you will usually see the hostile person cool off—he or she returns to a rational level.

–Once the person has returned to the rational level, you can begin to solve the problem that triggered the anger. People are in a mood to solve problems when they are rational, not when they are full of steam and at the top of the hostility curve.

–Finally, reinforce the importance of listening and showing empathy until the complaining party calms down and becomes clear-headed enough to work on solutions to the problem.

Skill Builder #3: Listening Practice
1. Form trios.
2. Give out instructions to trios. Give each member a chance to practice listening effectively using these scenarios.

Empathy Practice

For each of the following statements, look for the customer's "feeling" message. If you are person A, speak the statement with emotions that you believe would be appropriate. The task of person B is to try and mirror back to you what they think you are feeling.

1. "My insurance covers my hospitalization. Why do you keep sending me all of these outrageous bills?"
2. "I called and let the phone ring 22 times before you answered! This is ridiculous!"
3. "Why do you have to take blood again today? You took so much yesterday."
4. "This may sound silly, but I think I lost the forms you sent me to fill out. Is there anyone who can help me?"

Person C: Give feedback afterward.

- Did person B reflect back the right feeling before trying to solve the problem?
- What signs did you have that person B was really listening? Eye contact? Body language? Tone of voice? Words used?

3. Review these "Dos and Don'ts."

Do	Don't
Understand that the hostility is directed at what you represent, or at the situation, not at you as a person.	Take the hostility personally.
Recognize the anger and let the person know you hear it and can understand it.	Deny the anger or tell person to "calm down."
Listen carefully and fully to what the person says, waiting until their anger is out.	Refuse to listen to the anger or the reasons for it.
Keep an open mind about who is wrong and what should be done until you have a chance to investigate the problem.	Defend the organization or yourself until the person has calmed down and you have investigated.
Help the person save face when they realize they have behaved poorly.	Embarrass the person by pointing out the foolishness of their behavior.
If possible, gently steer the person to a private area where there will be less distraction and eavesdropping.	Carry on a screaming match in a public area.
Have both of you sit down, leaning on something (armrest, table) if you need support.	Have one of you standing and one sitting.
Keep your tone of voice calm.	Get caught up in the hysteria by talking in a hostile tone of voice.
Keep to yourself your judgments about what should and should not make people angry.	Jump to conclusions about what should and should not make people angry.
When the person's anger begins to slow down, support person without necessarily agreeing.	When the person's anger begins to slow down, take advantage of it by arguing and making excuses.
If you just can't handle a situation, find another staff person who can.	Continue trying to handle something when you're no longer able to.
After an incident, vent your own feelings with someone you trust.	After an incident, keep it all to yourself.

4. Recap that the key to handling people's emotions is listening—
   for both the content of people's messages using paraphrasing
   and also for the emotion in people's messages using active listening. We need to let people get complaints off their chests, then
   empathize with them so they know we understand. We must
   communicate by our words and actions that we want to help
   them and do care. After all, when someone is angry or complaining, *we* are the only person there. At that moment, *we* are
   our organization. And by the way we handle the complaint, we
   create the image they walk away with of our organization.

Skill Builder #4: Empathy

1. Divide people into trios. Ask them to fill out the following
   worksheet together, working together on developing good language that expresses empathy.

Common Complaint We Hear	Typical Customer Feeling	Words We Can Use to Express Empathy
1.		
2.		
3.		
4.		

2. Afterward, invite people to share their results. Invite comments
   to help people get better at empathetic statements.
3. Reinforce the importance of helping the customer feel understood through empathy.

Skill Builder #5: Problem Solving

Our model "10 Steps to Service Recovery" includes steps in which you need to ask questions so you're very clear about the nature of the problem and the situation that triggered it. You need to find out exactly what the customer wants. And then, you need to generate alternatives and solutions for the complaining customer and follow through on those alternatives.

1. As a job aid, provide staff a card with questions on it that they can use to help solve customer complaints. Walk through these questions with them.

   —Questions that gain additional information:

   –Can you describe the problem?

   –What do you mean by . . . ?

   –What is your name/time of appointment/and so on . . . ?

   –What is your doctor's name?

   —Questions that identify what the person needs and wants:

   –What can I do to help you?

   –What do you wish we could do for you about this?

   —Form trios and ask people to work together to identify three common complaints they hear on their jobs. Then, for each complaint, list the questions they can ask to clarify the details of the problem, so that they can respond more effectively.

Complaint Situation	Questions We Can Use to Clarify the Details
1.	
2.	
3.	

   —Afterward, invite people in the whole group to share their results.

   —Emphasize the importance of asking questions so that the customer sees that you care and so that you have the facts you need so you can intervene effectively.

2. Tell staff that once they have found out the customer's problem, there are three good ways to generate alternative solutions.
   —First, they can ask the customer for suggestions about what he or she sees as possibilities.
   —Second, they can equip themselves with alternatives for predictable complaints.
   —Third, they can ask the customer to excuse them for a moment, then consult a colleague for advice.
3. Ask staff to brainstorm the complaints they get repeatedly, including the real sticklers. List these on a flipchart or whiteboard.
   —Focusing on one complaint at a time, invite staff to brainstorm alternatives people have in that situation. Devote time to this, because this equips staff with important alternatives for the lion's share of the complaints your team hears.
   —Have someone take good notes and turn these alternatives into a tip sheet or job-specific protocols.
4. Have staff figure out what they can do and what they can't.
   —Help staff figure out the latitude they have to resolve people's complaints, since people stop short of solving problems because they assume the solution goes beyond their authority.
   —Ask people to work alone to list the complaints they hear repeatedly, no matter whether these complaints refer to situations within their span of influence or not. Then, working in pairs with each person serving as his or her partner's consultant, have people list for each situation three alternatives they have the authority to do and three options they think they do not have the authority to do.

Situations	I can't . . .	I can . . .
1.	• •	• •
2.	• •	• •
3.	• •	• •

—Afterward, in round-robin manner, have the whole group share situations and what they can and can't do. Discuss and untangle any misconceptions about people's latitude to act. Work out ways then and there to expand people's latitude to act.

 Skill Builder #6: Follow-Up
Most people intend to take action to follow up on a customer's complaint, but something gets in the way. Engage staff in looking at the obstacles that get in the way of follow-up and discuss how to overcome these obstacles together.

1. Pass out this worksheet and ask people to check the obstacles that get in *their* way.

Obstacles Worksheet

Obstacle	I can overcome this by . . .
I forget what I said I would do.	
I can't find the right people.	
I get distracted by other tasks and people.	
I just don't have time.	
I rely on other people who don't follow through.	

2. Get people into pairs to help each other complete the right-hand column as well as they can.
3. Convene everyone and go through one obstacle at a time, comparing suggestions about how to overcome the obstacle.

 Skill Builder #7: Practice in Handling Emotion and Problem Solving Together
1. Form groups of three with one person being "A," another "B," and the third "C."
2. Person A will be a complaining customer. Person B will be the complaint handler, and person C will observe B, looking to see how well the complaint manager handles emotion and solves the problem.

Sample Complaints

—Patient was charged for TV—TV was broken the entire time and no one responded to complaints to fix it.

—In an HMO, the tele-nurse said member did not need to bring sick child in and, not only that, no provider was available. The parent wants to bring the child in and is angry about the barriers.

—Member was moved twice in the middle of night from one floor to another in the hospital. She felt like she was treated like a number and was shown no concern or compassion.

—Physician is angry with slow lab test turnaround. Inquires and talks with surly employee.

—Customer is angry about a billing error that has not been corrected despite six phone calls and one visit.

—A patient experienced an unusually long wait after medical office receptionist had said, "It won't be more than one hour."

3. Switch roles after two minutes and allow each person to try on the different roles.

4. Discuss the exercise and learn from it by asking:
   —What went well?
   —What did you have difficulty with?

Skill Builder #8: "Glad but Sad" Practice

A key step in service recovery involves a "glad but sad" statement in which you express appreciation to the customer for speaking up and also express empathy that shows your regret for their disappointment. In practice, it's not always easy to think of the words that accomplish this double message. To get better at this aspect of service recovery, engage staff in practice.

1. Ask people to form trios and to work out what they think would be a good "glad but sad" statement in response to each of the situations listed on the worksheet. Then compare notes and see what people suggest.

Situation	"Glad but Sad" Statement
Patient was kept waiting.	
Member felt rushed by doctor.	
Billing person is pushy to patient with financial hardship.	
Primary care doctor is angry because specialist doctor didn't call to discuss a decision about patient.	

    2. Afterward, take turns hearing people's suggestions and inviting comments and suggestions.

 ### Provide Written Skill Builders to Reinforce Skills in Service Recovery

Consider a series of service recovery bulletins that include skill builders, case situations and their responses, reports on prevention initiatives, and the like.

Bulletin #1: Verbal Responses to Customers' Complaints

Defensive responses: Defensive responses should be avoided at all costs, even when you're tired or busy or occupied with other thoughts. For example:

- "It isn't *my* fault!"
- "That's not *my* job!"
- "You can't *possibly* be right about this!"
- "Our organization would *never* do such a thing!"
- "Why are you telling *me* this? I wasn't there!"

Helpful responses:

- "You seem upset. Please tell me more . . ."
- "Perhaps I've misunderstood. Can you please explain that to me again?"

- "I'm glad you brought this to my attention. I'd like to look into it."
- "If I understand correctly, you're saying that . . ."

Empathetic responses:

- "I can appreciate how you're feeling about this."
- "I can see how upsetting this is to you."
- "It certainly sounds as though we've caused you some inconvenience."
- "I know I'd be upset too, if that happened to me."

Thanks for complaining:

- "Thank you for speaking up about this. It gives us the chance to fix it and make sure it doesn't happen again."
- "Thanks for taking the time to tell us about this. If you hadn't, we might never have known about it."
- "Thank you for pointing out this problem to me. I'll take care of it within the hour and call you to tell you the result."

Bulletin #2: Skillful, Effective Apologies

Research by Ron Zemke and Kristin Anderson suggests that in more than 50 percent of obvious service breakdowns, no one apologizes to the customer for the breakdown. Why is that?

What stops people from apologizing? They think it means "It was my fault," or "I've failed," or "I am less than perfect," or "I am not paying attention," or "I'm not committed to my customers," or "If I apologize, somehow my boss will hold me responsible for a problem I didn't cause, and this could threaten my job."

The fact is, apologies go a long way to helping customers feel better when they think they've been wronged. And staff don't need to see apologies as an admission of guilt, because customers don't. When you apologize, you merely acknowledge that the customer sees something as having gone wrong. You communicate to the customer that you're taking responsibility for their dissatisfaction, whether it was your fault or not, and this impresses them.

Characteristics of effective apologies:

- They're sincere. If you somehow communicate that you don't care, even if you say the words "I'm sorry," your customer won't hear them.
- They're personal. In a good apology, the speaker speaks in the first person, saying "I," not "we."
- They're specific. They refer to the specific effect the problem had on the customer. They don't stop at canned lines.
- They're immediate. You apologize right away, even before finding out the details of the situation or the remedies.

What's wrong with these apologies?

- "I'm sorry you didn't think to call before you came in. Most of our customers do, so they learn that the doctor might be delayed."
- "My shift just began, so I don't know what happened before. I'm sorry you didn't check your mother's medicine before your last nurse left."
- "We are sorry for the problem that occurred on July 19th. We are deeply troubled that you experienced any problem with our service."
- "Problems happen. We're sorry this happened to you."

These are better:

- "I'm so sorry we kept you waiting. I realize we should have called you to alert you once we knew the doctor would be delayed. Let's see what I can do now that you're here."
- "I'm so sorry about the problem your mother had getting her medication. Through some oversight on our part, I don't see a note here about the situation. I want to take care of it for you. Would you mind if I take about five minutes to follow up with the nurse and the pharmacist and see what I can find out?"
- "I was so sorry to learn about the fact that, on July 19th, you called our advice nurse and couldn't get through for a very long time. I realize it must have been very upsetting waiting when you had concern abut your daughter's fever. I am troubled about us taking such a long time to answer your call and I'm going to look into it. Specifically, I'm going to . . ."
- "I'm so sorry this happened to you. While problems like this do happen from time to time, I do wish we could have prevented it and I'm particularly sorry you were inconvenienced by it."

Bulletin #3: What Drives the Complaining Customer Nuts?

Do you ever fall into these traps?

- *Become defensive.* If we take complaints personally and say things like "I only work here" or "It's not my fault," we make matters worse. We need to keep calm; stay objective; and avoid judging, acting superior, or making excuses.
- *Coldly cite "policy"* as our reason why we can't do what the customer wants. Phrases like "I'm sorry, but that's the way we do things here" or "It's our policy" infuriate customers, because it seems we care more about protecting ourselves than serving their needs. We need to somehow give the customer at least one option in line with policy or find ways to bend rules when we know we're acting in the customer's and organization's best interest. And when the rule can't be bent, we can at least listen intently and with great apology and sympathy explain good reasons why the rule exists.
- *Listen poorly.* When you fail to really listen to customers' complaints, when you interrupt them, act unconcerned, or minimize the complaints, you will almost always increase the customers' hostility. Listen to what customers are telling you. Fix your attention on your customers. Nod, look concerned, and do all you can to absorb the feeling and content of their message so that they will feel listened to and you can respond effectively.
- *Give a runaround.* When we pass the buck or tell the customer to see someone else or give an excuse that doesn't make sense, we further frustrate and alienate our customers. If we need to shift the complaint to someone else, we should hand off the complaint ourselves, instead of making the customer do it.
- *Show "off-putting" nonverbal behavior.* When we look annoyed, fidget, appear impatient or rushed, avoid eye contact, or keep working on our paperwork, we put off our customers, making them feel unimportant and aggravating their dissatisfaction.
- *Make false promises.* Sometimes in our fervor to make things right, we offer solutions we can't implement or promises we can't keep. It's better to stop at hearing the customer out and apologizing than it is to promise to do things that won't happen.
- *Putting down our own organization.* We really look bad to our customers when we make remarks like "We get complaints like this all the time" or "Sometimes I wonder what management thinks it's doing." The fact is,

when a complaining customer is interacting with any one of us, we are our organization's ambassador of goodwill. If we condemn our organization, we make our organization and ourselves look bad, and we kill our customer's confidence in us and our services.

Add to these bulletins by having staff develop other scenarios with possible responses and their analyses, using the complaints most typical of your setting.

Bulletin #4: How You Can Kill Customer Satisfaction When the Customer Complains

Killer words:

- "You must be mistaken."
- "You'll have to . . ."
- "I can't help you."
- "It wasn't my fault."
- "That's never happened before."
- "That doesn't sound likely (or possible)."
- "It's the computer's fault."
- "That's not my department."
- "That's against our policy and there's nothing I can do about it."
- "Are you sure about this?"
- "That's hard to imagine."

Killer actions:

- Silence or nonresponsiveness
- Moving slowly
- Chatting with a colleague while customer is waiting
- Pointing or using another gesture to direct a customer to someone else or to a seat
- Turning your back on the customer without apologizing and explaining
- Walking away from the customer with no explanation
- Acting tired, bored, or distracted
- Looking at your watch
- Muttering
- Interrupting the customer

Provide Practice in Handling Difficult Complaints and Difficult People

One good practice method is to run a biweekly complaint clinic, which can be a session of about one hour.

1. Ask your team, "Who has a complaint situation you want to discuss with the group?" If there are more than three hands raised, ask people to summarize in one line the nature of the complaint situation so that the group or leader can pick the most typical type of complaint to address first (in case there isn't time for all of them).
2. Focusing on one complaint at a time, complete the following tasks:
   —Have the person describe the situation and what he or she found difficult about it.
   —Invite the group to brainstorm alternative approaches.
   —If the difficulty had to do with the fact that solutions exceeded the authority of the person hearing the complaint, talk about who would have been appropriate to handle the complaint. And pinpoint how the person hearing the complaint could make an impressive handoff of the complainer to that person.
   —Then invite volunteers to play the situation live, trying out some of the alternatives suggested in role-play form.
   —Invite feedback:
     –"What language and/or behavior was effective?"
     –"What suggestions do you have for even more effective service recovery in this situation?"

 ### Tips

• Yes, there is an overwhelming amount of skill needed to be really great at service recovery with every individual customer. Chip away at the skills staff need. During your intense effort to improve service recovery, consider a skill builder every two weeks for many weeks. Alternate training modules with complaint clinics in which staff help each other come up with better ways to handle tough customers and tough complaints.

- Find people in your organization who are effective in handling complaints to serve as facilitators. Facilitators of these skill builders need to have considerable emotional intelligence in order to help staff sharpen their skills.
- Since good skill building related to service recovery takes several sessions, consider the idea of joining members of your staff together with members of the staff of other services, so you can send a few people at a time to training without depleting staff coverage. For instance, if you're in a medical practice, consider cosponsoring service recovery training with two or three other practices with whom you connect because you refer patients to them or vice versa.

Step 6: Do a Trial Run, Assess Performance, and Make Improvements Based on Feedback

 ### Key Actions

- Provide people with a self-assessment device.
- Institute a method for collecting difficult situations so you can address them with staff and fine-tune people's approaches.
- Solicit customer feedback.
- Make improvements in protocols and practices.

Now that everybody has a pretty good idea of what's expected of them and an introduction to the behavior and skills that will help them fulfill those expectations, it's time to practice. Step 6 involves testing the new protocols and offers a chance to correct any glitches that may have gone unnoticed in the development process.

 ### Provide Staff with a Self-Assessment Device

Because effective handling of complaints is a complex task that is new to many staff, it is respectful to provide people with a checklist they can use to assess their own performance after they've been involved in the heat of an interaction with a complaining customer.

Here's an example, or engage staff in designing their own.

Self-Assessment after Handling a Complaint

Did the Customer Want (circle one):   Did I meet this need?

To be taken seriously and
treated with respect . . . . Yes   No   Yes   No

Immediate action . . . . Yes   No   Yes   No

Compensation . . . . Yes   No   Yes   No

The responsible employee to be
reprimanded for their offense . . . . Yes   No   Yes   No

Prevention of the problem
in the future . . . . Yes   No   Yes   No

Someone to listen to them attentively
and with understanding . . . . Yes   No   Yes   No

Information to remember/note:

1. The customer's name.
2. How to contact them (address, room number, phone number).
3. Background on the situation (time, place, people involved, event).
4. How the customer defined the problems.
5. How you responded/options you described.
6. What you promised or agreed to do.
7. Any suggestions you have regarding the solution.
8. How you can be reached for questions or a report on results (your name, position, phone number, address).
9. Is the customer still angry? . . . . Yes   No
10. And how do you feel?
    —Gratified that you could help?. . . . . Yes   No
    —Frustrated because you couldn't help?. . . . . Yes   No
    —Resentful for having been placed in this position? . . Yes   No
    —Unhappy?. . . . . Yes   No

Have staff bring three examples of this to a staff meeting that you transform into a complaint clinic for helping people examine their behavior and work on making improvements.

Institute a Method for Collecting Difficult Situations

Have each work team create and centrally locate a service recovery box in their work area. Attach to it a pad of paper and pencil, and invite staff and customers to submit anything complaint-related into it. Specifically, encourage staff to enter into it complaints they fielded that they found hard to handle. These will be retrieved later and discussed at a complaint clinic where staff help each other strategize about how best to address tough complaint situations.

Solicit Customer Feedback

Provide staff with a method for collecting feedback from customers who have complained to them. Plan together how the staff member can tactfully ask for feedback.

Customer Feedback Request

Dear Customer:

Thank you for speaking up about your dissatisfaction recently. We learn a great deal from our customers' complaints.

In fact, we are in the process of learning to handle complaints more effectively. Will you please answer a few questions to let us know how we did recently in handling your complaint? Thank you.

On the following, how do you rate the staff member who handled your complaint?

	Poor	Fair	Good	Great	Suggestions?
Listening					
Showing concern/care					
Pinpointing problem					
Giving me alternatives					
Following up					
Overall responsiveness					

Make Improvements in Protocols and Practices

One good method for accomplishing this key action is to hold protocol improvement meetings. Encourage staff to convene in job-specific groups to review the protocols they tried out. They should bring their self-assessments and customer feedback. Together, have them make improvements by addressing these questions:

- What happened when we tried out the protocols?
- What did customers say about our methods?
- What did we think about our own approaches and performance? What common experiences did we have? What uncommon things happened?
- Looking at the protocol, what worked and what didn't?
- What changes should we make based on our experience?

 ### Tips

- Do this step in a way that aids people's development. Create an atmosphere of "getting your feet wet" by going further with handling complaints than you have before.
- Encourage people to have their job aids handy and go get them when in need. Even suggest that they politely say to customers, "Will you excuse me for just a moment so I can get a guide I have here to make sure I attend to every aspect of your concern?"
- People who provide staff with feedback (steering committee members, supervisors, coaches, and so on) should emphasize the difficulty of getting truly skilled at service recovery because of the many skills involved. They need to be very supportive of staff, or staff will retreat to patterns of trying to find *someone else* to handle the customer.

Step 7: Institute Improvements and Build New Habits

 ## Key Actions

- Provide daily reminders to use service recovery protocols.
- Reward successes.

In many ways, step 7 speaks for itself. Your job now is to monitor staff as they begin trying out their new service recovery techniques and to help them build the healthy habits that will make improved complaint handling automatic.

Provide Daily Reminders to Use Service Recovery Protocols

Ask your steering committee to get creative again. One idea that might help them think of better ones is to adapt the concept of a 21-day calendar to show progress through the 21-day habit-building period. For instance, they might use a thermometer picture with days instead of degrees, with day 1 at the bottom and day 21 at the top. They can hang these in prominent places and have team representatives mark off the days. Call it "We're getting better at taking the heat!"

 ### Reward Successes

Two proven methods for rewarding success are peer coupons and complaint collectors.

Method: Peer Coupons
Provide everyone with coupons so staff can recognize each other for successful interventions with complaining customers and for cooperation with or coming through for *one another* to help bring a complaint to resolution. Here are some examples:

THANKS
for coming through for me.

Together,
we satisfied a disgruntled customer.

CONGRATULATIONS
on turning a customer's dissatisfaction into satisfaction.

You did us proud!

Reprinted, with permission, from the Albert Einstein Healthcare Network © 1996.

Method: Complaint Collectors
Identify a group of people as "complaint collectors." Tell everyone to share their complaint-handling successes with these collectors. When they share a success, the collector gives them a coupon for something special (a free drink, sandwich, umbrella, who knows?)

And, the complaint collectors pool the service recovery success stories to display them during the learning and celebration in step 9.

Tips

- As always in the habit-building period, the emphasis is on helping people remember to play the active role in service recovery that they've been prepared to play.
- Steering committee members and people in management roles should focus on being supportive and encouraging.

Step 8: Check Performance against Targets

Key Actions

- Examine evidence of overall satisfaction with your services.
- Readminister any measures you have of complaining customers' satisfaction.
- Engage staff in evaluating the success of complaint-specific protocols.

Step 8 offers a chance to step back and see how effective your redesigned efforts have really been. As always, the participation of customers as well as the entire staff will give you the broadest perspective and most realistic view of how attitudes and satisfaction are changing as a result of this process.

Examine Evidence of Overall Satisfaction with Your Services

Examine any satisfaction survey data you have to see whether customers' overall satisfaction scores went up. In time, with every staff member nipping dissatisfaction in the bud by handling complaints on the spot, these scores should improve.

Readminister Measures of Complaining Customers' Satisfaction

Remember this from a previous step? Have staff use it again for a concentrated time period (like two weeks) and see how they do.

Customer Feedback Follow-Up

Dear Customer:

Thanks for speaking up about your dissatisfaction recently. We learn a great deal from our customers' complaints. In fact, we are in the process of learning to handle complaints more effectively. Will you please answer a few questions to let us know how we did recently in handling your complaint? Thank you.

On the following, how do you rate the staff member who handled your complaint:

	Poor	Fair	Good	Great	Suggestions?
Listening					
Showing concern/care					
Pinpointing problem					
Giving me alternatives					
Following up					
Overall responsiveness					

 ### Engage Staff in Evaluating the Success of Complaint-Specific Protocols

Staff members have accumulated experience using their newly explicit protocols, and they will have opinions about the effectiveness of these protocols. Respect that by asking staff (in work teams or as a group) the following questions:

- Having used your protocols, what worked and what didn't?
- What got in the way of their use?
- What needs to be changed?
- How can we make our system of protocols more accessible? More effective?

Tips

- This is a time to get analytical and fine-tune your service recovery systems as well as staff skills. Discussions here should help you figure out follow-up strategies that you will inevitably need.
- Since there is so much involved in effective service recovery, substantive discussions with staff are key. No quantitative data tell you enough to help you fine-tune the specifics that merit attention in your approaches. It is these specifics that will make the difference between mediocrity and excellence in your service recovery systems.

Step 9: Share Experience and Results— Learn From Each Other and Celebrate Successes

Key Actions

- Help staff share service recovery successes.
- Celebrate improvements in customers' overall satisfaction.

Time to celebrate! Congratulate everyone on a job well done so far. In the following sections we show you some useful tools that will allow staff to share their successes and setbacks and learn from each other's experiences.

Help Staff Share Service Recovery Successes

Two methods that accomplish this action are creating a storybook for service recovery and warming up meetings by sharing success stories.

Method: Service Recovery Storybook

This method helps people learn from each other while at the same time recognizing people for their successes. Remember the complaint collectors who helped to recognize staff during the habit-building stage? Convene them and engage them in figuring out a way to assemble the success stories they collected into a service recovery storybook that features specific staff members. In this book, tell their stories (which were success stories) and circulate it to all staff.

Method: Success Story Warm-up at Staff Meetings
Open staff meetings with a few minutes during which you invite staff to tell a service recovery success story. Encourage group support for the successes.

 ## Celebrate Improvements in Customers' Overall Satisfaction

If you have evidence of increased customer satisfaction (attributable in part to nipping complaints in the bud), have your steering committee acknowledge everyone on the team for contributing to these results by posting a large, computer-generated banner with a congratulatory message, such as, "Ta-daah to us for better satisfying our customers!"

Reprinted, with permission, from the Albert Einstein Healthcare Network © 1996.

 Tips

- Because service recovery skills are so hard to develop, avoid producing too great a sense of closure during this step; people will need to keep paying close attention to their service recovery efforts or their effectiveness will fade, not build. For that reason, it works better to celebrate and build in ongoing opportunities for the sharing of successes and learning.
- Provide some special recognition here for any people whose jobs include an inordinate amount of service recovery work, such as attorneys, patient representatives, member services representatives, and the like.

Step 10: Institute Ongoing Methods for Sustaining Top-Notch Performance

 ## Key Actions

- Institute a system for ongoing feedback.
- Build into the hiring process screening methods for service recovery skills.
- Add service recovery responsibilities to job descriptions and the performance appraisal process.
- Provide periodic education and reminders.

As you approach the end of your service recovery improvement process, it's time to ensure that the improvements you and your staff have so painstakingly devised, preached, and practiced will not fade into memory, but will instead become a constant in everyday life.

 ## Institute a System for Ongoing Feedback

To monitor the effectiveness of staff at service recovery, use your complaint-tracking system, satisfaction survey, and feedback devices presented earlier to evaluate customers' overall satisfaction and also their perceptions of staff behavior in response to their specific complaints. Channel the results to staff in staff meetings and use the feedback to generate new goals for improvement.

 ## Build into the Hiring Process Screening Methods for Service Recovery Skills

Build into your screening process the following two situations that are very effective in screening applicants on their competency at service recovery. You will learn a great deal from having each candidate respond to these two situations.

Situation #1

Ms. Riley arrived ten minutes early for an appointment with the doctor. She was scheduled to be the first appointment of the day. While she sat, time passed and other patients started filling the empty chairs.

At 9:30, Ms. Riley still had not been called. By that time, she was fidgeting nervously and glancing often at her watch.

At 9:40, impatient and uncomfortable, Ms. Riley stood up and walked to the reception desk and said in a sarcastic tone, "I *hope* I'm not inconveniencing anyone, but I *did* have a 9 o'clock appointment that I made three weeks ago. My time is as valuable as the doctor's, and I want to know why I wasn't taken yet."

Ask the following questions:

- What do you think is the problem here?
- What do you think Ms. Riley is feeling and why?
- What would you have done to prevent this?
- Let's say staff didn't prevent it. What would you say to Ms. Riley now?
- Now, imagine that the staff member said, "This is a very busy service, and you can't expect your doctor to see you the minute you walk in the door. I'm sorry, but you'll have to wait until she's ready for you." What do you think of this response?
- Now let's say this staff person had a habit of alerting patients to delays before the patient asks—they stop into the waiting area to update them if they think there will be a delay. If you did that, what might you say?

To rate the candidate on handling this situation, listen for the following:

- Thanks to the patient for speaking up
- An apology for keeping the person waiting and for not alerting them to the wait before they had to ask
- Empathy and acknowledgment of the patient's feelings of inconvenience
- A nondefensive response
- A comment that staff should have alerted the patient to the delay before the patient had to protest
- An explanation
- The taking of responsibility
- A concrete offer to help or a plan of action such as offering to call and check on the doctor
- An offer of options such as staying or rescheduling
- Suggestions to ease the customer's impatience

Raters, please note this example of a response that meets most criteria.

"Ms. Riley, I'm really sorry I didn't let you know why there's a delay. I meant to do that. I know you were on time, and I'm very sorry that you've been waiting so long. The fact is, Dr. Rhodes had a serious emergency this morning and is behind schedule. I'm going to call her right now and find out how much longer it will be. Then you can decide if you can wait or would prefer that I reschedule you. In the meantime, would you like a magazine or cup of coffee?"

Situation #2

Evelyn Jones, Dr. Simon's appointment secretary, handles a variety of phone calls every day. Although she gets billing information from patients during their visits, she isn't the person who issues their bills. The Outpatient Billing Department does that.

On this particular morning, she answers the phone and Mrs. Garrett is on the line. Mrs. Garrett says in a loud voice, "I just received a bill for $130 for tests that usually cost $30, and I want this fixed!"

Ask the following questions:

- What do you think Mrs. Garrett is feeling and why? How can you tell what she is feeling?
- Upon hearing her say this, what would you say to her?
- What, if anything, would you do for her afterward?

Listen for the following:

- Thanks to the patient for speaking up
- An apology
- Empathy and acknowledgment of the patient's feelings of frustration
- The taking of responsibility
- Initiative to address problem

Raters, please note that you *don't* want to hear responses such as, "I'm sorry but the mistake wasn't mine. The Billing Department wrote that bill. You'll have to talk to them about it. There's nothing I can do. Call the switchboard and ask for them."

The following response meets most of the criteria you should be looking for:

> Thank you for bringing this problem to my attention. I'm very sorry you received what looks to you like a mistaken bill. I'd like to connect you with Robin, our billing person. Would you mind letting me put you on hold while I try to locate her and explain the situation? And if she's available, I'll be able to transfer you to her. I'm sure she can help you.
>
> The individual should then locate Robin and perhaps continue in this manner: "Mrs. Garrett, I located Robin, and she'll be glad to help you. I'll transfer your call, but you might want to jot down her number in case we somehow get disconnected. Her number is 555-4625. And Mrs. Garrett, I'm sorry about this situation. Thank you very much for calling."

Add Service Recovery Responsibilities to Job Descriptions and the Performance Appraisal Process

Add statements like the following to all job descriptions:

- Takes responsibility for service recovery and is effective at handling customer complaints.
- Welcomes customer complaints, listens, shows concern, pinpoints problems, provides solutions, and follows through to ensure customer satisfaction.

Add similar statements to people's performance appraisal forms.

Provide Periodic Education and Reminders

Using an employee newsletter or special bulletins, keep communicating with staff about the importance of responsiveness to customer complaints and about the skills involved. Here are a series of inserts you can clip and copy in your communications with staff, or even include in their pay envelopes.

Clip 'n' Copy #1

Even if our members/customers are not consciously aware of what constitutes top-notch service, they know when they get it, and they certainly know when they don't.

That's why we hear complaints.

We owe it to our customers to listen, understand, respond, and follow through.

And when we do—we turn lemons into lemonade!

Clip 'n' Copy #2

At any given moment, 25 percent of your customers are annoyed enough to walk away and take their business to someone else. Even worse is the fact that only one of them will tell you about it before they do.

So invite people to complain, so you have a chance to make things right.

Clip 'n' Copy #3

Self-check: When you handle complaints, do you get defensive?

	Yes	No
Do you feel like the customer is insulting you?		
Do you disagree quickly with what the customer is saying?		
Do you find yourself arguing with the customer?		
Do you say something negative to the customer about their behavior?		
Do you ever lose control of your own behavior in response to a customer's words?		

If you answered "yes" to even one of these questions, you could benefit from help (training or coaching) on how to hear complaints without taking them personally or becoming defensive.

Clip 'n' Copy #4

Self-check: Do You Avoid Service Recovery Pitfalls?

Do you have coworkers who overhear you when you deal with a complaining customer? Ask them for feedback about your behavior.

Do You:	Never	Rarely	Fairly Often	Very Often
Become defensive				
Cite "policy" as reason to say "no"				
Listen poorly				
Give runaround				
Give nonverbal negatives				
Overreact				
Side against service, undermine customer's confidence				

Clip 'n' Copy #5: The 10-10-10 Principle

- It takes $10,000 to get a new customer.
- It takes 10 seconds to lose one.
- It takes 10 years for the problem to go away . . . unless you are good at SERVICE RECOVERY!

Clip 'n' Copy #6: We Benefit from Service Recovery

According to the TARP study on consumer complaint handling in America:

- 54 percent of the people who complain and are then satisfied by the response will keep giving their business to the organization.
- And 19 percent of people who complain but are not completely satisfied will return with more business.
- But, only 9.5 percent of the people who have complaints but don't express them will come back for more.
- So, ask customers how we're doing. Invite, even beg them to complain. Say, "Please tell me your concerns, so I can do what I can to make things better!"
- And you will build customer loyalty.

Clip 'n' Copy #7

When a customer complains, apologize on behalf of all of us. A few words of regret is a way of saying you care—a show of sensitivity to the ragged edge of another's emotion.

Clip 'n' Copy #8: Getting a Grip on Our Reputation

- When members/patients are dissatisfied with our service, they typically tell *20* relatives and friends.
- When they're satisfied, they tell only *5*.
- Fact is, a negative grapevine spreads like wildfire and hurts our business.

But, we can stop it with great service recovery!

Clip 'n' Copy #9: For a Big Organization

The fact that we are a multidivisional, multiservice, multifunctional, multisite organization is not the customer's problem.

When customers get lost in our system and complain about it, it's our problem.

Clip 'n' Copy #10: What Do *Complaining* Customers Want?

- *They want to be taken seriously and to be treated with respect.* That means we can't have any responses like "You're kidding" or "There's no way that could have happened."
- *They want immediate attention and action.*
- *They want compensation.* Customers want us to compensate them somehow for any inconvenience, pain, or time lost—with a written apology or special favor or effort to make things right and try again.
- *They want someone to be called on the carpet.* Sometimes customers want a staff member to get reprimanded or punished for what they did. And it *is* important for the people responsible for creating the problem to get feedback about their actions and the consequences.
- *They want us to clear up the problem so it doesn't repeat.* Most customers feel better if they know we're taking steps to prevent the problem from ever happening again.
- *They want to be heard.* This is very basic—to want someone to listen to their complaints and show empathy for their feelings.

Tips

- In the course of your strategy, you will see that some staff step forward, bringing to service recovery a great deal of energy. Engage them in planning your follow-through processes, since they obviously have the commitment it will take to persist in future efforts.
- Over time, you'll need to pay attention to altering the systems and staff performance that generate customer complaints. Patterns change over time, and you need systems that sense the emerging problems and trigger prevention initiatives. Be careful that you don't pin all responsibility on staff for creating solutions and solving problems. Systems and work processes often victimize staff and make it painfully difficult to deal with customers with calm and confidence.

Pitfalls and How to Address Them

Service recovery strategies are met with a wide variety of responses by staff. Some people are enthusiastic because they see themselves as responsible for satisfying customers. These people want all the help they can get to become more effective. Others resent responsibility for satisfying customers when they are already working hard and doing so much. The variety of responses to service recovery make it worth your while to anticipate and prepare to handle ruffled feathers among your staff. In a way, we're talking about helping you anticipate complaints and prepare your responses, much like protocols enable staff to do in service recovery.

So what kinds of resistance and complaints can you expect?

"What Am I to Do?"

Some people resist responsibility for service recovery because they expect to feel inept when a customer is in their face expecting resolution to problems. To address this fear, you need to make sure that your strategy includes substantial skill building and also that it provides resources to help staff resolve problems they feel unprepared or ill equipped to handle. They don't want to feel stranded or stuck speechless in the face of customer complaints.

"Don't Look at Me. I Didn't Do It!"

Some resist taking responsibility for service recovery because they resent being in a position where they need to apologize to customers for anything. They see service problems as results of systems problems or other people's neglect or inattention. And even if they see themselves as partly responsible, they think it reflects negatively on them as a person to apologize. Rather than apologize, they prefer to pass the buck to someone else. First of all, it's critical to help all staff see the difference between accepting blame and expressing regret. People need to know how to say "I'm so sorry you were inconvenienced." This does not accept blame. The irony is that people who humbly apologize when they are at fault or aren't at fault are perceived by most customers as humble and honest and therefore worthy of more, not less, respect.

"Patients Want the Impossible."

Some staff resist service recovery because they think most patient complaints are unjustified—that people expect too much. First of all, if there is a pattern of patients expecting more than your staff can deliver, you need to consider a preemptive patient education strategy that lets patients know up front what they can and cannot expect, given your resources. But if individual staff members have the attitude that patients' expectations are off the wall and therefore don't deserve their effort, these staff need coaching in the old adage "The customers are always right, even when they're wrong." Staff not amenable to coaching on this point are likely to create customer complaints, and they will certainly not be able to deal effectively with them. These attitudes show; don't allow them in your service. Build into your discussions opportunities to grapple with this way of thinking, or staff will persist in blaming the customer instead of absorbing the heat from customer dissatisfaction.

"This Is Beyond Me!"

Other staff resist service recovery responsibilities because they think systems problems make it impossible to deliver good service; they therefore they see customer complaints as predictable and inevitable. If they are right, and they frequently are, launch process improvement initiatives to tackle service problems at their root so that staff are not in the position of forever having to apologize for systems that don't work.

"I Did My Part, but Did You?"

Another source of resistance to service recovery—and a barrier to people's effectiveness—is staff's inability to rely on each other (or their manager) for coming through on promises. If a staff member handles a complaint but needs the cooperation of a coworker or boss in order to resolve it, that staff member has only so much capability to satisfy the customer. That person needs help from coworkers. If these coworkers don't come through, the person is left looking very bad in the eyes of the customer for having failed to keep a promise. If this issue is alive and kicking in your service, take it on at a staff meeting or team-building session. It is a killer of initiative and good intentions. Everyone needs a written or unwritten contract that they will come through for each other when someone needs help in order to satisfy a customer.

"I'm Not Gonna Get Hit with Their Anger!"

Another reason for resistance to active roles in service recovery has to do with a very rampant fear of conflict among many people in our culture. Some staff are afraid of people's anger and resist listening thoroughly to complaints. People's anger causes them to feel afraid, perhaps from their own family history or personal patterns beyond the scope of work. The result is that such staff tend to act in ways that shut the customer up or fend them off in the direction of someone else ASAP. The challenge here is to help people defuse others' anger, since they cannot necessarily prevent it. To do this, they need training and practice in calming the upset customer through listening, empathy, and nonverbal regard. Invest in assertiveness training or workshops on handling the irate customer for people who resist service recovery because of this conflict avoidance pattern. They can learn how to listen without defensiveness, how to calm an irate customer, and how to avoid taking personally the anger expressed by customers.

"I Don't Have Time!"

Many staff, as you know, complain that complaints from customers eat away at their already overloaded time and interfere with their productivity. While that is true in the short run, help people see how much time is spent unruffling ruffled feathers or dealing with very upset people whose initial words of complaint were handed off from one person to another without relief. The point to emphasize is that people usually aren't furious the first time they complain. It's more often the second and third time they tell someone that their anger reaches escalated levels.

Conclusion

All of this points to the fact that service recovery is not a short-term service objective. It is a long-term service objective. While you can reap gigantic benefits by focusing intense attention on it in the short run, you need to keep the pressure on and revisit this far-reaching responsibility over and over and over, or your staff will veer off the road to service recovery.

References

1. JCAHO, *Comprehensive Accreditation Manual for Hospitals* (Oak Brook Terrace, IL: JCAHO, 1996).

2. Liz Osborne, *Resolving Patient Complaints: A Step-by-Step Guide to Effective Service Recovery* (Gaithersburg, MD: Aspen Publishers, 1995). Reprinted with permission.

Other Resources

Books

• Wendy Leebov, *Resolving Complaints: For Professionals in Health Care,* 1995. Available from: Mosby Great Performance, 14964 NW Greenbrier Parkway, Beaverton, OR 97006, 503-690-9181. This 53-page booklet is full of examples, exercises, and tips that help health care staff handle effectively the complaints expressed by their patients, members, and other customers. It is designed for health care professionals in hospitals, networks, managed care organizations, medical practices, ambulatory care services, home care agencies, long-term care facilities, and other health care organizations.

- Liz Osborne, *Resolving Patient Complaints: A Step-by-Step Guide to Effective Service Recovery.* Gaithersburg, MD: Aspen Publishers, 1995. Available from: Aspen Publishers, 200 Orchard Ridge Drive, Suite 200, Gaithersburg, MD 20878. This is a terrific book that lays out procedures for handling all kinds of health care complaints and emphasizes the roles of patient relations representatives and member services departments in collecting, addressing, recording, and triggering prevention efforts relentlessly.

Films

- *Oops! Time for Service Recovery.* Santa Monica: Salenger Films, 1990. Available from: Salenger Films, Inc., 1635 12th Street, Santa Monica, CA 90404, 310-450-1300. This is a curriculum designed to help service workers handle complaints effectively. It includes a step-by-step process, case studies, and practice exercises. The film motivates staff to see complaints as opportunities to win over unhappy customers and demonstrates effective methods.

PART THREE

• • •

Help Clinic

• • •

In part 3, you'll find advice about how to make your service optimally effective.

- Chapter 7, "Special Considerations for Large Health Care Organizations," is especially for people in networks, hospitals, nursing home chains, health care systems, and the like. It addresses special considerations and recommendations to help large organizations orchestrate and coordinate strategies and also promote cross-fertilization, learning, and celebration in large organizations.
- Chapter 8, "Special Considerations for Medical Practices and Specific Service Lines," is especially for people in smaller health care organizations, whether independent services like a medical practice or a service line within a larger organization—services that tend to have fewer internal resources for support, but a much easier time achieving effective communication and group learning.
- And finally, chapter 9, "Your Questions Answered: Pitfalls and Pointers," poses the frequently asked questions about the approaches presented here and suggests answers to help you make your strategy purposeful, fruitful, and gratifying for your team.

Chapter 7

• • •

Special Considerations for Large Health Care Organizations

The bigger the organization, the greater the alignment challenge. If your organization is large, it isn't easy to address a service objective quickly, nor is it easy to mobilize people and help them support, learn from, and appreciate each other.

Your Five Greatest Obstacles

Large organizations face these obstacles in particular:

1. *Teams become lost or confused.* While the steering committee creates a plan and schedule, there is a distance between them and each work team, a distance reflected by several layers of management and also departmental boundaries. Communication is not easy and can break down. In the process, it's not unusual for work teams to become confused or lost. They ask, "Now, say this again. What is it we're supposed to be doing?"

2. *People reinvent wheels unnecessarily.* Because each team doesn't know what the other teams are doing, they each cover the same ground; they each expend effort doing what one team could have done if the other had known it.

3. *Team efforts are invisible, so people feel slighted.* Inevitably some teams give the objective their all and do terrific work, but their efforts and results go unnoticed. The result is that staff will feel unappreciated and disappointed.

4. *Important work that cuts across work teams doesn't get done.* Some work processes that relate to the service objective might not fall entirely within the domain of one work team, but instead may involve many teams or departments. The result can be that no one team feels ownership, and therefore no one initiates improvement related to it. For instance, if the goal is to improve first impressions, who is likely to design protocols for behavior in the elevators and cafeteria? If the goal is creating great explanations, who owns the challenge of creating directions to get to the organization by subway? Probably no one, because the need is not specific to their service and it doesn't occur to them that they can take it into their own hands and do it.

5. *Leaders lose track of what's really happening, and some teams count on this.* Also, with so many people doing so many things, senior management tends to lose track of what is really being accomplished and by whom. Teams fade into the woodwork, sometimes deliberately, knowing that administrators can't see what they're doing or not doing from their distant purviews. The result is that some don't get on board; they do nothing but prepare excuses in case anyone eventually notices.

The fact is, effective pursuit of a service objective is like creating a symphony from an orchestra. An orchestra has a written plan, clear to all. There are many parts, each with unique roles. They need to play together with their unique sound and artistry to create music. And they need leadership, coordination, and a signal system that helps them play the right notes at the right time. Meanwhile, behind the scenes, they need individual support so that they bring to the process an effective instrument, skills, stamina, and the quality of attention they need to play the right notes in the right way at the right time.

It's no different here. You need to coordinate and support your service improvement strategy with methods that have the effect of orchestrating everybody's efforts, creating contagious energy, cross-fertilization, and accountability, and also promoting the sharing of successes—all with the goal of creating a powerful cumulative impact that is, as with the orchestra, bigger than the sum of its parts.

Methods for Overcoming These Obstacles across Organizational Lines

You can minimize the extent and strength of these obstacles and engage teams in making beautiful music together in the form of service breakthroughs. This chapter describes several strategies that serve these functions, including:

- Strategies that help to synchronize your efforts
- Energy Infusions
- Cross-fertilization and troubleshooting methods
- Methods for pursuing priorities shared by many and owned by none
- Accountability methods
- Methods of reducing invisibility and highlighting successful teams

Strategies That Help to Synchronize Your Efforts

As described in chapter 2, big organizations require an infrastructure for your one-objective-at-a-time approach that is layered and enables every aspect of the strategy to reach people in every nook and cranny of the organization. This is hard to coordinate in a big organization like a large hospital, provider network, or system composed of different entities that are not even all on the same campus.

To focus attention on the breakthrough objective and provide support to work teams in an efficient, organized manner, it helps to have everyone going through the same process *at the same time*. By having everyone go through the same process steps at the same time, you can easily make the process visible and continuously raise people's awareness of what should be happening at any particular time. It also serves as a constant reminder of the importance of the objective as a shared priority.

Publish and Distribute a Calendar

To help synchronize efforts, publish and distribute a calendar that shows the timeline for every step in the 10-step improvement process. People can use a basic month-by-month calendar by marking when each step begins and showing its length, or they can get creative about the format, using perhaps a flowchart approach or calendar software that allows easy applications of graphics or icons to illustrate each step. The steering committee should distribute the calendar to core groups or team leaders and ask them to post it as a daily reminder of where they are in the improvement process. Teams can also be encouraged to mark off accomplishments and/or add notes onto the calendar designating team meetings, due dates, and the like.

Here are two excerpts from calendars used to help teams stay synchronized and aligned in their service improvement process:

Timeline for Improving First Impressions

	Task	Time frame
Step 1	Plan your department's approach to first impressions.	April 26–May 22 4 weeks
Step 2	Communicate expectations to staff: that they meet and greet people according to both our universal protocols and their job-specific protocols. Distribute protocols/job aids.	May 23–June 5 2 weeks
Step 3	Institute the designed process. Do a trial run. Try out both our universal and job-specific protocols.	June 6–June 12 1 week
Step 4	Measure: Check progress. Recognize people for following protocols effectively.	June 13–June 19 1 week
Step 5	Assess: Identify problems and pursue improvements.	June 20–July 10 3 weeks
Step 6	Implement improvements: Build habits to hold the gains through 21 workdays of habit building.	July 11–August 8 4 weeks
Step 7	Celebrate success!	August 9

Monthly Calendar Showing Steps in the Process

April 1998 Monthly Planner

Sunday	Monday	Tuesday	Wednesday	Thursday	Friday	Saturday
March S M T W T F S 1 2 3 4 5 6 7 8 9 10 11 12 13 14 15 16 17 18 19 20 21 22 23 24 25 26 27 28 29 30 31			**1** 9 A.M.–11 A.M. Coaching/Running Meeting—Elkins 1 P.M.–3 P.M. Coaching/Running Meeting—Elkins	**2** 9 A.M.–11 A.M. Coaching/Running Meeting—Elkins	**3** 9 A.M.–11 A.M. Coaching/Running Meeting—Elkins	**4**
**Step 2: Communicate Expectations**						
5	**6**	**7**	**8**	**9**	**10**	**11**
**Step 3: Trial Run**						
12	**13**	**14**	**15**	**16**	**17**	**18**
**Step 4: Measure/Check Progress**						
19	**20**	**21** 10 A.M.–4 P.M. Drop-In Help Clinic: Problem Solving— Korman Rm. B-6	**22** 9 A.M.–10 A.M. Style Clinic—Korman Rm. B-6 10:15 A.M.–11:15 A.M. Style Clinic— Korman Rm. B-6	**23** 1 P.M.–2 P.M. Style Clinic— Korman Rm. B-6 2:15 P.M.–3:15 P.M. Style Clinic— Korman Rm. B-6	**24**	**25**
**Step 5: Assess/Solve Problems/Make Improvements**						
26	**27** 9 A.M.–10 A.M. Style Clinic— Korman Rm. B-6 10:15 A.M.–11:15 A.M. 11:15 A.M.–12:15 A.M.	**28**	**29**	**30**	**May** S M T W T F S 1 2 3 4 5 6 7 8 9 10 11 12 13 14 15 16 17 18 19 20 21 22 23 24 25 26 27 28 29 30 31	
**Step 5: Assess/Solve Problems/Make Improvements**						

Reprinted, with permission, from the Albert Einstein Healthcare Network © 1996.

In this figure is an example of a way to help everyone track progress during the habit-building period:

"Tickler" System

A "tickler" system of fliers also helps people to stay on the same timeline. In one example of a tickler system, at each new step in the improvement process, the steering committee mailed to all teams a tickler reminding them of the dates associated with that process, along with how that step in the process fit with other steps. These ticklers became reminders to teams to get back on track if they were falling behind.

Following is an example of a tickler promotional flier:

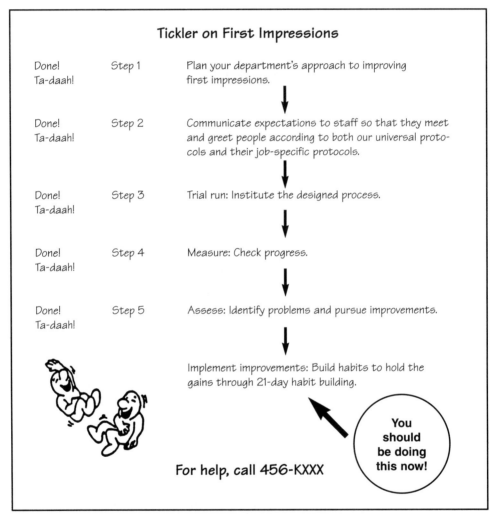

Reprinted, with permission, from the Albert Einstein Healthcare Network © 1996.

Energy Infusions

Since the 10-step improvement process can take many months, people need periodic energy boosts that spark their energy and stamina for working on the objective.

The "I'm Impressed!" Memo

Consider simple periodic "I'm impressed!" memos and also more ambitious rallies and events that refocus attention on the objective in a very positive, uplifting way.

To: Network Staff

From: President of Board of Trustees

Subject: Wow and Keep Up the Good Work!

On my way to a board meeting this morning, I couldn't help but notice your work in progress on our service goal of _____. This goal touches me personally because _____.

I realize that you're already working very hard to provide great care for our patients, and I realize that working on the service goal of _____ might feel like extra work and might produce extra pressure on you. All the more reason that I want you to know how impressed I am with what you're doing and how excited I am about what your work is going to do for our network. Thank you on behalf of our patients.

Rallies

Consider also developing a special team to plan a rally or two for each service objective. Rallies are creative events designed to attract hundreds of employees to see demonstrations, quiz shows, displays, and other methods of featuring people's accomplishments related to the service objective.

The following summarizes the details of rallies that the Albert Einstein Healthcare Network's rally team held for all staff when pursuing their objective on "first impressions last" and then their great explanations objective.

First Impressions Rally Flyer

**Come help us kick off
our first networkwide values goal
at the First Impressions Rally!**

When: May 25
Where: Braemer Auditorium
Times: 9:00 a.m.–10:00 a.m.
        11:00 a.m.–12:00 p.m.
        1:00 p.m.–2:00 p.m.
        6:00 p.m.–7:00 p.m.
        7:30 p.m.–8:30 p.m.
        1:00 a.m.–2:30 a.m. (third shift)
(Come to any session—no RSVP needed)

Play the first impressions game!

This is for everyone!

Prizes

Music

Food

Movie clips

Contribute to our giant Meeting and Greeting Collage

Send multicultural photos, magazine pictures, and other visuals to Julie Hyland,
Moss Administration, or bring them with you on May 25. Please include your
name and department so we can give you credit!

and

Find out who won the First Impressions Scavenger Hunt.

Questions?

Call the Values Hotline (456-KXXX).
Leave a message and we'll call you back.

Reprinted, with permission, from the Albert Einstein Healthcare Network © 1996.

Cross-Fertilization and Troubleshooting Methods

As work teams proceed through the 10 steps of service improvement, they develop products and ideas that can help other teams. They also encounter problems that other teams and individuals can help them solve, thus saving time and energy and reducing frustration that might otherwise stop them dead in their tracks. Here are several methods for promoting cross-fertilization during the 10-step process and also providing easy access to troubleshooting help along the way.

Core Group Leader Meetings

In an organization where you have different work teams working on the objective and you have designated leaders of each work team, convene the team leaders for a meeting about problems, plans, and sharing. At these meetings, you post a chart with three columns:

Problems	Plans	Sharing

One column is for "problems," one for "plans," and one for "sharing." Invite group leaders to enter their initials in the column on this chart next to whatever topic they want to share. So, someone with a problem to discuss writes his or her initials under "problems," someone with progress or a telling anecdote to share writes his or her initials under the column labeled "sharing," and so on. This shared agenda is then followed to create a very rich, mutually beneficial, and lively meeting that has the effect of helping people share across work teams and learn from each other.

Help Clinics or "Office Hours"

Line up resource people who can be available all day long to help staff members who drop in with any need related to the objective being addressed. In our work at Albert Einstein Healthcare Network, all kinds of people and needs have shown up to help clinics. During our network's pursuit of the great explanations objective, a six-person team from pathology wanted help developing explanation protocols for phone interactions with doctors who want to know "Where is my test result?" People from the heart center showed up to ask for feedback about evaluation devices they had drafted to determine the effectiveness of new face-to-face explanations they designed for family members. A nurse came with a draft of new patient education materials and asked for feedback and editing help. In order to provide staff the help they need, you must line up resource people with topics they can address expertly and encourage staff to use them.

Highlighting from Interim Reports

If you institute a system of interim reports (see next section), have managers or team leaders send a copy of each to your steering committee who, in turn, reviews the reports, compiles helpful highlights, and communicates these either in simple newsletter form or as is so that everyone can see what everyone else is doing and benefit from other teams' developments.

Methods for Pursuing Priorities Shared by Many, Owned by None

With nearly every objective, there are likely to be improvement needs that are not owned by any one team. For instance, when Albert Einstein Healthcare Network pursued the great explanations service objective, many work teams identified the need to develop an explanation for patients of managed care about how managed care affects decisions about lengths and stay, red tape, precertification, and the like. Some departments said in effect, "This isn't our job to create explanation protocols about this." Others identified this as a priority and began work on it. The same situation arose for explaining bills; for explaining informed consent; for explaining directions such as how to reach the hospital by car, bus, or train; for handling complaints about bills; and so on. So, instead of letting teams bow out of work on this because it didn't fall within their purview or having several teams work on it in a duplicative fashion, we organized interdepartmental teams, all of which had regular opportunities to give the same explanation to customers. And these teams developed protocols for a variety of situations all relating to the same subject. Then, these protocols were widely distributed to all departments who handled the situations covered by these explanations. This is efficient and creates far-reaching improvements.

Accountability Methods

With diverse teams working in diverse ways in a large organization, you also run the risk of having some work teams neglect to engage in the process, letting it fall through the cracks or blatantly disengaging from it. To protect against this, you might need to install some accountability methods that hook service improvement efforts into your regular authority structure, so that people's managers keep track of their efforts and hold them accountable. Helpful tools include a system of simple interim reports and also leadership prompts that remind the administrators to track and follow up on the activities of their direct reports.

Interim Reports

Consider building into your step-by-step plan certain "report" points at which team leaders need to submit to their boss a summary of their team's work at that point. For instance, there might be a report due that describes the job-specific situations they chose as priorities for making improvements. Another report might be due after teams should have developed their evaluation devices. Another might be due once they designed their improvements. Here's an example of a report due to administrators in one organization:

Interim Report Format

Which improvement priorities did you establish for your particular department/team/service? Why?

What tool(s) did you establish for testing your improvements?

Which improvements did you implement?

Enclose the protocols you designed that describe the changes you've made.

People in which functions are expected to adopt these protocols?

What are you doing as a team to ensure that people continue instituting these improvements? How are you "holding the gains" with your new standards?

What reactions does your team have so far to our work process on this objective?

Leadership Prompts

Consider also leadership prompts that, in a synchronized fashion, remind administrators to follow up with managers who report to them to find out the status of their work on your service objective. Here's a leadership prompt memo developed for Albert Einstein Healthcare Network's "first impressions last" objective:

Dear Administrator:

September marks the end of our systematic approach to improving first impressions. To help bring closure to this effort and prepare for the launch of our next objective, please take these actions:

1. Follow-up and accountability
   —Be sure to collect from your direct reports their summary report and evaluation form. The summary should include final protocols, prelims encountered and their solutions, and measurements. We will use these reports to evaluate the process overall and also to glean learning that we can share with everyone networkwide.
   —For people who did not turn in the report, please call them to express your disappointment and the expectation that they follow through, or write them a note to this effect. A sample memo might read: "If my records are right, I didn't yet receive the report of your team's first impressions process. I need this report so I can review your progress and identify any problems or insights that merit further attention so we can all meet high standards of first impressions with our customers and coworkers."
2. If they did turn in their summary report and it impressed you, please take a moment to send a thank-you note. For example, "Thank you for sending me your first impressions report. I had a chance to read it and found it thorough and interesting. I'm encouraged by the improvements in customer satisfaction that I'm confident will result from your team's efforts."

Methods of Reducing Invisibility and Highlighting Successful Teams

During the recognition and learning step in your improvement process (step 9), you have special opportunities to connect people from disparate parts of the organization and highlight the individuals and teams whose contributions to the objective deserve recognition. Because the organization is so large, you need to find ways to invite contributors to step forward and show their accomplishments.

Consider first of all the simple memo.

To: Everybody

Subject: First Impressions Recognition

We will be recognizing great first impressions work throughout September in a variety of ways.

Please help us identify departments, teams, and/or individuals whose work you think merits recognition. Call 555-8288 and say who you are, the team(s) or individual(s) meriting recognition, and a one-liner about why each deserves recognition for their work from your point of view. We'll highlight these star contributors in a big bulletin board display, in our employee newsletter, and also provide nominees with some special memento celebrating their contribution.

Also, use leadership prompts such as the following. This one asks administrators to nominate teams whose efforts merit recognition.

To: Administrators

Subject: Suggestions to Help You Bring Closure to Our First
           Impressions Objective with Your Direct Reports

September marks the end of our systematic approach to improving first impressions. To help bring closure to this effort and prepare for the launch of the next one, please help:

- Identify teams and/or individuals whose work you think merits recognition and call 555-8288 to give the details. The steering committee will then see to it that the team or individuals get special recognition.
- Encourage your direct reports to encourage their work teams to have the guts to enroll in the "First Impressions Dare." This is a golden opportunity for people proud of their first impressions work to step forward, show off their work, and be recognized for it. Details are coming soon.

And although it's more work, it's spirit boosting to develop splashy, attention-getting recognition methods that invite teams proud of their accomplishments to step forward to gain recognition, perhaps in a competitive manner.

Here's one example, called the "First Impressions Dare," developed by the first impressions recognition team at the Albert

Einstein Healthcare Network. Our goal was to evaluate how well people were actually implementing their new greeting protocols. The team considered having mystery guests do observations without telling people that they would be observed. However, because this might have undermined trust and possibly created negative feelings, the team decided instead to create an opportunity for people *proud* of their first impressions results to step forward to be recognized for their work by taking the "First Impressions Dare." Teams who took "the Dare" were alerted that mystery guests would call and visit in order to check the quality of their greetings. Teams that met a standard of 90 percent great greetings would win prizes. Every team could enter and win if they met the standard. The recognition team then made sure that winning teams were recognized in their employee newspaper, on a "Great Wall of Fame" in the cafeteria, and with a token prize for each individual. Here are materials that explain the Dare further, in case you want to adapt it to your organization. It begins with the invitation designed to recruit mystery guests or observers needed in the Dare.

The First Impressions Dare

Will You Help Out in Evaluating First Impressions by Serving as a Mystery Guest?

Here's the plan:

We're daring each team, department, and unit in the organization to submit to an intensive examination of how well they are doing with their first impressions protocols. We want to know how well our first impressions goal is working, and we want to recognize individuals, departments, and units who are meeting and greeting stars! Teams that accept the dare will do two things:

1. Submit the "story" of their first impressions work
2. Agree to be evaluated by "mystery guests" who will visit the unit or department in person or by calling on the phone

This is where individuals can help. We need a large group of people to serve as mystery guests. Between August 25 and September 16, each mystery guest will need to visit and phone the departments who accept the dare and, using a simple checklist, observe whether or not the staff are using the protocols. If you think you might be willing to be a mystery guest, please come to one short meeting so we can give you the details.

Here are the instructions to teams accepting the Dare:

Congratulations! Your Team Has the Guts to Accept the First Impressions Dare!

Here are your instructions. By September 16

1. You must tell us the "story" of your first impressions work (how you organized yourselves to do it, what was involved, how you measured progress, how you identified and overcame problems, and your action plan for making sure great first impressions last! This story can take any form: posters, songs, a written report, videotape, or audiotape—be creative!

2. You must prepare your team to be visited by "mystery guests"—a select group of people who will, unbeknownst to your staff, observe your first impressions in action, both in person and over the phone. Here's how it will work:

   - Between August 25 and September 16, mystery guests will visit and call your team on the phone. They will experience a minimum of 20 greetings by your staff.

   - Using the attached checklist, mystery guests will evaluate each greeting. These checklists will be turned into human resources, who will tally the results. If your department/unit creates great first impressions 18 out of 20 times, you and your staff will meet this daring requirement.

   - Also submit two of your own team-specific protocols on which you dare to be evaluated. Please fill in the attached form and return or fax to human resources. As an additional incentive, when the mystery guest visits your team, he or she will give your greeters a coupon that informs them that they have been visited by a mystery guest. Collect 5 of these coupons and redeem them for a prize!

We will announce all winners during the week of September 26. And, hats off to you for boldly accepting the dare!

Reprinted, with permission, from the Albert Einstein Healthcare Network © 1996.

And here is the checklist mystery guests use to check compliance with protocols:

Mystery Guest Checklist

Date/time _____ Protocol _____	Yes	No	Comments
In Person Acknowledged the customer's presence right away, even if on the phone			
Made eye contact			
Smiled			
Said hello or other greeting			
(If a stranger) Introduced self, stated role and purpose			
Offered assistance like "How may I help you?"			
Patient Rooms Knocked before entering			
Telephone Greeted caller (Hello, Good morning, etc.)			
Identified self			
Identified department/service			
Offered assistance like "How may I help you?"			
Team-specific protocol followed?			

Names of stars observed

1. _____

2. _____

3. _____

4. _____

5. _____

6. _____

7. _____

Here are the instructions to the mystery guests:

Instructions to Mystery Guests

Note: Before arriving, make sure you have the team's greeting protocols, so you'll know whether people are following them.

When You Visit a Team in Person

Part 1
1. Walk into a work area.
2. Look pleasant, but don't say anything.
3. Approach the reception area.
4. Wait for a staff member to acknowledge you.
5. After the acknowledgment and greeting, identify yourself: "I'm your mystery guest—thanks for accepting the dare!"
6. Hand them the coupon.
7. Fill out the checklist as soon as you leave.

Part 2
1. Circulate—see several people (at least three), so not only the receptionist is observed.
2. Follow same steps as above.

When You Visit a Nursing Unit

1. As nonchalantly as possible, walk up and down the halls for a few minutes, observing whether or not staff members knock on patient doors before going in.
2. If asked what you are doing, say: "I'm a mystery visitor and am conducting research on first impressions."
3. Go up to the nurses station and follow the same instructions as listed under "When You Visit a Team in Person."

When You Telephone

1. Call each number listed in the phone directory for that department/unit. Listen for the items on the checklist.
2. When each caller has completed their greeting, say "I'm a mystery caller—thanks for accepting the first impressions dare!"

And finally, here is a blurb about what happened. It was publicized widely.

We Dared You and You Accepted!

Twenty-two teams from across the network accepted the First Impressions Dare during our work on the first breakthrough objective. The "daring" teams first had to tell the story of how they developed their first impressions greeting protocols, measured their progress, and overcame any problems. Then, they agreed to accept an unannounced mystery guest into their department. Mystery guests arrived in person and called on the phone. They observed such details as whether or not employees greeted them politely, made eye contact, smiled, and offered assistance. They also noted if employees knocked on patients' doors before entering, identified themselves, and followed their department-specific greeting protocols.

The results: Spectacular!

Teams who accepted the dare and won:

- Emergency Department
- Radiology
- Environmental Services
- Information Services
- Orthopedics
- Willowcrest Dietary
- Moss Telecommunications
- Moss Medical Administration
- Physical Therapy
- Quality Management
- Patient Services
- Premier Years
- AEHN Executive Office
- Willowcrest Business Office
- Moss Maintenance
- Organization/Staff Development

Reprinted, with permission, from the Albert Einstein Healthcare Network © 1996.

Conclusion

Large organizations need glue to hold together the multitude of teams and miniprojects that become active during pursuit of any service objective. Why go to the trouble? Because methods that provide this glue foster alignment throughout the organization with the service objective, create a powerful group learning effect, and mobilize energies across organizational lines—all in the direction of your objective.

Chapter 8

• • •

Special Considerations for Medical Practices and Specific Service Lines

Service enthusiasts in medical practices, service lines, and other smaller provider organizations also need to pursue service improvement in an organized fashion. On the one hand your job is simpler. On the other hand, your job is harder.

Why is your job simpler? Because in a small service, you can easily communicate with all staff, even on a face-to-face basis. That's impossible in a large organization. And because you can communicate more easily, you can cut corners, bypassing the need for so many formal communication methods. You can call people together to focus them, to find out what and how they're doing, and to foster mutual problem solving, recognition, and support. Also, in a smaller service, service processes are likely to be less layered and less complicated, making it somewhat easier to redesign, streamline, and improve service processes.

Your job is, however, harder in some ways than that of a large organization, and you will have to compensate for these aspects. For instance, few small organizations have staff whose specific job it is to support strategies like this. Bigger organizations might have marketing people, public relations people, training professionals, management engineers, and the like, all able to provide expertise to support their colleagues in every part of the service. And they can do this during their work time; it's not really a deviation from their main job, but part of it. In some small services, you have to do this yourself or call on people for whom it will be an addition to their daily work—an extra demand. In order that all functions can be served and support can be provided for aspects of the work on which coworkers need help, you have to invite people to share their special talents—talents that might not be part of their everyday work. Also, in a smaller organization, you might not exist in a vacuum. Perhaps you represent one service line in a large organization or network or one site in a chain of small service sites. You might need to connect to other sites and engage the cooperation of other departments in order to make your strategy effective, even while these other sites and services do not share your objective.

Pointers for Small Organizations

Your service's small size can accelerate your process improvement efforts. The following subsections discuss these four important pointers:

1. Simplify and speed up.
2. Identify your own internal talent pools.
3. Reach out to other departments whose help you need to reach your goal.
4. Take advantage of the ease of communicating when you have a small staff.

Simplify and Speed Up

The do-it-yourself kits in this book include a variety of tools to help organizations deal thoroughly with each service objective. For smaller organizations, you might find more than you need. If your colleagues are quick to embrace an objective, don't employ multiple methods up front to sell the objective. Move instead right to the design phase. If you have a talented and gung ho steering committee interested in doing design work such as protocol development, have them do it with input from coworkers, instead of forming subteams and any additional infrastructure for your work. If you have small numbers of people to influence, consider replacing the training components of the tool kits with a coach who works with individuals. In other words, don't feel wedded to these tools. Here are other examples of ways to simplify support and communication during key steps in the 10-step improvement process. During the trial run step, on the first day, do the following:

- Gather all staff for a quick pep talk. Remind them of the powerful impact they can make by implementing the designed changes.
- Remind them of your expectations. Review the changes to be implemented and respond to staff questions and concerns.
- Throughout the day, have a coach or steering committee member circulate to address concerns, remind people to do what they're supposed to do, and ask how it's going.

On the second day of the trial run, gather all staff to discuss "What happened yesterday?" Ask the following questions:

- What went well?
- What was awkward or didn't work?
- What changes/revisions in the protocols do we need?
- Any reactions yet from customers? What do they tell us?

Thank people for their efforts so far and urge them to focus on using their protocols consistently. Consider also pairing people up in a buddy system to encourage use of the new protocols and mutual help. And all week, you and steering committee members can provide on-the-spot recognition for people by wandering around your site.

During the habit-building step of the 10-step process, simplify the process by providing the following support—which you can do easily because your service is small:

Support during Habit Building

- Have a coach or steering committee member check with people every day to make sure they're implementing the new protocols. Invite people to identify problems and help solve them so that these problems don't become an excuse for abandoning the changes. Coach, help, and support!
- Track progress through the 21 days. Post a progress-plotting chart or calendar in a central location. As each day ends, mark it off in an attention-getting way—celebrating progress toward

the new habits. Every day, extend the line to reflect where in the 21-day habit-building process people are.

In other words, simplify and streamline everywhere you can out of respect for staff's precious time.

Identify Your Own Internal Talent Pools

If you have no specialists (for instance, no corporate support services) devoted to functions needed to support your strategy, consider having your steering committee inventory the skills and talents that would be helpful to people during your pursuit of your particular service objective. Then, poll *all* staff to see who is willing to volunteer which talents in support of their colleagues and the objective. Then, harness these people to provide help clinic support, being careful to thank them profusely for this generous sharing of their expertise. And if at all possible, relieve the productive pressure on them so that they have a little spare time within their work to devote to helping colleagues pursue the service objective.

Reach Out to Other Departments

If your service is dependent on or interdependent with other service sites or support departments who have not embraced your service objective, draw them in and ask for their help. Inform them about what you're doing and take steps to identify and address with them any special needs you have in order to be successful with your strategy. See if you can negotiate up front to receive any special attention, arrangements, or latitude you need in order to pursue your goal. Why should they cooperate? Appeal to the mission you share having to do with serving your ultimate customers—patients. Offer to share your findings. And fuss over them, pouring on appreciation as they help you meet your service objectives.

Take Advantage of the Ease of Communicating

Working with a smaller staff, you can replace formal communications with easy, off-the-cuff methods. For instance, you can use a central bulletin for communications. You can assign a "point person" from each work team whom you can call to convey important messages back to the team. Also, you can use steering committee members in an "each one, tell some" approach. In these ways, you can reach everyone while keeping the communications feeling natural and informal.

If your practice is small enough to make face-to-face communication easy, you have many opportunities to speed up and simplify your improvement process with an even greater likelihood of achieving significant, visible results.

Conclusion

No matter what the size of your service or organization, you can adapt your strategy to make it reach everyone in an efficient way. Consider the ideas provided here and engage your planning team in the discussion, "How can we do this *here* to make it effective with our people and services?" Pooling everyone's wisdom, there is always a way.

Chapter 9

• • •

Your Questions Answered

No doubt, you have questions! We've tried to anticipate your questions and address them. Here you'll find answers to three kinds of questions:

1. Questions about implementing the one-goal-at-a-time approach.
2. Questions about employee resistance and how to approach it.
3. And other questions about the nature and philosophy of the one-goal-at-a-time approach.

Questions about Implementing the One-Goal-at-a-Time Approach

Here are pointers about follow-up, staff motivation, the pace of your strategy, and what to do when people find the results of their efforts disheartening.

What Pace Do You Suggest for Pursuing These Breakthrough Service Objectives?

You need to figure out what your staff can handle. Engage your steering committee in a discussion of the appropriate schedule and pace, asking how long teams should have to complete each step in the process given the mix of activities you decide to include at each step. We also suggest at least a one-month gap between one objective and the next so that you and others have a short breather between objectives and have time to savor what is hopefully a sense of accomplishment from the previous work. Of course, to begin a new objective after a one-month hiatus, you will need to stagger your planning process so you select your new objective and decide on strategy steps before you complete your previous objective.

After You Finish Pursuing an Objective, How Do You Make Sure People Don't Backslide in Their Performance?

You're certainly right that you have to keep watch or you're likely to see slippage on hard-won gains. After the intense period of pursuing each objective, as specified in step 10 of the improvement process, you need to institute some method of monitoring performance and customer perceptions of performance so that you can feed back the results and pinpoint slippage that needs attention. Also, people in supervisory roles need to keep paying attention. If they stop paying attention to any service factor, some employees will let it slip. Like any foundation you build, this one needs periodic maintenance checks and preventive maintenance. While this might sound like ever-increasing work for people in leadership positions, it shouldn't be because, as you approach each service objective, you will redesign elements of service that should from then on be much easier to maintain at a high standard. Every service objective you take on becomes one more building block you're putting in place as you create a sustainable, service-oriented culture and service. Because you'll need periodic spot-checks, troubleshooting, and preventive maintenance, consider developing an ongoing team called something like *service watch* to serve this watchdog function.

Also, when you're launching a new objective, take steps to build a strong connection between the new objective and the one just addressed. Staff need to get a sense that the improvements you're making in service are cumulative—that one focus builds on and extends the previous ones, and that none is ever forgotten or replaced by the next. This is also important because otherwise staff view each new objective as a new "program" with a start and finish. If they think there is an end to it, there's no doubt that your effects will slip. We're talking about making permanent improvements and continuously monitoring and ensuring those improvements until the next time you decide to raise the bar and reach for an even higher standard.

How Do We Motivate Staff to Participate Wholeheartedly?

This is not easy, because staff already tend to feel so busy, even over-worked. The best way is really to appeal to their altruism. Most people enter health care because they care. They want to do good for people. You don't do good for people when there are service breakdowns. Not only that, you don't make a significant difference to people when service is average or mediocre. You need to impress customers in order to build their appreciation and loyalty. And that takes excellent service. Only by methodically working to improve service quality can you achieve excellent service. Appeal to people's pride in their work and their strong, although perhaps temporarily buried, altruistic desire to make a difference in people's lives. In today's high-pressure, often demoralizing environment, it is by setting ambitious goals and reaching high to provide great service that we elevate staff spirits above the everyday pressures and insecurities that drag them down.

What If We Pursue One Objective and It Doesn't Go Very Well?

First of all, debrief as you go. Don't wait until the end of the process to evaluate your efforts. Constantly ask "How are we doing? What's working? What isn't? What course corrections do we need to make in our approach?" And in all communications with staff, create the atmosphere that cultivates ongoing learning: "Let's see if we can improve customer satisfaction by pursuing this objective. We'll try the following approach, stop along the way to see how we're doing, and make course corrections so we get where we're going. Sometimes, we'll no doubt make false starts and mistakes. But this is a process, and by evaluating and learning as we go, we can make it work."

Questions about Employee Resistance and How to Approach It

Inevitably, some employees resist service improvement work with a wide variety of excuses such as the following:

- "We don't have time! I can't fit one more thing into my day!"
- "I can't see how this will benefit customers any more than what we're already doing."
- "I already do this!"
- "My manager doesn't do it, so why should I?"
- "We've tried things before, and they didn't work."
- "This is common sense. Why are we making such a big thing of it?"

You can certainly expect excuses why this doesn't make sense or why it is unrealistic or unfair to expect. The fact is, resistance is inevitable. But if you give in to it, you need to resign yourself to status quo service quality.

What Are the Main Kinds of Resistance Employees Will Be Likely to Express toward This Kind of Approach?

Some people will resist the standardized, lockstep process. But if you abandon this, you will have trouble tracking and supporting people's efforts. Point out the many options along the way and the fact that this standard process is designed to help people develop job- and team-specific improvements—improvements that really make sense for their specific services and roles. It also helps to create a "breakthrough." Other people will resist by saying, "We don't have the people to do this!" It's true that it takes people's time and energy, beyond the time and energy you ask of people in their everyday tasks. But many people view engagement in service improvement as enrichment, as welcome breaks in routine, and as opportunities to contribute to the greater good. Acknowledge this and appeal to these people. Also, remind people that to ignore improving service is to let service slip, which will cost your organization dearly and ultimately threaten your service's competitiveness and people's jobs.

Overall, What's the Best Way to Deal with Employee Resistance?

It's no surprise that the best way to deal with it is to prevent it! Employees sometimes perceive service improvement work and especially the one-goal-at-a-time approach as programs that, like buses, if they miss one, another will come along. That's why it's so important to include staff in as many of the decisions as possible and to focus up front on effective communication surrounding every aspect of your strategy. Specifically, make sure you do the following:

- Involve employees in selecting your service objectives, and as soon as you've made the decision to go ahead with a particular objective, communicate that decision to the people who were involved in helping to select it. And ask them to spread the word.
- Ask for their reactions.
- Listen to their reactions. If resistance is present, listen to it and ask questions to get clear on why they're resisting. Get everything out in the open. It's better to do this now than later. Acknowledge as much as you can and ask for suggestions about what to do in the strategy itself to reduce the issues they're raising and engage them. Often, the most resistant people will rally and have a change of heart when you invite them into the design phase of your planning process.
- Keep the lines of communication open throughout the process. When you see resistance cropping up at any point, talk openly about it with the person or team involved.
- If one of your employees is really resistant during the process, don't let this person's repeated expressions of resistance drag everyone else down. Let this person opt out of most of the process, but tell them that they will be held accountable for implementing the changes and improvements that are developed during the process. Say, "Okay, step back. Don't participate at this point. Just know that I'll expect you to deliver service in whatever ways the rest of your team determines to be better for our customers." At this point, most people will stop resisting and either bow out quietly or become anxious about not being part of your strategy. In any case, they tend to stop infusing the rest of your team with negative energy.

Questions about the Nature and Philosophy of the One-Goal-at-a-Time Approach

Also, some readers might have questions about the one-goal-at-a-time approach, its dynamics and its rationale. Hopefully we anticipate and address your questions here.

What Do You See as Critical Success Factors in Getting Results from Service Objectives?

First and foremost, you need a service champion with energy and authority—ideally the head of your service—who is willing to share a determined commitment to upgrading service quality for the sake of building staff pride and customer loyalty. This champion has to keep paying attention to the service and your strategy, because when attention slips, so do service standards and people's efforts to make improvements.

The second critical success factor is that key people need to realize that great service is a matter of design. It doesn't happen by accident or by itself, which means it will take *work* to make service consistently better.

And third, you need to develop and empower planning teams in the form of a steering committee who steep themselves in the service objective and approaches to achieving it and who develop a careful plan and timeline for getting there. There needs to be clarity around the process so people don't get lost and frustrated and therefore dwindle their efforts.

What If These Aren't Our Objectives?

Then apply the 10-step process to pursuing the service objectives of your choice. Also, if you read the techniques used here, they might help you design tools for your chosen objectives—tools that serve the same functions for those objectives.

This Looks Like a Lot of Work. How Can People Do This on Top of Their Hectic Jobs?

It's not easy to take on any additional projects. The fact is, can your organization afford to relegate service improvement to the status of "something extra"? We don't think so. The challenge then becomes dividing up the work, which we think these tool kits help you to do, and building into the process spirit-boosting fun elements and also markers and recognition methods that reinforce people for going the extra mile to make service improvements for their customers' sake.

Are These Breakthrough Objectives All You Have to Do to Improve Service?

No. These *augment* your efforts to ensure that every service process is designed well from the start and improved in process. These engage all staff in a united effort to improve service and earn customer loyalty.

What if Our Service Problems Have to Do with Systems, Not Individuals' Behavior?

In this book, we establish one criterion for breakthrough objectives: *Everyone must be able to contribute to them.* That means that many systems problems aren't likely to come up as breakthrough objectives, because typically not all employees play a role in running any one system. But you have two choices. One is to define your objective more broadly so that there are ways everyone can contribute. For instance, focus on speeding up service as the breakthrough objective, and within your approach, include the tackling of systems problems involving sluggish systems. Or, work on the service systems as a separate objective, a process improvement project, rather than within the framework of your breakthrough service objectives. You will, after all, certainly have staff working on objectives other than the one you set as your current breakthrough objective.

Why Not Make *Service* the Breakthrough Objective and Work on All Aspects for a Longer Time?

There are many aspects to achieving and sustaining great service, so adopting service as a breakthrough objective is too big, too ambitious an objective. It works better to break it down into key components, the vital few aspects your service needs to improve in order to earn customer loyalty and a competitive advantage. If you set service as your objective, what usually happens is that different people and teams improve different aspects of service, usually the easiest but not necessarily the most important aspects.

Conclusion

Hopefully, this book will help you embrace the one-goal-at-a-time approach and help you mobilize your team to pursue service improvements in a coordinated and effective manner.

Please stay in touch. Let us know how you're doing. Tell us what other do-it-yourself kits you wish you had (one on access? speed? privacy? respect? coworker relationships?). Don't hesitate to call with your reactions to this book or with questions, and we'll try to be your own *personal* help clinic. Also, share your learning so that we can all refine our approaches to service—one goal at a time.

How to contact us with questions or comments about this book:

Wendy Leebov, Susan Afriat, Jeanne Presha
Albert Einstein Healthcare Network
Sheerr Building
5501 Old York Road
Philadelphia, PA 19141
215-456-7063
Fax: 215-456-8353
E-mail: Leebovw@aol.com

Index